Witches, Rakes, and Rogues

True Stories of Scam, Scandal, Murder, and Mayhem in Boston, 1630–1775

D. BRENTON SIMONS

COMMONWEALTH EDITIONS

CARLISLE, MASSACHUSETTS

In memory of my mother,
Mary Hoyt Fitch, and in gratitude
to my friends and family

ISBN: 978-1-933212-47-0

Library of Congress Cataloging-in-Publication Data
Simons, D. Brenton.
Witches, rakes, and rogues : true stories of scam, scandal, murder, and mayhem in Boston, 1630/1775 / D. Brenton Simons.
p. cm.
Includes bibliographical references and index.
ISBN 978-1-933212-47-0
1. Boston (Mass.)—History—Colonial period, ca. 1600-1775—Anecdotes. 2. Boston (Mass.)—Social life and customs—Anecdotes. 3. Boston (Mass.)—Biography—Anecdotes. 4. Scandals—Massachusetts—Boston—History—Anecdotes. 5. Crime—Massachusetts—Boston—History—Anecdotes. 6. Witches—Massachusetts—Boston—Biography—Anecdotes. 7. Rogues and vagabonds—Massachusetts—Boston—Biography—Anecdotes. 8. Swindlers and swindling—Massachusetts—Boston—Biography—Anecdotes. 9. Criminals—Massachusetts—Boston—Biography—Anecdotes. I. Title.
F67.S57 2005
974.4'6102—dc22   2005016325

First published in hardcover, 2005
Cover design by Dean Bornstein.

Interior design by Ann Conneman, Peter King & Company.

Cover image: Woodcut by Paul Revere from *The Speech of Death to Levi Ames,* 1773, courtesy of the Historical Society of Pennsylvania.

Bonner's 1722 map of Boston, used courtesy of the New England Historic Genealogical Society. Icon used in front matter, Part One, and end matter: detail from a 1770 woodcut from *The Prodigal Daughter,* courtesy of the New England Historic Genealogical Society. Icon in Part Two: detail from a woodcut from *The Prodigal Daughter,* courtesy of the Massachusetts Historical Society. Icon in Part Three: detail from "Bostonians Paying the Exciseman," from *Stark's Antique Views of ye Towne of Boston.* Icon in Part Four: detail from Coat of Arms, Joseph Dudley, from the *Gore Roll of Arms,* courtesy of the New England Historic Genealogical Society.

On page 140, the portrait of Elizabeth Greenleaf is used by permission of The Metropolitan Museum of Art, Partial and Promised Gift of Marc Holzer, 2002 (2002.612); the portrait of Priscilla Greenleaf is from a private collection (photograph by Coleman Sellers); the portrait of John Greenleaf Jr. is used by permission of The Metropolitan Museum of Art, Gift of Stuart and Rhoda Holzer, 2002 (2002.611).

COMMONWEALTH EDITIONS, AN IMPRINT OF APPLEWOOD BOOKS, INC.
Carlisle, Massachusetts 01741
www.commonwealtheditions.com

Printed in the United States of America

10 9 8 7 6

Witches,
Rakes, and
Rogues

Contents

Part Three
A Miscellany of Miscreants

Part Four
Family Skeletons, Dangerous Liaisons, and Black Sheep

Introduction

BOSTONIANS ARE JUSTIFIABLY PROUD of our city's place in the annals of American history. Many are, however, perhaps more familiar with the Revolutionary War period than with the hundred and forty or so years that preceded those tumultuous times. Innumerable events and people from this earlier period (from the 1630s to the early 1770s) have been almost forgotten: women accused or convicted of witchcraft, diabolical possessions that seized the town with fear, upstanding citizens swindled by con artists, the kidnapping of young heiresses, innocents murdered, acrimonious divorces, and other stories that made tongues wag throughout the town. This book gathers for new examination the stories of individuals whose lives were forever altered by scams, scandals, murder, mayhem, and other disturbances now long faded from memory.

Many written sources and local records help provide a picture of colonial life. Diaries offer tantalizing views of local happenings and stories that circulated in town. Sometimes these accounts are detailed, but all too often they are oblique and offer only hints of events that will now never be fully understood. One of the great chroniclers of early Boston history was the first governor of the Massachusetts Bay Colony. In addition to weighty matters of state, John Winthrop captured in his journal small events that had major consequences, such as the conflict between Robert Keayne, a merchant, and a local woman, Mrs. Sherman. "There fell out a great business upon a very small occasion," as Winthrop put it. This squabble over the disputed ownership of a barnyard animal reached monumental proportions—and had the unlikely effect of dividing the colony's government into two branches. A host of other men and women, both famous and obscure, kept diaries or journals or wrote histories, though not all chroniclers were as meticulous as Winthrop. One of those more oblique accounts appears in the diary of townsman John Marshall. In September 1710, he offered a cryptic note on the death or disappearance of the disreputable wife of Christopher Vail: "Toward the end of this month a woman at Boston, a person of bad report, either drowned herself or was carried away by the devil. Her maiden name was Joan Heiferman." Mrs. Vail's fate—the devil or the deep blue sea—remains a mystery.

Early Boston newspapers are another rich source of stories, frequently carrying items about runaway wives, the identification of scoundrels, public quarrels, and other human failings. Sometimes newspapers spread rumors or were used to counteract the damage of gossip. In September 1728, chocolate grinder James Lubbock felt it necessary to advertise that his business had suffered from the "false reports and defamations" circulated by Margaret Belcher. Lubbock assured readers of the *Boston News-Letter* that his business, located near the Reverend Benjamin Colman's meetinghouse, was reputable and continued to supply "the best chocolate, well prepared and at a reasonable rate." Lubbock's reassurances of a stable business were unfounded: dogged by Margaret Belcher's rumors, the chocolatier absconded from Boston the following spring, carrying away with him "four Negroes and sundry affects to a considerable value."

Other events we can reconstruct through the first-person accounts of visitors to Boston or by the stories written about these visitors. Ironically, one of the most colorful accounts of a visit to Boston in the twilight of the seventeenth century was written by a man who may never have set foot in town. Flushed with success from his 1698 book *A Trip to Jamaica,* Englishman Edward "Ned" Ward (1667–1731) published *A Trip to New-England* in London the following year. Experts think that Ward may have prepared his account by cobbling it together from earlier published travelogues. His fanciful, larger-than-life descriptions of Boston and its residents, nevertheless, were widely read and offer an amusing, and sometimes risqué, view of what he called the "metropolis of New-England."

Ned Ward's commentaries give us an animated, opinionated view of the churches, clergymen, and religious character of colonial Boston. The town, he said, possessed four clapboard and shingle-clad churches overseen by the same number of ministers, "who some," he quipped, "very justly, have applied these epitaphs, one a scholar, the second a gentleman, the third a dunce, and the fourth a clown." He observed that in Boston there were "more religious zealots than honest men," and although the townspeople appeared religious and as innocent as doves, in their business dealings they were "as subtle as serpents." Their priorities, he alleged, were not religious: "Interest is their faith, money their god, and large possessions the only heaven they covet." He unflatteringly described Bostonians as being preoccupied in "detecting one another's failings," that a "meritorious Christian" is one who "betrays his neighbor to a whipping post." He related the anecdote of two busybody deacons mortified by the sight of a woman relieving herself in public:

> *A couple of deacons marching along the street espied a woman in a corner relieving nature from the uneasiness of a burden she could keep no longer, one of them cried out to the other, pointing to the stooping object, "Brother, Brother, what a shameful thing, what a beastly thing is this? I vow, Brother, this is a thing that ought to be peep'd into." The other being a more sensible man, "Prithee Brother (said he) do thou peep into it then, for I care not to run such a hazard of my eye-sight. Besides (said he) the thing's too deep for our inspection; and therefore we shall only be laughed at for meddling with the matter."*

Visitors had a habit of passing through Boston and leaving marks, or at least traces, of infamy or curiosity. In 1731, for example, merchant Benjamin Walker Jr. noted that an Irish parson named Christian arrived in Boston from England with a woman "well advanced in years" he identified as his wife. But according to his friend Jonathan Clarke, "said Christian has another wife and two children in England . . . he had preached several times in this town." With this brief glimpse, Parson Christian then disappeared from view.

MY ADVENTURE WITH EARLY BOSTON SCANDALS began in the late 1990s when Barbara Luck of the Abby Aldrich Rockefeller Folk Art Museum asked me to look into the mysterious demise in the mid-eighteenth century of the children of Dr. John Greenleaf. What emerged was a surprising tale of poisoning and murder that was undeniably true, despite attempts by some writers in the twentieth century to discount the story as an impossible folktale. Over time, I collected similar stories, and before long it was obvious that they might make an intriguing anthology.

For clarity, I have standardized dates as well as spelling and punctuation in original quotations wherever possible. Also, I am solely responsible for any errors that may have crept into this work.

This examination of colonial Boston reminds me of both the uniqueness of its people and the universalities of human nature and proclivities that, I would venture, could with a little digging be uncovered in almost any city in any age. In 1660, Thomas Hobbes wrote in *The Leviathan* that the life of man is "solitary, poor, nasty, brutish, and short." While Hobbes may have been somewhat more pessimistic about human nature than warranted, I might agree, based on the following stories, that at the very least many people are inventive, deceptive, highly imaginative, and capable of more than a little chicanery. At least early Boston's men and women were.

Part One

Witch's Brew: Witchcraft and Possession in Early Boston

OVERSHADOWED BY THE HYSTERIA that gripped the towns-people of Salem in 1692, Boston's considerable witchcraft record has received relatively little attention. From the late 1630s to the 1690s, the town intermittently fell into witch-hunting fervor as accusations coalesced around individual women. The consequences were often deadly, as witchcraft was then a crime punishable by death. Especially vulnerable to charges were widows, female medical practitioners, and outspoken matrons. Men in Boston were seldom the subject of witchcraft accusations; most of the few claims or rumors about male suspects occurred at the time of the Salem events. By the close of the seventeenth century, concern over witchcraft had generally subsided in New England. However, in 1741, decades after Boston's last case, a young local woman, Martha Robinson, experienced what was described as a diabolical possession—a last gasp in the town's legacy of such occurrences. In all, four local women were convicted and executed in Boston witchcraft trials. Many others endured accusa-tions, and a number of women and children claimed to be afflicted by satanic possessions. Their stories reveal aspects of long-forgotten Boston history and the perils of life in a puritanical society that believed in the possibility of such events.

In 1638, Jane Hawkins, a midwife and medical practitioner, became the first person in Boston publicly suspected of witchcraft. Jane had previously been banished from the Massachusetts Bay Colony as a result of her sympathies during the religious conflict known as the Antinomian Controversy, when orthodox Puritans persecuted Anne Hutchinson and her followers. A further mark against her was that she assisted in the birth of a monstrously deformed baby to Mary Dyer, later the famous Quaker martyr hanged on Boston Common in 1660. This incident was seen as signal of "God's displeasure with the Antinomians." Governor John Winthrop noted in his journal that Jane was suspected of witchcraft even before her arrival in New England. She "had much familiarity with the devil" in England, and ministers there, Winthrop wrote, had examined her and "found it true." In 1641, Jane Hawkins was again banished from the colony, an act that probably helped to preserve her life.

The first witchcraft trial in Boston involved Margaret Jones of Charlestown, another medical practitioner deemed suspicious by the establishment. In May 1648 she was convicted of practicing witchcraft and the following month became the first woman in Boston to be executed for the crime. When the accusations arose, the court ordered Margaret and her husband to be placed in seclusion and separately watched for signs of witchcraft. Mr. Jones was cleared in this process, but Margaret was less fortunate. The principal source for Margaret's story is once again John Winthrop, who left a substantial account of the case in his journal. Winthrop gave six reasons for Margaret's conviction: (1) she possessed a "malignant touch" that caused people to become violently ill and sometimes even deaf; (2) her medical treatments "had extraordinary violent effects"; (3) she warned ill persons who declined her services that they would never recover unless they used her "physic," and "accordingly their diseases and hurts continued"; (4) she was able to accurately predict events and knew details of private conversations she had "no ordinary means to come to the knowledge of"; (5) during a forced search of her body, a freshly sucked witch's teat was discovered in her "secret parts" and a second one soon began to appear; and (6) while in prison she was visited by an imp that witnesseses saw before it vanished into thin air. Any one of these circumstances, if believed, might have been sufficient to sway the court against her; taken together they formed a body of evidence Margaret Jones was unable to overcome.

According to Winthrop, Margaret did not help herself in court. Behaving "intemperately," railing against the jury, and "lying notoriously," Margaret was her own worst enemy. In the end, she was convicted and sentenced to death. Winthrop noted in his journal a distant omen that took place at the day and hour of her execution in Boston: a "great tempest" struck Connecticut and caused much damage. To the Puritans of New England, this storm represented more than a coincidence: it was further evidence of Margaret's guilt. As a boy, John Hale, later the author of *A Modest Inquiry into the Nature of Witchcraft,* was among Margaret's visitors in jail shortly before her execution. He had a quite different explanation for the charges. Her case had come about, he alleged, because of "some angry words passing between her and her neighbors" and "some mischief" that befell the neighbors' livestock.

About 1650, Alice Lake of Dorchester became the second person tried and executed in Boston as a witch. While few details of her offenses survive, she had two potent strikes against her: she had committed fornication prior to marriage, and she was reputed to have killed an infant she was carrying. The source for these particulars was again John Hale, who wrote that Alice "played the harlot" when she was single. After Alice became pregnant, he wrote, she "used means to destroy the fruit of her body to conceal her sin and shame." At least one known sexual episode occurred between Alice and her future husband, Henry Lake. In 1643, some time after the couple married, word of their premarital transgression came to the attention of the Court of Assistants. Before that body, Henry and Alice Lake were charged with fornication and "enjoined to appear the next Lecture day, at Dorchester, and to acknowledge their fault." Many years after her execution, Nathaniel Mather wrote his brother Increase to ask why he had not included Alice's story in his recent publication, *An Essay for the Recording of Illustrious Providences.* "I have heard the devil drew in," Nathaniel wrote, "by appearing to her in the likeness and acting the part of a child of hers then lately dead on whom her heart was much set." Increase Mather's reply does not survive. Alice's execution had a divisive effect on the remnants of her family. Her surviving children were sent to other families to be raised, while their father relocated to Rhode Island.

Engraving of John Dunton, who visited Boston in 1686 and recorded the story of "Mrs. D——." Courtesy of the Massachusetts Historical Society.

In 1673, Ann Martin Edmonds, a healer from Lynn with Boston associations, was brought before the Court of Assistants on witchcraft charges. One of her medical cases appears to have been at the root of accusations by Samuel and Sarah Bennett of Boston. After hearing the evidence, however, the Court of Assistants dismissed its case against Mrs. Edmonds and instead tried the Bennetts for the neglectful care of Alice Wilson and the "clandestine" burial of her son. The chief witnesses against the Bennetts were Ann Edmonds and her husband, William. The Court of Assistants fined the Bennetts and ordered them to reimburse the Edmondses for court expenses. When she died in October 1686, Ann Edmonds took the details of the spurious witchcraft charges against her to her grave at the Copp's Hill Burying Ground in Boston's North End.

Oil portrait of diarist Samuel Sewall by Nathaniel Emmons, 1728.
Courtesy of the Massachusetts Historical Society.

One of Boston's last and most elusive witch suspects is known only as "Mrs. D——." When English bookseller John Dunton made an extended visit to Boston in 1686, he recorded his impressions of noteworthy Bostonians. Because he borrowed so liberally from earlier printed sources, we may never be sure who Mrs. D—— was, or if she even existed. Nevertheless, Dunton gave a vivid account of a woman who played some remarkable tricks and possessed "a bad face, and a worse tongue; and has the report of a Witch":

> *Whether she be one or no, I know not, but she has ignorance and malice enough to make her one. And indeed she has done very odd things, but hitherto such as are rather strange than hurtful; yea, some of them are pretty and pleasing; but such as I think cannot be done without the help of the Devil—as for instance, she will take nine sticks, and lay them across, and by mumbling a few words, make them all stand up on end like a pair of nine-pins. But she best have a care, for they that use the Devil's help to make sport, may quickly come to do mischief. I have been told by some, that she has actually indentured with the Devil; and that he is to do what she would have him for a time, and afterwards he is to have her soul in exchange! What pains poor wretches take to make sure of Hell!*

One of the final references to the possibility of witchcraft in Boston came in 1694. After making a mundane entry in his diary on January 19, 1694, about the installation of a new kitchen floor, Samuel Sewall noted the following tantalizing item: "This day Mrs. Prout dies after sore conflicts of mind, not without suspicion of witchcraft." Elizabeth Upsall Greenough Prout would have been one of the last women in Boston to be considered a witchcraft victim, but the episode at the close of her life remains an unsolved mystery of early Boston history.

Unlike the more famous events in Salem in 1692, episodes of suspected witchcraft or diabolical possession in Boston were mostly unrelated events occurring over the course of a century. Many women and a few men escaped with their lives. Women and children who experienced what they claimed were possessions gradually returned to normality. However, for four Boston-area women—Margaret Jones and Alice Lake, as we have seen, and Ann Hibbins and Mary Glover, whose stories follow—witchcraft charges leveled by their neighbors exacted the ultimate toll.

Chapter 1
Hanged for a Witch:
The Turbulent Passions of Ann Hibbins
1656

MEMORABLE FOR HER ENCOUNTER with Hester Prynne
in *The Scarlet Letter,* Mistress Hibbins was not simply a figment of
Nathaniel Hawthorne's imagination. Long a controversial woman
in Boston, she was a real person who in May 1656 was sentenced to
death for the crime of witchcraft. The widow of an affluent merchant
and office holder, Ann Hibbins was, in the words of historian Samuel
Adams Drake, a "person of superior quality in life," and not, as the
popular imagination conceives of a witch, a "wretched hag," In spite
of her privileged position in Boston society, Ann was unable to stave
off strong public sentiments against her. No details of her witchcraft
offenses survived, but some account of the troubled years leading up
to her execution can be reconstructed. Ann's most serious conflict in
town stemmed from a dispute with joiner John Crabtree over what
she considered to be extortionately high charges for his work. This
disagreement sparked in Ann rumor-mongering behavior later criticized by the elders of the First Church of Boston. Finding this
quarrelsome and accusatory conduct intolerable, the elders in 1641
excommunicated her from the church. But perhaps the strongest
mark against Ann was the "natural crabbedness" of her temperament,
a trait exacerbated when her husband, William Hibbins, suffered a
significant financial reversal shortly after the couple's arrival in Boston.
In time, Ann became a pariah in town and after her husband's death
was rendered vulnerable to witchcraft claims offered on what may
have been thin evidence. An outspoken woman of turbulent passions,

Ann Hibbins was later said to have "been hanged for a witch, only for having more wit than her neighbors."

Before marrying William Hibbins and moving to Boston, Ann had another, altogether different life. Her maiden name and origins are not known, but various associations indicate that she was from a family of substance and had received more education than most women of her time. For our purposes, Ann's story begins a number of years before her arrival in New England. She was at this time married to a gentleman named Moore by whom she had three sons. After Moore's death, Ann married a well-connected widower, William Hibbins, the son of a prominent family in Shropshire, England. His first wife was Hester Bellingham, a sister of Richard Bellingham, who was later the governor of the Massachusetts Bay Colony. Sometime after marrying, William and Ann decided to emigrate to New England and arrived in Boston by 1639. As a respectable couple in their middle years, they were soon received as members of the First Church. In recognition of his prominence, William was selected as a deputy for Boston to the General Court the following year. From this promising beginning great troubles unexpectedly arose.

One of the first problems to beset the couple in Boston was a transaction made in England with mariner Nicholas Trerise that went awry. Trerise, later recalled by some of his contemporaries as a scoundrel, was entrusted with four parcels of gold (valued to almost £500) by William Hibbins in May 1638. The funds were to support the expenses of 180 passengers who would accompany Trerise on his ship *Planter* from Gravesend to New England. The gold was later lost, seized, or stolen. When Trerise arrived in Boston the following year, he was promptly brought before the General Court by William Hibbins and his brother-in-law, Richard Bellingham. Hibbins later sued Trerise for £500, but the mariner seems to have escaped a judgment against him. The murkiness of the business between Hibbins and Trerise led one author to speculate that perhaps the two were engaged in illegal activities together. In all likelihood that was not the case, but the episode is cited as one of the causes of Ann's subsequent mental turmoil. According to a nearly contemporary historian, William Hubbard, the Trerise imbroglio "so discomposed [her] spirit that she scarce ever was well settled in her mind afterward, but grew very turbulent in her passion." In time, Ann's passions would cost her dearly.

The next incident soon followed. With her husband's permission, Ann engaged joiner John Crabtree to perform some carpentry work in their new house near the south side of town. It is safe to say that Crabtree, a native of Yorkshire who had been in the colony only a few years, had not encountered a client in Boston as unpredictable as Ann Hibbins. After he completed his work the joiner asked for payment. Bitterly unhappy with his fees, Ann claimed that the bargain was for forty shillings. In the end Crabtree demanded the far greater sum of £13. Ann carried word of her discontent far and wide. After the recent failure suffered at the hands of Nicholas Trerise, it is possible that Ann felt victimized. She and her husband were again on the losing end of a transaction, albeit one on a much smaller scale. William allowed his wife to argue with Crabtree over the price and "order the business with him as she thought good." When it became clear that "the work was too much for the price," he proposed to pay Crabtree a sum decided upon by two independent appraisers. William Hibbins selected another joiner, John Davis, to help establish a new price. In his visits to the Hibbins house, Davis received conflicting information from Ann about Crabtree's work and before long concluded she was lying. Ann was unhappy with Davis when he and others recommended Crabtree's fee be only slightly reduced to about £10, an amount she found unacceptable. In addition to spreading rumors about John Crabtree, Ann now began bad-mouthing John Davis about town. Before long, this seemingly pedestrian conflict became a major controversy. Because Ann's querulous behavior reflected poorly upon her as a member of the First Church, the matter was taken up by its elders. Merchant Robert Keayne was a member of the body and recorded the testimony of several of the proceedings.

On September 13, 1640, John Wilson, first minister of the First Church of Boston, stated that Ann had charged John Davis "with a confederacy, and divulging and publishing it all abroad to ministers, magistrates, neighbors and others." This she had done, according to Wilson, in an effort to bring "infamy, disgrace, and reproach" upon the joiner. Davis appeared at the meeting and offered that in the process of appraising Crabtree's work, Ann had told him "a lie or two." Worse still, Ann was publicly accusing him and all the joiners of Boston in conspiring against her. On one of his visits to her house, Ann declared to Davis that "the timbers of the room would cry for judgment against [him]." The elders soon turned their attention to Ann herself. Unwisely remaining silent, Ann did not respond when directly questioned by the churchmen on the excuse that it might not be "lawful for her to speak in the church." Assured that no such obstacle existed, she still refused to answer them. Her obstinacy infuriated several of the men who believed it an act of sheer contemptuousness. John Wilson excused her temporarily, offering that perhaps a "bodily infirmity" might be interfering with her ability to communicate. During the course of the meeting it emerged that Ann had previously admitted some of her wrongs against John Davis in an emotional encounter with him. According to William Hibbins, Davis was satisfied at the time and blessed God that he had "so much humbled her spirit, she confessing her error with tears." Now unwilling to utter a word, much less show repentance again, Ann left the first meeting with a severe admonition for her conduct.

She did not remain silent for long. In the second meeting held the following week, Ann finally addressed the charges against her. "I desire you all to take notice of my fall," she said before the elders, "that you may stand." Not convinced that she had committed anything wrong, she acknowledged "how far the Lord hath withdrawn Himself" from her and offered to explain herself in writing the following week. This suggestion was rejected by John Cotton, who stated that "the practice of writing is uncouth in the church and we have no precedent for it in Scripture." Realizing the elders would not accede to such an unusual request, she then launched into the history of her conflict with John Crabtree. This tack dismayed the churchmen who, having heard it all before, eventually interrupted her. "I desire to proceed, that I may clear myself," she replied in frustration, "[from the] many aspersions that have been laid upon me in this business." Refusing to admit her fault, Ann was, in the eyes of the elders, simply making excuses for her irregular conduct. William Hibbins stated that he was satisfied with the results of Davis's appraisal and that he wished with all his heart that his wife would go along with it. Elder Thomas Oliver told an unyielding Ann that she should have been satisfied with the reduced charge of about £10. Unwilling to let the matter rest, she replied that she had identified a joiner in Salem, among others, who thought the fee should have been even lower. With no clear resolution, the matter now subsided for several months.

In February 1641, Ann's conduct was raised again in a special meeting of the congregation. John Wilson stated that the Lord had "not yet broken her spirit" and called for discussion on whether another admonition should be passed. Especially offensive to the elders was the perception that Ann did not appear to be subservient to her husband. Captain Edward Gibbons summarized this sentiment, asserting, "She hath usurped authority over her guide and head, whom she should have obeyed and unto whom God hath put her in subjection; yet she hath exalted her own wit and will and way above his." In the end, the elders decided that only excommunication would do. Directed to stand and accept Wilson's judgment, Ann listened as her "many and gross sins and offenses" were reiterated before the assembled parishioners. Before the meeting broke up, William Hibbins, in his usual humble and respectful manner, asked to be heard. Requesting the prayers of all assembled, he hoped his wife would eventually be restored to her faith and to membership in the congregation. His wish was never realized.

No details remain regarding Ann's behavior during the decade following her expulsion from the First Church. Her husband was in 1643 elevated from a deputy to the General Court to the more important office of an assistant of the colony. However, his death in 1654 marked a significant turning point in the story. The passing of this influential and diplomatic gentleman eased the way for Ann's detractors to take serious aim at her. A despised woman to many in town, Ann was considered "so odious to her neighbors as to cause some of them to accuse her of witchcraft." When the accusations mounted, Ann was brought before authorities, who concluded that she should stand trial. Regrettably, no court records or firsthand accounts remain to tell us of the evidence presented against her or the names of witnesses who testified on her witchcraft activities.

If Ann was as stubborn and disobliging a witness as she was in her excommunication hearings years earlier, it is likely she did herself considerable damage during the trial. According to historian William Hubbard, she was found guilty by a jury, but the verdict was not accepted by the colony's magistrates, who referred the case to the General Court—the same body in which Ann's husband had formerly served. "*Vox populi* went sore against her," Hubbard noted, "and was the chiefest part of the evidence against her, as some thought." After deliberations, the General Court, perhaps responding to a clamoring public, found her guilty and sentenced her to be hanged:

> *Mrs. Anne Hibbins was called forth, appeared at the bar; the indict-ment against her was read, to which she answered not guilty, and was willing to be tried by God and this court. The evidences against her was read, the parties witnessing being present, her answers considered on, and the whole court, being met together, by their vote, determined that Mrs. Anne Hibbins is guilty of witchcraft, according to the bill of indictment found against her by the jury of life and death. The Governor in open court pronounced sentence accordingly, declaring she was to go from the bar to the place from whence she came, and from thence to the place of execution, and there to hang till she was dead.*

The General Court set the date of execution for June 19, 1656, to take place after the lecture—a sermon that undoubtedly focused on Ann—in a public setting. The Marshall General was called upon to have a sufficient guard at an event likely to be attended by a large percentage of the town. Ann's reaction to the verdict was never recorded, but as a woman of substantial means, she soon moved to set her affairs in order. On May 27, 1656, she wrote a will naming her sons, at least two of whom were living as gentlemen in Ireland, as her beneficiaries. Her estate included property and personal effects in Boston, a three-hundred-acre farm called Stanford on the Muddy River near town, and other lands. To her eldest son, John Moore, she bequeathed a double portion of her estate and specified two chests and a desk he was to receive. Her sons Joseph and Jonathan would be given equal portions of the other half of her assets. Because her sons lived abroad, she enlisted the aid of several prominent Bostonians as administrators of the will, including Thomas Clarke, Edward Hutchinson, William Hudson, Joshua Scottow, and Peter Oliver. This indicates that Ann still had some supporters in town, perhaps men who had been friends or associates of her late husband. Thomas Clarke, for example, was one of the wealthiest merchants in town, and Edward Hutchinson, a son of religious dissenter Anne Hutchinson, had served as town treasurer. Another interesting selection was Peter Oliver, a son of Elder Thomas Oliver, who had been instrumental in Ann's excommunication many years earlier. One administrator, Joshua Scottow, was critical of the General Court's handling of Ann's case but later apologized for his comments.

On June 16, 1656, a few days before her execution, Ann added a codicil to her will including two more gentlemen, styled as "loving friends," to be among the overseers of her will: Captain James Johnson, a leather merchant, and Edward Rawson, secretary of the colony. In Captain Johnson, Ann appears to have found a sympathetic friend whom she entrusted with some of her most important possessions. She specified that Johnson should safeguard her chests and desks and all the papers contained in each. Among the other bequests of note in the second document was a gift of forty shillings to a cousin in England, Captain Mark Coe, a merchant from Essex prominent in London affairs during the Cromwellian period. This bequest and other provisions in the will indicate that Ann had significant connections there and perhaps was a Londoner herself. Finally, Ann made a pathetic request that the overseers would have been unlikely or unable to keep; she asked that respect be shown to her "dead corpse" and that they endeavor to see that it be "decently interred and if it may be, near my late husband."

The second codicil also reveals that in her final days, Ann received, or expected to receive, a visit by one of her younger sons, Jonathan Moore. If Jonathan made the trip in a last-ditch attempt to assist his mother in her case, his efforts were unsuccessful. For his "pains and charge" in coming to see her, Ann bequeathed him an additional £20. Three days later, the last day of her life, she added a third codicil for the purpose of leaving him a further £10, given, she said tenderly, out of "my sense of more than ordinary affection and pains for my son

Jonathan, in the times of my distress." These words were the last utterances by Ann Hibbins that survive. Later that day, Ann was taken from jail to hear the public lecture and from there to the place of her execution. According to lore, it occurred on the Boston Common at the site of the Great Elm, not far from the present-day site of the Frog Pond. Before a huge concourse of onlookers, this wealthy woman of unstable emotions was hanged from a branch of that venerable tree. The place of her burial is not recorded, but Samuel Adams Drake speculated that her remains were "probably thrust into some obscure hole."

According to Thomas Hutchinson, at some point after Ann's death a search for telltale signs of witchcraft was "made upon her body for teats, and in her chests and boxes, for puppets, images, etc., but there

The Old Elm or Great Tree on Boston Common, where Ann Hibbins's hanging is said to have taken place, as it appeared prior to its destruction in 1876. From Antique Views of ye Towne of Boston.

is no record of anything of that sort being found." In keeping with the terms of her second codicil, Edward Rawson gave Captain James Johnson the keys to the chests and desk mentioned so prominently in her will. On July 16, 1656, he opened them to make an estate inventory. Among the valuables were New England currency, gold, and English and Spanish silver. Heirlooms intended for John Moore included numerous silver and gilt serving pieces, ten silver spoons with pictures of the Apostles in gilt, a diamond ring, a gold wedding ring, and a Bible and case. Other items were an immense assortment of fashionable clothing, fine linens, and sundry household goods.

Ann's execution did not close the controversy surrounding the claims of witchcraft. An unsettling postscript to the story occurred years later when the Reverend Increase Mather received a letter from a minister named Beach in Jamaica. The letter recounted Beach's recollection of a story the Reverend John Norton supposedly told to the Reverend John Wilson, Elder James Penn, and others:

> You may remember what I have sometimes told you your famous
> Mr. Norton once said at his own table, before Mr. Wilson the pastor,
> Elder Penn, and myself and wife, &etc., who had the honour to be his
> guests. That one of your magistrates wives, as I remember, was hanged
> for a witch, only for having more wit than her neighbours. It was his
> very expression, she having, as he explained it, unhappily guessed
> that two of her persecutors, whom she saw talking in the street, were
> talking of her; which proved true, cost her her life, notwithstanding
> all he could do to the contrary, as he himself told us.

At least some people believed that evidence of Ann Hibbins's witchcraft had been detected. Increase Mather received a letter from his brother Nathaniel, who, after reading Increase's 1684 *An Essay for the Recording of Illustrious Providences,* queried why he had not included the story of "Mrs. Hibbons witchcrafts, and the discovery thereof." Was Ann Hibbins practicing something resembling witchcraft, or was her downfall more obviously a case of retribution against a blunt and unpopular woman? As Thomas Hutchinson said, with some license, "It fared with her as it did with Joan of Arc in France. Some counted her a saint and some a witch."

Chapter 2

Mary Hale and the Death
of a Bewitched Mariner
1680

AMONG THE WOMEN involved in the practice of herbal medicine who were accused of witchcraft is the widow Mary Hale, whose story has received little notice in the pages of Boston history. In the late 1670s, Mary operated a boardinghouse that sometimes admitted sick people for nursing. During one smallpox outbreak, for example, she took in a black man, Zanckey, who "had the small pox coming out all over him." Zanckey's master later paid her more than £5 for his care. Like Ann Hibbins, Mary was a controversial woman prone to quarreling. In the summer of 1677 Dennis MackDaniel brought two suits against her. In one case, Mary was found guilty of striking and struggling with MackDaniel's wife, Alice, and was fined. MackDaniel's second suit alleged that Mary had defamed both him and his wife by saying MackDaniel was a "cuckoldley old rogue" and that his wife was a "whore and that she had several children by other men." Mary was found guilty in this case, too, and was ordered to acknowledge her crime before the Suffolk County Court or be fined the steep amount of £10.

Three years later, at age seventy-four, Mary faced public accusations of witchcraft. Her story can be reconstructed from depositions regarding the strange death of Michael Smith, a young mariner who lodged at Mary's house. It seems that Mary promoted the mariner as a suitor to her teenage granddaughter, Joanna Benham, and a smitten Michael began pursuing Joanna with the intent to marry her. The seed of courtship did not flower in Joanna, however, and after a time the young woman informed Michael that she "could not love him." The impasse was temporarily relieved when Michael went to sea, but when he returned he attempted to revive the relationship. Joanna held her ground, telling Michael that "absolutely" she "would not have him." Soon afterward, Michael turned his attentions to another young lady in town, twenty-three-year-old Margaret Ellis, and found new lodgings in the nearby house of Goodwife Everill.

Mary Hale, however, was not as willing as her granddaughter to let the young mariner drift away. On several occasions while Michael lodged at the house, a "jealous" Mary supposedly crept up to the window and eavesdropped on her former lodger and his new girlfriend. One night Michael encountered Mary loitering at the door. He accompanied her back to her house, where she railed against Margaret Ellis and called her a whore. Mary did not keep her feelings about Michael's new liaison a secret in the neighborhood. On one occasion she asked shopkeeper Hannah Manning if she thought Michael would marry Margaret Ellis. The shopkeeper suggested that a wedding seemed likely and might even take place before Michael's next voyage. Mary snapped back that Margaret Ellis was "a hunchbacked jade" who would never "enjoy" Michael Smith.

A short time later, as Michael prepared to undertake another voyage, he stopped at Mary Hale's house to meet two of his fellow seamen who boarded there. During his visit, Michael drank a concoction prepared by the widow. By the time he arrived at the Isles of Shoals, he was seriously ill and suspected he had been poisoned. After a few days he made an unexpected recovery. His trouble, Michael told a doctor there, was that he was "bewitched" and that Mary Hale was haunting him. Upon returning to Boston, Michael moved once more, this time to Hannah Wakeham's house. There again, he fell ill. Prior to his illness, he told a number of people in town that the rift with Joanna Benham was at the root of his problems. In an attempt to clear her name, Joanna visited him during his illness. To determine the cause of his malady, two doctors were summoned. According to Joanna, Dr. Johnson could find no disease present in Michael other than being

Witchcraft suspects were seen as being in league with the devil, as seen in this 1770 woodcut from The Prodigal Daughter. *Courtesy of the New England Historic Genealogical Society.*

lovesick for her. Joanna's rival, Margaret Ellis, later demanded that Joanna call for a "couple of fresh doctors."

Michael Smith lingered on. In his final days, Michael's new landlady, Hannah Wakeham, made an interesting experiment that threw suspicion squarely upon Mary Hale. Hannah collected some of Michael's "water" (urine) in a bottle and locked it in a cupboard. Mary Hale, during a visit to Hannah's house that day, "did not cease walking to and fro about the house." Later, when Hannah retrieved and unstopped the bottle, Mary's agitated movements suddenly ended. To seventeenth-century Boston women, this was a sure sign of witchcraft.

On his last day of life, Michael consumed another preparation by Mary Hale. Margaret Ellis claimed that Mary had prepared a caudle, or warm drink, for Michael, which Joanna brought to her in the morning. Margaret warned him that "it would be his death if he drank it." That evening, however, she had a change of heart and brought him Mary's preparation, claiming that she had made it. Michael consumed the beverage and soon fell asleep. At midnight he began moaning so loudly Margaret thought "the walls of the house would have fallen on us." After waking, Michael began complaining that Mary Hale was "halvinge out his bowels" and demanded that Margaret fetch a constable to arrest her. He wanted "some of her blood," which he claimed "would be a speedy remedy for his recovery." He then told Margaret and others assembled at his bedside a remarkable tale of witchcraft: in the hours since he fell asleep, Mary had magically transported him to a banqueting house near Dorchester. There he claimed to have been in the presence of a coven of twenty witches sitting at a round table drinking wine. Among the witnesses present during Michael's outpouring was Hannah Wakeham's grandfather James Everill, a reputable man in town affairs and a past selectman of Boston. Soon after making these accusations, Michael Smith died. On the strength of his accusations, Mary Hale was formally charged with witchcraft. Tried before the Court of Assistants, she was found not guilty.

Mary Hale's last days, whether in Boston or elsewhere, go unrecorded, but accusations of witchcraft ran in her family. In subsequent years Mary's daughter and granddaughter, both named Winifred Benham, were accused of witchcraft in Connecticut. Like Mary Hale, they escaped conviction.

Chapter 3

The Pitiful Spectacles of Haunted Children: Cotton Mather's Account of a Possession 1688

BELIEVING SOME LINENS TO BE MISSING, thirteen-year old Martha Goodwin unwittingly took steps that led to the execution of a neighbor for witchcraft—the fourth and last Boston woman so convicted. Martha suspected that her family's laundress, a woman named Glover, had stolen the items, and in midsummer 1688 Martha confronted her. The laundress's elderly mother, Mary Glover, did not respond well to the charges against her daughter (whose first name is not known) and "bestowed very bad language" upon Martha, who promptly became ill and began experiencing "strange fits." Before long, three of Martha's younger siblings were similarly afflicted. In time, suspicions fell upon Mary Glover, who was soon put on trial. The case attracted much attention and the involvement of the Reverend Cotton Mather, who made it the centerpiece of his 1689 *Memorable Providences, Relating to Witchcrafts and Possessions.*

Martha Goodwin was the eldest daughter of John Goodwin, a mason and a "sober and pious man" originally from Charlestown, and his wife, the former Martha Lothrop, a granddaughter of the eminent Puritan minister John Lothrop. Goodwin, a god-fearing man, had no way of knowing that his move from Charlestown to Boston would expose his family in one of the town's most sensational witchcraft cases. When his daughter Martha faced the laundress about the missing linens, she triggered a chain of events that affected her and three of her siblings, John Jr., Mercy, and Benjamin. Few details survive about Martha's subsequent encounter with the laundress's mother, Mary Glover, but the elderly Irishwoman's unseemly reputation preceded her. Considered an "ignorant and scandalous old woman" in the neighborhood, Mary had made even her late husband suspicious. According to Cotton Mather, Mary's "miserable husband before he died, had sometimes complained of her, that she was undoubtedly a witch" and that after his death "she would quickly arrive unto the punishments due to such an one." If Glover really said that, it was a prescient observation.

Little is known of Mary's origins. According to one source she and her husband had "in the time of Cromwell" been "sold to the Barbados," presumably as servants, and in due course made their way from the Caribbean to Boston. By 1688, Mary Glover was considered a disreputable woman in Boston, and her words to Martha Goodwin that summer had a devastating effect. Before long Martha and three of her siblings were experiencing exquisite torments. Dr. Thomas Oakes was called to examine them. He was amazed to see all four affected in the same parts of their bodies at the same time, even when they were not in each other's company. Their pains traveled in unison "swift like lightning" through their necks, hands, and backs. The only cause of this malady, the doctor concluded, could be witchcraft.

The children's fits ended when they went to bed at nine or ten o'clock at night, but every morning John and Martha Goodwin faced a fresh onslaught of histrionics from their children. Described by Cotton Mather, the effects of the "possession" were extreme but varied:

> Sometimes they would be deaf, sometimes dumb, and sometimes blind, and often, all this at once . . . their tongues would be drawn down their throats; another while they would be pulled out upon their chins, to a prodigious length. They would have their mouths opened unto such a wideness, that their jaws went out of joint; and anon they would clap together again with a force like that of a strong spring-lock. The same would happen to their shoulder-blades, and their elbows, and hand-wrists, and several of their joints.

On top of this, the children were seen stretching backwards in such extreme positions that it was "feared the very skin of their bellies would have cracked." They shrieked that they were being cut by knives, their neck bones seemed to disappear and then become rigid, and their heads appeared to almost twist all the way around. The children remained in this deplorable state for several weeks, and, as a result, a group of local ministers decided to hold a daylong prayer vigil at the Goodwins' house. The prayers appeared to result in at least one victory: the youngest child, Benjamin, was released from the clutches of possession.

In the meantime, authorities initiated an inquiry in the neighborhood. On John Goodwin's advice they focused their attentions on Mary Glover. Under questioning, she gave "a wretched account of herself" and was jailed. "The hag," wrote Mather, "had not power to deny her interest in the enchantment of the children." Attempting to detect signs of witchcraft in Mary, the questioners asked if she believed God existed. Her answer was "too blasphemous and horrible" for Mather to print. When asked to recite the Lord's Prayer, she made a nonsense of it, further revealing her dubious character. At the instigation of the governor, Sir Edmond Andros, a trial under the direction of Joseph Dudley ensued. Mary frustrated the court by answering questions in her native Gaelic, even though she spoke fluent English. This stance was seen as another example of her strange manner and necessitated the presence of two interpreters in the courtroom. In time, Mary confessed her involvement in the enchantment of the Goodwin children. A search of her house turned up a cache of damning artifacts, including "several small images, or poppets, or babies, made of rags, and stuffed with goat's hair." Her method of tormenting the Goodwin children, she purportedly confessed, was by wetting a finger and "streaking" it over these objects in a voodoo-doll-like manner. A demonstration of this practice was made in the courtroom. One of the Goodwin children who was present fell into fits as Mary clutched a rag puppet. The judges asked to see this experiment again, and the same thing happened. The following night in jail, Mary was heard in a discourse with a devil, whom she chided for deserting her. According to Mather, the judges wanted to have Mary examined for any signs of mental illness to ensure that she "were not crazed in her intellectuals, and had not procured to herself by folly and madness the reputation of a witch." A group of physicians was sent to interview her one night. During the session Mary professed to be a Roman Catholic "and could recite her Pater Noster in Latin very readily." In the end, the doctors determined Mary to be sane, thus clearing the way for her conviction and death sentence.

Before her sentencing, another matter arose. A woman named Hughes came forward to say that a neighbor, Mrs. Howen, had on her deathbed six years earlier fingered Mary Glover as the cause of her illness through a bewitchment. Mrs. Howen even said she had seen Mary come down her chimney on occasion. As Mrs. Hughes prepared to testify in the current case, she reported that her young son fell ill in the same "woeful and surprising" manner as the neighboring

Cotton Mather, who recorded the story of the "possession" of Martha Goodwin and her siblings. Engraving by Peter Pelham, 1728; courtesy of the Massachusetts Historical Society.

Goodwin children. One night while Mrs. Hughes's son was lying in bed, he saw a "black thing with a blue cap" enter his room. The creature approached him and tried to "pull out his bowels." The attempt failed, and Mrs. Hughes, sensing that Mary Glover was somehow to blame for this frightening event, confronted her the following day at the jail. She asked why Mary was torturing her son. Mary supposedly replied that she was doing it because of the wrongs done to her and her daughter. She went on to say that she had been in Mrs. Hughes's house the previous night. "In what shape?" asked the bewildered visitor. "As a black thing with a blue cap," Mary replied, and "with my hand in the bed I tried to pull out the boy's bowels, but I could not." Mary offered to make the boy better if Mrs. Hughes would bring him by the jail. Mrs. Hughes complied, and after receiving good wishes from Mary the boy suffered "no more indispositions" or visits from "black things" in the night. Cotton Mather also visited Mary in jail where, he said, she "never denied the guilt of witchcraft charged upon her." He attempted to elicit more information from her about her "confederacies with the Devils." Mary was not forthcoming and, again, spoke mainly in Gaelic, a language Mather acknowledged he had "not learning enough to understand without an interpreter." Mary thanked Mather "with many good words," but after he left she took a long, slender stone and began stroking it with a wet finger in the manner she had with her poppets to torment the Goodwin children.

As Mary was brought to her execution on November 16, 1688, she declared that her death would not relieve the children. Mather reported that the three children continued in their malady after Mary's death and that their symptoms became even more extreme. Martha Goodwin reported to Mather that Mary had fellow witches in Boston, but the clergyman never disclosed their names. At this point the Goodwin children began "barking at one another like dogs, and again purr like so many cats" or said they were trapped in a "red-hot oven" one moment and severely chilled the next. John Goodwin Jr. shrieked that he was about to be roasted on an invisible spit that had been run through his mouth down his body to a foot. Other times he claimed that his head was being invisibly nailed to the floor. Mather wrote that Martha, John, and Mercy could "fly like geese." Carried "with an incredible swiftness through the air," their feet made little contact with the ground. A neighbor, Mr. Willis, confirmed this phenomenon by stating that one of the children flew twenty feet across a room in his house, landing in an infant's high chair without having touched the floor once. Throughout these horrible fits, the children cried out for help.

In the aftermath of Mary Glover's death, Cotton Mather intervened by bringing young Martha Goodwin into his house to help effect her spiritual restoration. There she passed some time behaving normally, occupied with pious and industrious activities. But by late November 1688, she returned to her former condition. "Ah, they have found me out! I thought it would be so!" Martha cried. This declaration was followed by fits and other strange ailments. Mather observed that, before falling into histrionics, Martha would begin "oddly looking up the chimney, but would not say what she saw." One of her most peculiar symptoms occurred when she coughed up and nearly choked on a "ball as big as a small egg" that emerged in the side of her windpipe. Only by stroking her neck and forcing her to drink water could the Mathers coax the mysterious ball into descending. Martha continued to be tormented with visions of Mary Glover. One day she reported that Mary's chains were upon her leg, and was able to demonstrate the identical postures "such as the chained witch had before she died." When trying to read the Bible, Martha's eyes would be "strangely twisted and blinded." She would also sometimes mount an invisible horse and amble, trot, and gallop about on her "aerial steed" while talking to a host of unseen demons. "Her fantastic journeys," wrote Mather, "were mostly performed in her chair without removing from it; but sometimes would ride from her chair, and be carried oddly on the floor, from one part of the room to another, in the postures of a riding woman." These and a multitude of other incidents consumed the young woman throughout her stay with the Mathers that winter. After many weeks, Martha's fits subsided, as did those of her younger siblings still at home. The following year, a triumphant Mather published his *Memorable Providences,* which offered a lengthy account of the possession and included a statement by the children's father, John Goodwin, corroborating the events.

To a modern mind, the possession of the Goodwin children may be viewed as a case of unbridled misbehavior and vengeful finger pointing by children at a spiteful old woman. Exacerbated by neighbors and clergymen wishing to root out evil, the situation spun out of control. Mary Glover's role in the affair is seen largely through the lens of a detractor, Cotton Mather. It is possible that this elderly woman was suffering from dementia or was, in some of her activities, drawing upon Celtic folk practices or pseudo-Catholic rituals misunderstood by her Puritan neighbors. Whatever the reasons for the "possession," its ramifications for Mary Glover were deadly. The episode had less discernible aftereffects on the Goodwin children. Martha, for example, became a church member and married five years later, in a ceremony performed by Mather. The "pitiful spectacles" of a "possession" long behind them, Mary Goodwin and her siblings gradually receded into obscurity.

Chapter 4
Devil in the Damsels:
The Afflictions of Mercy Short
and Margaret Rule
1692–1693

BOSTON IN THE EARLY 1690S was the setting for two further possessions Cotton Mather recorded in detail. The first concerned Mercy Short, a young servant who had been the victim of incredible violence only a brief time earlier. In March 1690, Mercy and her family were kidnapped from their home in the Salmon Falls settlement (near present-day Dover, New Hampshire) by Wabanaki Indians. She witnessed the brutal murder of her parents and several siblings and, taken with her surviving siblings to Canada as captives, she experienced untold horrors. Later that year, Mercy was among those captives redeemed and brought to Boston. In town, the young orphan found employment as a servant. When her mistress (probably Margaret Webb Sheafe Thacher) sent her to the jail on an errand, Mercy was asked by Sarah Good (later jailed in Boston and executed as a witch in the Salem trials) for some tobacco. Mercy replied by flinging a handful of shavings at Sarah, saying, "That's tobacco good enough for you." According to Mather, Sarah Good then "bestowed some ill words" upon the young girl, an act that sent Mercy into a spiral of fits and torments that lasted for weeks. Enduring a "world of misery," Mercy eventually recovered after a twelve-day fast.

The following winter, Mercy's fits resumed. Cotton Mather, in *A Brand Pluck'd Out of the Burning*, offered a firsthand account of Mercy's possession: she soon began seeing a devil in the shape of a short, tawny-colored man with a high-crowned hat, straight hair, and a cloven foot. Frequently she saw other specters at the same time. On several occasions, this supernatural band presented Mercy with a "Book of Death" that featured red lettering and told of their service to Satan. The specters endeavored to have her sign it, so that she, too, could become a vassal of the Devil. Even touching it, the specters said, would cure her of her torments. Mercy refused these and other "allurements," and so they heightened her miseries: stabbing her incessantly with invisible pins and pouring poisonous liquor down her throat that bloated her in the manner of ratsbane. The most excruciating torture, however, was when the spirits attempted to burn her. During these "fiery trials," Mercy claimed that the specters whipped her with invisible flames in torture sessions that lasted up to a quarter of an hour—and once even drove a hot iron down her throat. Mather claimed that blisters sometimes appeared on her skin during these episodes. "The agonies of one roasting a faggot at the stake were not more exquisite than what she underwent," he wrote, "in the scalds which those hell-hounds gave unto her." Mather and other witnesses believed that Mercy was genuinely experiencing all these nightmarish tortures and a host of others.

Mercy's afflictions continued unabated through the winter. In time, the specters told her of the whereabouts of a second "Book of Death," information she considered grave enough to communicate to the governor, Sir William Phips, when he paid her a call. The book, Mercy said, was located in the garret of a prominent neighbor's house. A few days later a servant was sent to look for the book, but was instead spooked by a big black cat that had never been seen in the house before. When the cat jumped over the servant, Mather wrote, it "threw him into such a fright and sweat, that altho' he were one otherwise of courage enough, he desisted at that time from looking any further."

Over several months neighbors prayed for Mercy's deliverance from her troubles. In the last stages of her affliction, the demons blinded her, but she soon recovered her sight and regained a measure of peace.

Her possession, according to modern-day scholars, may have been a hysterical reaction to the trauma of her captivity. In 1694 she was well enough to marry Joseph Marshall of Nantucket (though she was later found guilty of adultery and excommunicated). Today, Mercy's gravestone at the Copps Hill Burying Ground in the North End stands as the sole remaining artifact associated with one of Boston's most startling cases of possession.

ABOUT SIX MONTHS AFTER Mercy Short's recovery, another young Boston woman, Margaret Rule, experienced remarkably similar afflictions. Again Cotton Mather was witness to the woman's turmoils. Margaret, who lived with her parents in the North End, fell into a fit in the midst of a public assembly in September 1693. She was carried home, and suspicions soon fell on one of her neighbors for giving rise to this preternatural "mischief." Mather called this neighbor a "miserable woman" who had formerly been imprisoned on suspicion of witchcraft and who had "frequently cured very painful hurts by muttering over them certain charms."

Margaret's afflictions began the day after an encounter with her disreputable neighbor, who, in Mather's words, "very bitterly treated her." She was soon being tormented by eight specters, some of whom she recognized. Margaret later told Mather the names of the specters she knew; he declined to name them in his manuscript but acknowledged that they were the "sort of wretches who for these many years have gone under as violent presumptions of witchcraft, as perhaps any creatures yet living upon Earth." Like Mercy Short, Margaret claimed that her diabolical visitors brought her a book, which they asked her to sign in order to become a servant of the Devil. Margaret, like Mercy, refused, and for six weeks she was confined to bed while complaining that she was being pricked by invisible pins and experiencing other tortures.

One night in the midst of her malady, Margaret foretold the drowning death of a neighbor. And a short time later the young man did indeed drown in Boston Harbor as he attempted to swim from an anchored ship to the shore. The drowning, Mather alleged, took place only a minute or two after Margaret made her nocturnal prediction.

Gravestone of Mercy Short (later "Marcy Marshall"), who died in 1712, at Copps Hill Burying Ground in Boston's North End.

And Samuel Aves and four other townspeople—who later signed depositions as witnesses—testified to another astounding symptom of Margaret's possession, claiming they saw her levitate in midair. According to Aves, Margaret was lifted toward the ceiling of her chamber in spite of efforts to hold her down:

> *I do testify that I have seen Margaret Rule in her afflictions from the Invisible World, lifted up from her bed, wholly by an invisible force, a great way towards the top of the room where she lay; in her being so lifted, she had no assistance from any use of her own arms or hands, or any other part of her body, not so much as her heels touching her bed, or resting on any support whatsoever. And I have seen her thus lifted, when not only a strong person hath thrown his whole weight across her to pull her down; but several other persons have endeavored, with all their might, to hinder her from being so raised up, which I suppose that several others will testify as well as myself, when called unto it.*

In addition to the evil specters that visited her, Margaret soon encountered a "White Spirit," who, wearing "shining and glorious garments," stood at her bedside and implored her to maintain her faith in God. The White Spirit visited her periodically and, after five weeks, predicted that she would soon be delivered from her afflictions through the pastoral care of Cotton Mather. In a short time, Margaret did return to normality.

Mather, a controversial man in the best of times, did not escape the Margaret Rule episode unscathed. One of his harshest critics was Bostonian Robert Calef, who believed that the recent Salem witchcraft trials, in which Mather had so actively participated, were an abomination. Claiming that Mather was trying to agitate another such crisis in Boston, he took fire at the minister, making the sensational claim that in front of witnesses Mather rubbed Margaret Rule's stomach as she lay in bed with her breasts exposed. This accusation and others led to a heated correspondence between the two men. For Margaret Rule, like Mercy Short, the experience does not appear to have had lasting effects. Over the course of her life, Margaret married three times. Widowed by Joseph Page and Thomas Johnson, Margaret married Benjamin Snelling in 1708 and had four children. Long after her afflictions subsided, Margaret remained a parishioner of Cotton Mather at the Second Church of Boston.

Chapter 5

An Encounter with Satan:
The Diabolical Possession
of Martha Robinson
1741

DURING A BRIEF SOJOURN in Boston in January 1741, Captain
Joseph Pitkin, a prosperous merchant from East Hartford, learned
that a local woman was said to be possessed by the Devil. Part of the
story, as Pitkin heard it, was that a visiting clergyman had attempted
to perform an exorcism on her. Pitkin could not have envisioned that
only two months later, on a return business trip to Boston, he would
encounter the possessed woman, Martha Robinson, and record for
posterity one of the last and most complete accounts of a "diabolical
possession" in colonial New England.

During his Boston visits, Pitkin, a devout member of the New Light
movement, a group of evangelical Calvinists, rejoiced in the atmos-
phere of a town then experiencing religious revivalism. In March
1741, he returned to Boston and, finding himself "entertained in public worship," later wrote in his diary that "I found it profitable to my
soul to be there." The exact purpose of his business in town is not
known, but it was important enough to involve Governor Jonathan
Belcher. Word of the stranger's presence eventually got back to
Martha Robinson. On a Friday afternoon as he concluded his business
and prepared to return to Hartford, Pitkin was interrupted by the
wife of innkeeper Captain Josiah Shelton. Her young daughter, she
explained, had just returned from a neighbor's house, a young woman
wanted to meet him. Mrs. Shelton said that the woman had been
"under great trouble in her mind and had strange kind of fits." At this

point, Pitkin still did not know that the person in question was the supposedly possessed woman of whom he had heard so much in January. He told Mrs. Shelton that he knew nothing of the woman or her case and that he was just about to begin his homeward journey. But in spite of his reservations, Pitkin, "not knowing what might be the design of providence," agreed to meet the young woman if Mrs. Shelton would accompany him. The two crossed over to the neighbor's house and were shown upstairs into a chamber where two or three women were sitting. Moments later Martha Robinson joined them.

Appearing partly out of breath and somewhat surprised to see Pitkin, Martha invited her visitor to sit down and said she was glad to meet him. Then in her early twenties, Martha was the daughter of Samuel and Mary Robinson, parishioners of the Old South Church. Before long, Pitkin asked Martha why she had sent for him, a complete stranger. Martha said she had heard that a visitor, meaning Pitkin, had been noticed at a service on the Sabbath and that it was supposed he was a clergyman. He must be a good man, Martha concluded, because he had later been received by Governor Belcher, whom she contended "the Devil is enraged more against . . . than anybody in the world, because he is one that is zealous in promoting religion." She subsequently had seen Pitkin entering Captain Shelton's inn and passing in the streets. Surmising that he was "one of the precious servants of Christ," she sought to meet him. Now Martha warned Pitkin that diabolical forces were stirring within her: "The Devil is disturbed at your coming, he knows you are a good man and hates all such and he will roar in me anon." When Pitkin asked what she meant, Martha replied that for fifteen weeks the Devil had been speaking from within her. She related how her religious convictions had fluctuated over the years; however, the preceding fall, when the famous itinerant minister George Whitefield had come to town, her desire for salvation had been stimulated: "I begged heartily of God that if ever he designed my conversion this might be the time; and this man might be the instrument by which I might be converted." Before she even heard Whitefield, Martha detected a change in her soul, a feeling that was accentuated when she attended one of Whitefield's sermons. "After exercise was over," Martha continued, "[I] got as near him as I could and let him know I was pierced by the word: he turned to me and said he prayed God to set home my conviction to saving conversion; and said little more to me." The following month, she became a member of the Old South Church.

The young woman continued to recount her history to Pitkin. Her conversion, it seemed, only exacerbated her struggles. She explained to Pitkin that some time later, when Gilbert Tennent, a thirty-eight-year-old evangelical Presbyterian from New Jersey, came to preach in Boston, her life took a dramatic turn. Having attended one of Tennent's sermons with friends, Martha asked to meet with the visiting clergyman. Leaving a small gathering of other ministers, Tennent led Martha and her friends into another room and asked if she would let her friends hear what she had to say. Martha consented but, inexplicably, within seconds she was consumed by her first diabolical upwelling: "The Devil filled me with such rage and spite against [Tennent] that I could have torn him to pieces and I should have torn his clothes off if my friends had not held me." Tennent immediately left the room to find the other ministers. He told them that "one possessed with the Devil" was present and asked them to join in prayers for the young woman. As the clergymen gathered to pray for her, Martha stated that she had a "dismal night of it," was uncontrollably tossed about the room, and was "filled with rage and spite against all good people." Since that time, Martha told Pitkin, the Devil had spoken in her, blasphemed in unpardonable ways, committed unclean talk, and sung "all manner of foolish songs."

While relaying these events to Pitkin, Martha repeated several times that the Devil was disturbed at his presence. Before long, she issued "a loud shriek, as loud as her voice would carry it," which greatly startled her visitor. Pitkin knew that Martha had noticed his reaction, and a few moments later she said, "Pray, Sir, don't be surprised. The Devil endeavors to scare everybody from me that is good." Asked if she had been offended by anything he had said, Martha answered, "Not at all but the Devil can't stand it." Her facial expression changed a moment later "into the most dismal form of rage and disdain." The Devil "with her tongue broke forth in the most hideous outcry, contradicting, denying, and mocking, as if he would spit in my face." The sudden change in Martha's countenance genuinely shocked Pitkin, who later wrote that the incident caused him to feel as if the blood in his veins had stopped for a moment.

Once he gathered himself, Pitkin felt empowered with divine strength "raised to a double degree of courage" and began to offer Martha Biblical verse. He asked if she could hear him, even when the Devil was using her tongue. She replied that she could and that his message was

"The Devil is disturbed at your coming . . . and he will roar in me anon," cried
Martha Robinson. A woodcut from The Prodigal Daughter.
Courtesy of the Massachusetts Historical Society.

reviving to her soul, but the Devil was angered and would roar louder yet. Before long, she rose up with a fist doubled as if to strike Pitkin in the face. He continued to press Martha in reciting scripture in order to refute the Devil's "falsehoods and to quench his fiery darts." The young woman then began sharply fluctuating between speaking on behalf of the Devil and recovering herself and praising God.

Eventually, Martha's mother asked Pitkin to pray with her daughter. Pitkin later wrote that the Devil responded through Martha, saying he would not let her "ask anybody to pray with her." The women present told Pitkin that sometime earlier the ministers of Boston had conducted a day of fasting and prayer on Martha's behalf, but the effort had been ineffectual and "Satan afterwards made a great outcry in prayer time." Rising to the opportunity to battle with Satan, Pitkin invited Martha to ask him to pray with her, a proposition that sent the Devil into mocking and hissing at him. Pitkin refused to back down and kept trying to persuade Martha to ask him to pray, offering that "the Devil would not always have such power over her."

Finally, Martha acceded, saying, "Sir, I should be heartily glad if you could pray with me." Pitkin then asked Martha if she could keep herself from making noises during the prayer. She knelt by the side of a bed and the two prayed. Martha was silent for a short time, but before long she barked in a devilish voice, "Hold your tongue! Hold your tongue!" In spite of the interruption, Pitkin continued praying. Martha shortly recovered herself and he heard her "softly say Amen." After a long diabolical outcry, a teary-eyed Martha composed herself once more.

At last, Pitkin decided to excuse himself to get ready for his return to Hartford. As he left the Robinson house, Pitkin decided instead to stay another night at Captain Shelton's inn. Learning that he would be staying longer, the Robinsons asked him to visit Martha once more. He returned, along with Colonel Timothy Dwight, another traveler staying at the inn. An enthusiastic Martha greeted Pitkin— "She was exceeding glad to see me"—and before long, a crowd of friends and neighbors gathered around them. Now, however, it was Colonel Dwight who became the focus of what appeared to be the

Devil's wrath. When he mentioned the name of God, Martha's tongue snapped, "There is no God." As earlier in the day, Martha made disdainful expressions, clenched her fists, made blasphemous outbursts, and went into diabolical histrionics. After a time, she began weeping and said, "The Devil reproaches me that I have been so impudent." Pitkin asked Colonel Dwight to say a prayer, an action that quickly elicited great noises in Martha. Staying until about nine o'clock, the men listened to Martha as she launched into long, uninterrupted soliloquies. As they started to leave, Martha recovered herself and began "blessing God."

Colonel Dwight later told Pitkin that the incident astounded him: "He was never so surprised in all the days of life, nor never met with anything like it." During their call, Martha told the men of an omen that occurred the previous night presaging their visit. Martha and her aunt had heard a noise like the bleating of a goat emanating from Captain Shelton's inn. All of a sudden, the troubling sound was swept away by a "violent gust of wind as if it would have taken the top of the house off." This extraordinary incident was witnessed by Martha's aunt, Mrs. Sylvie.

The following day as he returned home to Hartford, Pitkin could not help but ponder Martha's condition: "[It] filled up my meditation great part of the way. I pitied her case as under great affliction by the power the Devil seemed to have over her tongue." It was not his final encounter with Martha. Two years later, once again in Boston on business, Pitkin decided to revisit her. Returning to the Robinsons' house, Pitkin was greeted warmly by a more humble Martha: "She was glad to see me and behaved very decently." She "acknowledged her obligation" to Pitkin for the kindness he had shown her on their last visit, and said that "God had gradually delivered her from that distress." Upon further questioning, she explained that some of her words had come from her soul but "sometimes I was almost all Devil." Asked if she could be provoked to speak such words now, Martha answered in the negative: "No, if I might have the world for it." Pitkin expressed his desire that all who read his narrative about Martha Robinson devote their "souls and tongues to the service and glory of God."

This was not the last evidence of Martha's religious fervor. In 1744 George Whitefield returned to preach in Boston. Colonel John Phillips noted in his diary that many at Whitefield's New North Church sermon "cried out, Robinson's daughter and others." Two years later Martha married Michael Mallet of Charlestown and shortly thereafter receded, as one author put it, "into the anonymity of normality," having survived what she and many others believed was a satanic possession.

Part Two

Rogues' Gallery: Scoundrels, Impostors, and Schemers

TELLING TALL TALES, offering make-believe backgrounds, and peddling counterfeit business deals, some of colonial New England's most infamous confidence men (and women) operated in and around Boston. Several of the schemers created identities from whole cloth: Thomas Rumsey pretended he was the son of an English baronet; Dr. Seth Hudson posed as an affluent traveling Dutchman; and Robert Palmer played the heir to a vast fortune. John Pierpont of Roxbury traveled to England in a vain attempt to secure favors from titled kinsmen and was said to have behaved as a "knavish villain" and perhaps even committed highway robbery. Some scoundrels invented positions of trust to fool their victims. Dick Swayn, Eleazer Kingsbury, and Samuel May all masqueraded as evangelical ministers in Boston in order to swindle (or, in May's case, seduce) members of their flocks. Others perpetrated notorious frauds. Miriam Fitch, for example, tantalized three Bostonians with the false prospect of finding a horde of gold. Some villains portrayed themselves as being down on their luck. John Hill, a man who claimed his tongue had been cut out by the Turks, was a rambling vagabond looking for handouts from sympathetic passersby. "No Mouth'd Moll" begged her way to town all the way from Philadelphia and by the time of her arrest was said to possess "pockets full of money." In colonial Boston, impostors seemed constricted less by the law than by the limits of their imagination.

ENGLISHMAN THOMAS RUMSEY'S imposture as "Sir Thomas Hale" was the earliest major deception of its kind in town, but the most important con man in colonial America was a native son, Tom Bell. Born in Boston in 1713 to parents of middling stature, Bell attended the Boston Latin School and in due course was accepted at Harvard. His educational career was cut short by repeated incidents of thievery; a "scandalous neglect" of his studies and "notorious, complicated lying" were two of the final factors leading to his expulsion from the college. Bell's career as an impostor began early, extended through much of his adult life, and spread throughout the colonies. A dazzling actor, he was able to change his identity on a moment's notice and was particularly adept in using aliases. He sometimes selected regionally appropriate names from the native gentry where he happened to be traveling. In Virginia, for example, he might take the name of Fairfax; in New York, Livingston; or in the Carolinas, Middleton. His intellectual capacities, taste for fine apparel, and air of refinement in speech and manner all added luster to his performances and enabled him to portray an array of high-born characters with remarkable authenticity. Time and again, Bell eluded authorities and escaped punishment. On the occasions he was caught, he used his talents as a brilliant escape artist and fled.

Bell's most famous caper occurred in 1739 in Barbados, where he presented himself to the local society as Gilbert Burnet Jr., son of the late governor of Massachusetts, and came bearing a Burnet coat of arms painstakingly copied from a map of Boston. While attending a Jewish wedding on the island, Bell feigned a headache and was taken to a place to rest by his host, Mr. Lopus (or Lopez). Later, after members of the Lopus family realized their guest was a thief, they confronted, stripped, and beat "Burnet." That a respectable Gentile of high standing should be attacked by Jews infuriated local residents and sparked what has been described as the first known anti-Semitic riot in the Americas. During the melee, the synagogue in Speightstown was burned and the Jewish population driven out of town. The incident was reported in newspapers in America. The publicity helped to blow Bell's cover, and he was quickly fingered as an impostor. Sentenced to be branded with a capital "R," possibly for "Robber" or "Rogue," on each cheek, Bell was granted clemency by a lenient governor and left Barbados unscathed.

Bell's intrigues continued for years to come and were regularly chronicled in newspapers throughout the colonies. In 1743 he escaped from the prison in Philadelphia, an act that elicited the following description:

> He is a slim fellow, of thin visage and pale complexion: had on when he broke prison, a dark blue cloth coat, black silk jacket, black cloth breeches, black silk stockings, new pumps, with black steel buckles; and 'tis supposed he'll wear a new castor hat or velvet jockey-cap and grey wig; he stole a great coat of lightish brown color, with brass buttons. . . . Among his other tricks and villainies he is very dexterous in picking locks, having obtain'd his liberty from confinement by this means.

On several occasions, Bell promised to reform his ways and write a sensational memoir, but the publication (for which he sold advance subscriptions) never materialized. In the end, Tom Bell appears to have finally met justice. In 1771, after being found guilty of various acts of piracy in the Caribbean, "Thomas Bell," the chief mate of a Jamaican sloop, was hanged at Kingston. Boston's most famous Colonial-era criminal export died, by one account a repentant man, far from his hometown.

John Hill, meanwhile, concocted a cunning charity scheme that preyed on people's sympathies. Presenting himself as the victim of brutal treatment while he was a prisoner overseas, Hill preyed upon the charitably disposed people of Boston and surrounding communities. Encountering "such persons as he had any prospect of receiving money from," a silent Hill would hand them a piece of parchment telling a tale of his gruesome torture and other "moving circumstances." The paper claimed that he had for seven years been held a prisoner. On attempting to escape from his Turkish captors, he had received "barbarous treatment," including having his arms burnt with hot irons and, most horrifically, his tongue cut out. Having aroused the sympathy of his victims by this woeful account, Hill would then gratefully accept their money and move on. In his scheme, Hill was accompanied by a woman who claimed to be his wife—Rachel Hill, alias Fig. Their luck ran out in Abington, Massachusetts, where he and Rachel arrived in early April 1733. As Hill began his routine for the townspeople there, a local minister arrived on the scene and, sensing a rogue, began questioning Hill "as to the truth of the facts related in his parchment." Then, without any warning, the minister jabbed his finger into Hill's mouth. This obliged the beggar "to produce his tongue or be choked, it being lodged clear out of sight." With Hill's undamaged tongue now revealed, the charity scheme collapsed. The minister promptly notified Habijah Savage, a justice in Boston, who apprehended Hill. On questioning the scoundrel, Savage found that Hill had tongue enough "to confess the whole mystery," thereby concluding one of Boston's strangest cases of imposture.

Another peripatetic swindler was Mary Kemp. Arriving in Boston from Philadelphia in 1736, Mary earned the nickname of "No Mouth'd Moll." Having by some accounts pockets lined with money and a taste for gold jewelry, Mary was the subject of a warning published in the November 29, 1736, issue of the *Boston Evening Post:*

> *A woman called Mary Kemp, but commonly known by the name of No Mouth'd Moll: she formerly came from Philadelphia, resided in this town some time since, and was sent to bridewell as a vagabond, but being discharged and forced out of town, she has lately been at Marlborough and the adjacent towns begging as an indigent and weakly person, by which she has got a great deal of money, (some say pockets full) and has lately bought her a gold necklace and two gold rings. (Very necessary and decent ornaments for a beggar). She was in Charlestown last week, and in this town a few days since; but a warrant being out against her, 'tis thought she is fled to the country, and is not imposing upon the credulity of honest and charitable people, to prevent which this account is now published.*

Another rogue who inspired a generation of American impostors visited Boston a few years later. Known variously as the "King of the Beggars" and the "King of the Gypsies," Bampfylde Moore Carew was one of England's greatest scoundrels. He left an autobiography recounting his extraordinary career as a vagabond, dog thief, and adventurer. He was so famous in his native land that in the nineteenth century William Makepeace Thackeray presented the character of Becky Sharp in his classic novel *Vanity Fair* to be "as restless as Ulysses or Bampfylde Moore Carew." Bampfylde did not slip easily from American memory either. In 1818, John Adams wrote to Thomas Jefferson in reference to the possibility of a Jesuit revival with the comment: "Shall we not have swarms of them here, in as many shapes and disguises as ever a king of the gypsies, Bampfylde-Moore Carew himself, assumed?"

Disguises were, in fact, one of Bampfylde's specialties. He liked to pretend he was a shipwrecked sailor looking for charity. On other occasions he pretended to be "a lunatic called 'Mad Tom,' a seaman, a zealous clergyman, a rat catcher, and even an old woman." Bampfylde was twice convicted in England and twice transported to Maryland as a convict. In his autobiography, written in the third person, he describes passing through Boston, a town he found picturesque:

> Mr. Carew was surprised at the grandeur of it; and seeing a green hill, at the end of the great street, much like Glastonbury Torr, he goes up it, and had a most beautiful prospect of the city from the top of it, where was placed the mast of a ship, with pullies to draw up a lighted barrel of tar, to alarm the country, in case of an invasion.

After enjoying this view, Bampfylde descended Beacon Hill and was recognized by some English soldiers. They "persuaded him to go along with them to one Mother Passmore's, a house of rendezvous, where they were very merry together." After a night of merriment, Bampfylde departed Boston without perpetrating any crimes during his brief visit. In a narrow brush with a criminal mastermind, the town was, for once, spared a major scam.

Money was not the only motivation in cases of imposture. In the summer of 1771, two young Bostonians, Lendall Pitts and John Gray, came to blows outside a barbershop in the center of town. John, who received two scalp wounds in the clash, later sued Lendall, the son of a wealthy family, for the steep sum of £300. The cause of the quarrel was a scandalous episode in which John, or possibly someone under his direction, masqueraded as a young woman and publicly solicited the attentions of Lendall and another man. The deception was so convincing that one witness, William Molineaux Jr., son of the Boston

Lendall Pitts, who attacked John Gray for deceitfully dressing as a woman.
Engraving by an unidentified artist from Tea Leaves *by Francis S. Drake, 1884.*
Courtesy of the Massachusetts Historical Society.

patriot of the same name, observed the hoodwinked men "gallanting" the enticing girl. "I saw him dressed in women's clothes," offered Molineaux. "He had the outward appearance of a woman, a gown and women's clothes." Having been openly "very loving" to the girl, Lendall became incandescent with rage when it was revealed that the object of his attentions was really a man. After attacking an unrepentant John, Lendall was defended by John Adams in two ensuing trials. An ardent patriot, Lendall Pitts later played a significant role in the Boston Tea Party in December 1773.

It is possible that the "gallanting" took place near the prominence called "Mount Whoredom" (a location otherwise known as Mount Vernon on Beacon Hill), a spot where men may have been accustomed to picking up unfamiliar women. Deeply embarrassed that his misguided attentions had been lavished on a man in front of so many townspeople, Lendall was consumed with fury toward John Gray.

The impostors who visited or lived in Boston were a colorful lot. Whether they pretended to be well-to-do, down on their luck, or pious preachers, they were all inventive, calculating, and sometimes even ingenious. In most cases, however, even the most carefully executed schemes did not fool the people of Boston for long.

Chapter 6
Abominable Villainy:
The Cruel Deception of Rebecca Rawson
1679

MARRYING THE SCION of a wealthy English family in the summer of 1679, twenty-three-year-old Rebecca Rawson could not have imagined what fate had in store for her. The marriage she had just undertaken was a sham, her husband an impostor, and her life would reach its tragic conclusion far from home. But, not knowing any of these things, Rebecca was likely filled with joy and high expectations as she accompanied her husband, Thomas Hailes, to England. There Thomas's scheme was revealed. He had lured Rebecca into marriage using false charms and the pretense of being "highly bred." Not only had he hoodwinked Rebecca, but he had also deceived several important men in the colony, including mint master John Hull and merchant Theodore Atkinson. Having now returned to England, Thomas, whose true name was Thomas Rumsey, promptly decamped with Rebecca's possessions (and presumably her marriage portion from Edward Rawson) and returned to his real wife in Canterbury. According to lore, this revelation was neither the last nor the greatest misfortune that would befall the young lady from Boston.

When Thomas Rumsey arrived in Boston in 1678, he found work as a bookkeeper to Theodore Atkinson, a hatter and feltmaker. Atkinson, then in his mid-sixties, had lived in Boston since 1634 and was a well-known and respected member of the community. Thomas gave the Atkinsons some account of his background. His father had been a prosperous yeoman, with a substantial estate of about £400 a year, who died when Thomas was a boy. This income would come to him, he explained, after his stepmother's death. Having passed muster as a pious and earnest young man, Thomas was accepted into the Atkinson home and began what was intended to be a one-year term of managing accounts and collecting debts on the hatter's behalf.

About a month into his employment, however, Thomas's story began to change. According to Atkinson, the young man alluded to being "one that had been highly bred, but he would not say further what he was." Four more months passed before Thomas divulged his secret: his late father was a baronet and his stepmother a lady. "So he lived and carried himself," recalled the hatter, that "he was highly bred." Atkinson believed the story and made a decision he would come to regret. He consented to suspending the young gentleman's employment and assuming his expenses. Thomas promised he would satisfy his former employer for all charges and expenses he had incurred to date. Atkinson soon noticed a further change in his "high born" lodger: Thomas's "religion did seem to wear away."

Within a year of arriving in Boston, Thomas added further details to his remarkable story. His name, he revealed, was actually Hailes and he had been "a great traveler in the Straights for about two-and-twenty months." His mother (formerly his "stepmother") was called Lady Hailes and she "paid him his money by bills of exchange from time to time." Lady Hailes, he said, had an income of £300 a year of her own that she had brought to her marriage. On top of this, Thomas now put his late father's income at £800 per annum, part of a "vast estate" that he hesitated to even mention to Atkinson or others "lest he should be laughed at and not be believed." Upon his mother's death this fortune would devolve to him. Having laid out the essential points of a new, affluent background, Thomas Rumsey, or Thomas Hailes (or Hale), as he now preferred to be called, set his sights on more lucrative targets in town.

One of Thomas's most important calls during his sojourn in the Bay Colony was to John Hull, the mint master and treasurer. Seeking credit, Thomas approached Hull and obtained a £250 advance in silver based upon bills to be drawn upon a lady he called "Sarah,

Portraits of Rebecca Rawson, who was deceived by Thomas Rumsey, and her father, Edward Rawson (facing page). Portraits by an unknown artist, 1670; courtesy of the New England Historic Genealogical Society.

Viscountess Croyden." Hull later concluded that this noblewoman was a myth invented to advance Thomas's scheme. The episode reveals the young man's ability to make even wise and powerful men believe the stories of his prodigious wealth and titled associations.

Deceiving the mint master was not Thomas's ultimate ambition. In the person of Rebecca Rawson, the unmarried daughter of the colony's secretary, he found an opportunity to advance his imposture to greater heights. Born in 1656, Rebecca was at this time, according to Rawson family lore, "one of the most beautiful, polite and accomplished young ladies in Boston." With or without these attributes, she was, given her status in Boston society, eminently marriageable. A three-quarter-length portrait painted in 1670 confirms that she was, almost a decade before her marriage, an elegant, if not beautiful, young lady. Richly attired, the teenaged Rebecca wears a dark dress with lace-edged puffed sleeves and a hood that almost completely

obscures her reddish brown hair. A string of beads adorning her neck, she holds a card in her right hand and, with a slightly tilted head, looks out toward the observer with a plaintive expression. The ninth child and sixth daughter of Edward Rawson and his wife, Rachel Perne, Rebecca grew up in a privileged Puritan household. Edward Rawson, the son of a "highly respectable family," came from Dorsetshire to the Massachusetts Bay in the late 1630s, settling initially in Newbury. In time, be became a deputy to the General Court from Newbury and in 1650 was elected to his most recognizable office, secretary of the colony, a post he held for thirty-six years. During his gradual ascension to the leadership circle of the colony, Rawson gained a reputation as a shrewd businessman and acquired a substantial fortune. In Boston, he settled on a thoroughfare that became known as Rawson's Lane, later renamed Bromfield Street.

While the circumstances of Thomas and Rebecca's meeting are now lost to posterity, a version of the story entered the realm of "romantic" New England fiction through the pen of John Greenleaf Whittier. In 1849 Whittier wrote *Leaves from Margaret Smith's Journal in the Province of Massachusetts Bay, 1678–9,* a beautifully crafted work purporting to be a travelogue written by Rebecca's (supposed) young cousin, Margaret Smith. Rebecca and Sir Thomas Hale (the style and spelling preferred by Whittier) are featured as key background characters in *Leaves.* In his work, Whittier established Rebecca as "very tall and lady-looking" and possessing a "not unpleasing waywardness, as of a merry child, that which make her company sought of all." Sir Thomas Hale was presented as a more stereotypical "dashing gallant" fashionably dressed "in rich stuffs." In Whittier's book, Sir Thomas meets his future wife in May 1678 at Newbury, and quickly lets it drop that he is a nephew of Sir Mathew Hale, the famous English jurist. This particular detail of Thomas's family origin has subsequently been repeated in various accounts of the story. But in fact, no known period document makes that lofty assertion, and this notion may have originated with Whittier. Perhaps Thomas introduced himself to Edward Rawson as a member of one of the Kentish "Hales" or "Hailes" families. Charles II made Sir Robert Hales of Kent a baronet in 1660. It is possible this or another member of one of the local Hales families served as Thomas's inspiration.

More than likely, Thomas and Rebecca first met in Boston. Having peeled away the identity of Rumsey, Thomas successfully convinced Boston society that he was a wealthy, high-born gentleman. This ruse enabled him to set about courting Rebecca as an appropriate suitor. In time, Thomas not only gained Rebecca's affections but, more critically, obtained permission from Edward Rawson to marry her. The journal of the Reverend Peter Thacher implies that the marriage was arranged through discussions between the couple, the Reverend Samuel Willard, and Thacher on June 26, 1679. The wedding itself took place on July 1 in "the presence of near forty witnesses," according to Theodore Atkinson, perhaps at Secretary Rawson's house in Boston, and was conducted in the presence of one of Rebecca's kinsmen, the Reverend John Wilson Jr. of Medfield. Interestingly, both of Peter Thacher's journal entries refer to Thomas as simply "Mr. Hales," evidence that he may have stopped short of calling himself "Sir Thomas." Nonetheless, some authors have speculated that Rebecca may have been enticed into the marriage by her suitor's status. Perhaps she harbored a desire to be known as the "Lady Hale" and may have been "much elated with the idea of becoming a *lady* of distinction." The matter of courtesy titles aside, Rebecca had her father's approval for an advantageous match that would return her to England to live among near relations, including some of her siblings. Rebecca and Thomas sailed to England and, according to the family historians, Rebecca's story then took an unexpected turn:

> Being handsomely furnished they embarked for England, where, in due time, they safely arrived. Anxious to set foot on land after such a long and tedious confinement on board ship, they went immediately on shore en dishabille, *leaving their trunks on board vessel; passing the first night at an inn, and the next at the house of one of her relatives. Early next morning he rose, took the keys, telling her he would go down to the vessel and have the trunks sent up in time for her to dress before dinner. The trunks came, and she waited patiently for him to come with the keys until two o'clock in the afternoon. When, upon breaking open the trunks, to her inexpressible surprise, she found herself completely stripped of everything. He had taken all articles of value out of the trunks, refilling them with worthless trash and combustible matter.*

After this alarming discovery, Rebecca visited the inn where she and Thomas had spent their first night onshore. Here she learned that her husband, "Sir Thomas Hale," was really Thomas Rumsey and that he had departed for his wife in Canterbury. By all accounts, Rebecca never saw Thomas again, and he appears to have successfully escaped apprehension or punishment for his crimes. Adding to the drama of the story, legend states that Rebecca was carrying a child by Rumsey. In this desolate position, she purportedly chose to remain in England for the next thirteen years. The Rawson family histories suggest that she "learned many curious arts, such as painting on glass" and was thus able to eke out "a genteel subsistence" for herself and the child.

Word of Rebecca's misfortunes was carried back to Boston quickly. Theodore Atkinson was deposed and stated that Thomas Rumsey's "unheard of stories" possessed "not the least shadow of truth." Thomas used his deceptions "as a delusion to put a cheat on Mr. Edward Rawson" and by "abominable villainy," Atkinson charged, Thomas deceived Rawson of his daughter. Rumors about the scandal must have spread like wildfire through town.

After thirteen years of artistic pursuits in England, Rebecca, according to the Rawson historians, decided to return to Boston, a determination that led to the tragic epilogue of her death. By this time her father was nearing the end of his life. The shock of her ill-starred marriage to a scoundrel had presumably diffused. Rebecca is said to have left her child in the custody of a sister living in England, who was married to "an opulent gentleman." Rebecca then embarked for Boston on a vessel owned by one of her uncles bound initially for Port Royal, Jamaica. If accounts are correct, this journey was her last. Port Royal, a town on the south coast of Jamaica, had the unseemly reputation of a "haven for buccaneers." Rebecca apparently arrived there in early June 1692, and was delayed for a few days before undertaking passage to Boston. What might have been an innocuous delay turned deadly shortly before noon on June 7, 1692, when an earthquake hit the island. The effects were particularly devastating in Port Royal, a town built entirely on sand at the end of a lengthy spit. As the quake rumbled, the town's sandy foundation turned into something resembling quicksand. Scores of people, buildings, and animals were consumed by the liquefied sand. A witness recorded the horror:

> *The sand in the street rose like the waves of the sea, lifting up all persons that stood upon it, and immediately dropping down into pits; and at the same instant a flood of water rushed in, throwing down all who were in its way; some were seen catching hold of beams and rafters of houses, others were found in the sand that appeared when the water was drained away, with their legs and arms out.*

In the ensuing mayhem two-thirds of Port Royal slipped into the sea and more than two thousand people were killed. A number of New Englanders died in the disaster and only a few miraculously survived by clinging to floating objects until rescued by passing vessels. Word of the earthquake reached Boston by August 1692; Lawrence Hammond noted in his journal the arrival of John Balston from Jamaica with news that Port Royal had been "overflowed by the sea in the space of 2 or 3 minutes" and that the town was now submerged at least four or five fathoms beneath the surface. The circumstances of Rebecca's death in Port Royal are not documented, but Rawson family records state that she perished in a tidal wave spawned by the quake. A young lady born to privilege, Rebecca Rawson was dealt the unhappy blow of marrying colonial Boston's most clever confidence man; added to that misfortune, she was apparently killed in frightful circumstances in a foreign port and never reunited with her family in Boston.

Chapter 7
Wolves in Sheep's Clothing:
A Trio of Impostors Disguised as Ministers
1699

HAVING GATHERED SEVERAL cautionary tales of mischief perpetrated by "false teachers of the Gospel" in Boston, the Reverend
Cotton Mather in 1700 published *A Warning to the Flocks Against Wolves
in Sheeps Cloathing*. Recalling a passage from the Sermon on the Mount,
Mather wished to warn the people of Boston of false prophets who
appeared godly but were really "ravening wolves." Twelve local clergymen endorsed Mather's publication, including the author's father,
Increase Mather. In a show of unity, the ministers stood together
against a series of blasphemous impersonations that had plagued the
town. In his *Warning*, Cotton Mather recounted the exploits of several
"wolves," three of whom—Dick Swayn, Eleazer Kingsbury, and
Samuel May—posed as ministers in and around Boston during a two-
year period at the close of the seventeenth century. The three impostors were men of humble backgrounds with little formal education:
the dismissed servant of a Boston mariner, a tailor's apprentice from
Wrentham, and a brick maker from England. During their cons, two
of the men abandoned their wives and one of the two consorted with
a woman who masqueraded as his wife. In the end, all three "wolves"
eluded capture and punishment in Boston. The men either changed
their identities or settled into quieter lives, and their subsequent
histories are unrecorded.

The first "wolf" was Dick Swayn, a young man employed by a Boston
mariner. After committing "a thousand rogueries," he was released

early from his service by the mariner's widow. According to Mather, Dick's misbehavior had been the prelude to a criminal career sufficient to "fill a volume." In due course Dick traveled in "miserable circumstances" to Virginia and from there gradually made his way to Providence Island in the Caribbean. There he conceived and hatched his roguish plan: to pose as a preacher and win the affections and financial support of a group of followers. Mather stated that Dick put on "a mighty show of religion" and soon developed an admiring flock of worshipers, who treated him with "more than ordinary liberality." After a spell, and perhaps suspecting his identification as an impostor loomed near, Dick concluded that it was time to leave the island. Forging letters to the effect that his father in England had died and left him a fortune, he embarked on a vessel bound for New England.

Dick began itinerant preaching in southern New England and eventually returned to Boston, where in 1698 he conducted his fraudulent ministry in private houses. According to Mather, his manner of delivery was loud and exaggerated. Being "ridiculously forward in thrusting himself upon prayer," Mather alleged that Dick "would manage with a noise that might reach all the neighborhood." Dick was not without personal charms, however, and the "fire and brimstone" style Mather criticized captivated many Boston townspeople. High on his initial successes, Dick soon began courting opportunities to preach throughout town.

Dick's decision to return to the town of his earlier troubles was a poor one. Most carelessly, he failed to change his name or appearance—mistakes that soon contributed to his exposure as an impostor. By chance, the widow of his former employer came into the house where Dick was lodging. Hearing that a "worthy, able, eminent" minister by the name of Dick Swayn was in the house, the surprised widow asked to see him. To her "astonishment she found it was Dick—even that very scandalous Dick," the young man who had "played so many abominable pranks in her own family some years ago." The widow could hardly believe her eyes. Dick was unable to give her an intelligible account of how he had become a believer, much less a clergyman. Dick begged her to forgive him for his former "knaveries," but seeing that he was up to his old tricks and on a much grander scale, the widow revealed Dick's true identity. After swindling "some credulous folks of considerable sums of money," the erstwhile preacher "marched off," abandoning his Boston flock, never to be heard of again.

NOT LONG AFTERWARD, in 1699, the second "wolf" Mather described arrived in Boston. Mather learned of the many misdeeds of Eleazer Kingsbury in a letter he received from an unnamed correspondent, "an honest and a discreet man in the country" who had encountered the twenty-six-year-old "minister" and quickly realized something was amiss. The gentleman quickly formed suspicions about the alleged clergyman, and so decided to reveal to Mather details of Eleazer's background. A devout man, the letter-writer feared that through Eleazer's imposture God would be dishonored and the Gospel scandalized.

When this gentleman questioned his credentials, Eleazer claimed to have been preaching for four months. To prove it, he produced a certificate with twelve names on it, which, the correspondent said, were all "written by his own hand." Eleazer boasted that he had recently preached on the last Sabbath at a location between Taunton and Freetown "before a considerable assembly," a fact verified by a Taunton resident.

Mather's informant probed further and uncovered a few details of Eleazer's early slide into disrepute. Eleazer was formerly a tailor's apprentice. Born in Wrentham in 1673, he was the youngest son of Joseph Kingsbury, head of an otherwise respectable family of that locality. Eleazer's troubles began during his apprenticeship, where he was "but so vicious a servant, that his master could do no good with him." After breaking free from the tailor, Eleazer rushed into a doomed marriage. In April 1696 he married Sarah MacCane at Wrentham, a woman he quickly abandoned and later professed to despise. The correspondent told Mather that after Eleazer discarded Sarah, the scoundrel went west only after adding "to his felony several other vicious tricks." Sometime later Eleazer offended some of his former neighbors by sending them a shocking letter that consisted "chiefly of lies and curses."

Having gained some knowledge of Eleazer's squalid background, Mather's informant pleaded with the young man to return to the tailor's trade, provide for his wife, and not dishonor God by such evil deceptions. The young man offhandedly dismissed the advice. He would never reconcile with his wife, whom he considered a "devilish jade." If he eventually had a house, he might take Sarah back as a servant. If she dared to disobey him, he rashly added, he would kick her into the fire. Finally, Eleazer boasted that he had no intention to stop preaching and wagered the gentleman "twenty pieces of eight, he would get money and credit in a short time." The gentleman wrote that a sheet of paper could be filled with Eleazer's further transgressions. He then closed his letter to Mather by seeking the Boston clergyman's intervention.

Mather rose to the bait. He stated that one of the ministers of Boston (almost certainly meaning himself) immediately wrote a letter to Eleazer charging him to abandon this blasphemous course and return to his family and trade. Mather further warned that justices everywhere would be informed of his activities as a "vagabond." Having thus been exposed as a "wolf in sheep's clothing," Eleazer, like Dick Swayn, hastened to leave the Boston area. The last that was heard of Eleazer, Mather noted, he had changed his name to "Berry," a convenient phonetic abbreviation of Kingsbury, and run away to Cape May. In New Jersey, it was said, he bewitched new followers so effectively that "they were almost ready to tear in pieces any man that should speak diminutively of him."

MATHER'S THIRD AND FINAL "wolf" was the most successful of the trio and the only one able to wreak some revenge on Mather by causing him considerable public criticism in Boston. While the first two impostors were unmasked by other individuals, Mather targeted Samuel May almost from the moment of his arrival in Boston in July 1699. Mather was eventually vindicated in his suspicions of Samuel and eagerly published his account of the "smutty, filthy, wanton fellow." In *A Warning to the Flocks* the clergyman devoted considerable space to "A Letter Containing a Remarkable History of an Impostor," the narrative of Samuel May, who so effectively enchanted some Bostonians that they came to believe, as Mather put it, that "all was gold that glittered."

Samuel May embarked from England professing to be a mendicant or beggar. During the long voyage, however, he altered his story and let it be known that he was a preacher, traveling to visit his uncle in Virginia. Accompanying him was a woman, whose name has not survived, who pretended to be his wife. Samuel's treatment of his "wife" during the passage to Boston was the first thing to cause skepticism. Treating her with great "crabbedness," he scandalized his fellow passengers.

Upon his arrival, Samuel sought the aid of Cotton Mather, and the clergyman, who later claimed to have formed almost immediate doubts about the authenticity of the stranger's story, gave him some assistance. He recalled Samuel as a needy foreigner in "ragged, wretched, forlorn circumstances"; Mather helped by obtaining for him two opportunities to preach at private meetings. In these trial engagements, Samuel performed with "plausible delivery," and many days passed before Mather had cause to form deeper suspicions. The tide had turned by August 9, 1699, when Mather noted that the Englishman, a "wondrous lump of ignorance and arrogance," possessed the marks of an impostor. He set about praying and fasting as he brought the disturbing matter "unto the Lord."

Samuel made one of his first missteps when he showed one of the ministers of Boston a testimonial about his prospects as a "man of a sweet Gospel spirit." The document was supposedly signed by two men, John Earle, a nonconformist minister (who would later help to unmask Samuel as a fraud), and another, whose name is not known. The latter minister, according to Mather, had previously made a "scandalous" impression upon the churches of New England. Correctly perceiving that the certificate worked against him for this reason, Samuel never produced it again, despite requests by various Boston

clergymen. Samuel aroused further suspicion when he was unable
to name for Mather a single clergyman in London. When Mather
inquired about Samuel's origins, education, or "former circumstances,"
the young preacher became "unaccountably shy." Most troubling to
Mather was the fact that he could not elicit from Samuel any information about his livelihood for the first twenty-six or twenty-seven years
of his life. Mather formed the opinion that Samuel was really a barber
by occupation.

Although he harbored deep suspicions, Mather did not yet act upon
his doubts. "If this be a honest man," Mather later recalled having
thought, "he is a humble man. If he be a faithful servant of Christ,
he'll plainly let his fellow servants know what he is." Instead of gradually revealing himself as Mather believed he might, Samuel continued
in his ruse. Mather's suspicions intensified when he learned that
Samuel was barely literate (having made eighteen "horrid" spelling
mistakes in a note sent to Mather) and yet claimed to be skilled in
Latin, Greek, and Hebrew. When Mather and others asked to sample
these talents, they were astonished to hear Samuel pronounce "exotic
words in a manner so ridiculous as to render it plain that he knew
nothing of them." When Samuel spoke in Hebrew, Mather believed
they were hearing "Welch or Irish or the vagabond's cant." It is possible that Mather was correct in the latter suspicion. Samuel may have
been conversant in the language of the English criminal class known
as "Canting tongue" or "Peddlers' French," which as a beggar or
vagabond he almost certainly would have encountered before his
departure from England. Another minister present, presumably
Increase Mather, knew that Samuel was not speaking in any of the six
or seven languages familiar to him. In spite of his claims as a linguist,
at some point Samuel admitted he had "never been one year under
any education." While local ministers detected these marks of fraud,
the impostor deluded the public. Samuel, it was clear, put "a strange
enchantment" upon many of his public listeners.

Before long, Samuel was loudly complaining that the ministers of
town had not "immediately invited him into their pulpits," a claim
that riled many Bostonians into criticizing Mather and the local
clergy. Mather by now had concluded that Samuel was a "blade"

whose "arrogance equaled his ignorance." If his plan was to cause trouble for the ministers of Boston, then Samuel was succeeding handsomely. Mather recorded some of the public's criticisms, which included the opinion that the local clergy was "always uncivil to strangers" and that "here was come a better workman than themselves, whom therefore they would not suffer to stay in the town, if they could help it." The local ministers decided to respond to the criticism and composed a "loving" and "tender" letter to Samuel inviting him to appear before them and better explain his credentials.

The ministers, who—as Mather expressed it—had now done the duty of watchmen, received a reply from Samuel, saying that he knew of no authority on their part to place him under examination and that he "was not bound to give them an account of himself." Standing behind Samuel, a group of followers galvanized public opinion against the "meddlesome" local ministers, especially Mather. Not only did a group collect money to reimburse the expenses of Samuel's passage to Boston, Mather recalled, but they "also filled the town with so much lying and outrage against their faithful ministers." The ministers "bore with patience all the contempt" of an angry populace.

The next indignity Mather and his fellow clergymen suffered was Samuel's invitation to preach before a local body of Anabaptists, a small group Mather had endeavored to add to his own flock. Samuel's proselytes, Mather feared, were not only slighting the "learned ministers" in town but had actively become their "enemies and revilers." In Mather's opinion, his enemy was preying on the "weaker people" in town, such as the Anabaptists.

At some point, fearing that Samuel would sneak into his church during a service, Mather went to Samuel to forbid him from making any such attempt. His plan backfired. To Mather's dismay, Samuel and his supporters subsequently "made more than ordinary noise" to the effect that the clergyman had invited Samuel to worship at the Second Church.

On the heels of this incident, Mather finally discovered concrete evidence of Samuel's criminality. During a visit with his father, Increase, the two clergymen realized that Samuel had lifted a recent sermon straight out of Dr. Samuel Bolton's new book *The Royalties of Faith*. Consulting others with "better memories" than he, Cotton Mather was delighted when they concurred that Samuel had plagiarized his sermon from the book. Comparing his copy of Bolton's text to the recollections of those who had heard the Boston sermon, Mather effused that the "exact agreement between Samuel the Doctor, and Sam the Dunce, was a diverting surprise to all that saw it."

Having uncovered hard evidence, Mather promptly confronted Samuel with Dr. Bolton's book. Offering Samuel a piece of eight for every original sentence he could recount from *The Royalties of Faith* without using Bolton's text, the young preacher began making peculiar flourishes and expressions. He denied that he had ever seen this or any other work by Dr. Bolton. To clear himself, Samuel offered to preach on any biblical text his accuser should specify. Mather, who concluded that Samuel had stolen three or four other sermons from the same text, did not back down. He told the younger man he had been "as plainly detected as ever any thief that was taken with the stolen goods about him." Finally, Mather concluded his accusations by accepting Samuel's challenge. "Miserable man, do you ask me for a text to preach upon?" he asked. "I have a text, more than one for you to think upon." The minister started with "he that telleth lies, shall not tarry in my sight," and three more texts that alluded to sins he saw in the actions of the young impostor. This performance, Mather wrote, induced trembling and quivering in Samuel but no admission of guilt. After the heated interview ended, Samuel dispatched his angry Boston followers to rail against Mather. There was even talk of arresting the man who had "defamed" such an "excellent person."

Mather decided that he now had sufficient evidence to carry before the officials of the Anabaptist church to ensure Samuel's dismissal. To his astonishment, the Anabaptists immediately renewed their arrangements with Samuel and sent Mather a message to the effect that as he was not a member of their church, they had no need for his advice. Mather, shocked that an impostor should be employed as a public preacher in a Boston pulpit, decided to completely withdraw from the issue, confident that Samuel would shortly expose himself as a fraud. From about September to December, Mather avoided the subject of Samuel while withstanding the criticism of the impostor's followers. Rather than subsiding, the public ill sentiments boiled toward rage. Samuel's followers "flew upon" Mather for "reviling an eminent worthy stranger." Mather's enemies included the Church of England contingent in town. Having been agitated by the Anabaptists, they were, according to an informant, planning to "ruin" Mather. This allegation resulted in a sharp reply from Mather: "Go tell the Church of England men, tell them from me, that as for them, God has made me a defensed city, an iron pillar, and a brasen wall. . . ." In the meantime, Samuel continued his calling before large assemblies and professed to some that he had for four or five years been leaning toward the theological practices of the Anabaptists. In this setting, the inevitable unraveling of Samuel's imposture scheme—Mather's dearest wish—drew closer.

Samuel's tumble with the Anabaptists came quickly. According to Mather, Samuel was impetuous when it came to money. The clergyman was informed of a remarkable incident in which Samuel stormed out of a service having not received expected funds: "[W]hen upon their Lord's day, wherein he preached not, he flew out as I am told, like a dragon, spitting this among other fire at them, 'I see, no longer pipe, no longer dance!'" As the Anabaptists grew worried that the man they had embraced might indeed be a fraud, Mather decided to write fellow clergymen in England for any word of the history of Samuel May. Like his predecessors Dick Swayn and Eleazer Kingsbury, Samuel timed his flight from detection well. Having fleeced his followers for "incredible scores of pounds," Samuel rejected offers to continue his ministry in New England and hastily shipped out for England.

No sooner had he quit Boston than rumors of Samuel's predilections for female congregants soon began to swirl in town. A "virtuous and laudable" gentleman dropped the bombshell that Samuel had committed "uncivil carriage" toward a parishioner. Later, the same person alleged that Samuel had "gotten her with child." Samuel's supporters, evidently still quite numerous, became obstreperous and tried to paint the rumors as falsehoods. The situation intensified, and "horrid things" were muttered about Samuel in succeeding weeks. In a further blow to Samuel's character, on December 9, 1699, several women of "unblemished reputation" appeared under oath before a magistrate to reveal the Englishman's attempts to seduce them:

> He would often watch opportunities of getting them alone, and then would often affront them with lewd, vile, and lascivious carriages, which rendered it a dangerous thing to be alone with him, and abundantly assured them that he was a great rogue and that if they had for his turn, he would have stuck at no villainy towards them. That he would also talk at a vile rate and among other things he would plead that there is no sin in adultery.

The public acknowledgment of Samuel's "lewd, vile, and lascivious carriages" opened a floodgate of claims. Mather noted scenarios by which Samuel, with Bible in hand, would solicit young women "to wantonness," and after inebriating them, attempt to have sexual relations. Another tactic, Mather alleged, was to seek out a woman known to be "affected by his ministry" and "spend several hours together in rude actions and speeches . . . urging her to lie with him, which he said was no sin, for David and Solomon did as much." On these occasions Samuel reassured women that they would not become pregnant by him, "for none ever were so!"

Mather's desired outcome had come to pass: the man he had long suspected, and who had caused him much personal grief, was finally exposed as a scoundrel. He rejoiced in the news, regretting only that the discovery had not been made before Samuel's hasty departure. By the end of the month, Mather had compiled *A Warning to the Flocks on Wolves in Sheep's Cloathing* for publication. In February 1700, however, Mather was once again taking heat from the stubborn residue of Samuel's flock in response to his "little book":

> Satan being exceedingly enraged at what I have done, stirs up a wonderful storm of clamor and slander against me from a numerous crew in this town, which ('tis astonishing!) are not able to bear the

detection of the folly they discovered in following one of the impos-
tors and the remarkable story I have laid before the churches.

The final word from Samuel May came in May 1700, when Mather
noted in his diary that, to the surprise of many, the impostor sent his
Boston followers a letter from London. The contents of the letter
remain unknown, but judging from the maelstrom that ensued, its
purpose was at least in part to foment further attacks on Mather.
"[T]hose bewitched creatures began a new storm of railing and raving
against me," noted Mather, "for my scourging that thief out of the
temple."

Mather's patience in the matter was soon vindicated. On May 28,
1700, a small packet of letters arrived from England, confirming
Samuel as an impostor. One letter was from John Earle, a nonconformist minister at Gosport in Hampshire, who reported that
Samuel May's true name was Samuel Axel. After committing some
"immoralities," Axel quit England, leaving behind "a wife and family
in deplorable circumstances . . . [and bringing] it seems a whore with
him hither, under the name of a wife!" The letter presented the proof
that Mather relished—he called it "a marvelous answer of prayer. The
arrival of it was highly seasonable and serviceable."

No further word on the fate of Samuel Axel alias Samuel May, provincial Boston's most convincing "wolf in sheep's clothing," was recorded
in the diary of his nemesis, Cotton Mather.

Chapter 8
Sign of a Rogue
1701

RATHER THAN COMMITTING a run-of-the-mill burglary, Elias
Purrington concocted a more complex scheme for looting the home
of a prosperous Boston merchant. His plan, according to the deposition of Elizabeth "Betty" Corbison, a servant he courted and jilted,
was to gain access to the house of John Campbell by romancing Betty,
even though he was already married and lived in town with his wife.
In February 1698, Elias succeeded in his ruse and, after an evening of
hospitality in the cellar kitchen of Campbell's house, absconded with
a valuable silver tankard and spoons, leaving a bewildered Betty to
explain the theft to her master the following morning. Elias might
have been successful in the robbery if he had not later contacted Betty
again. Knowing him to be a thief and startled by the interchangeable
names he used, Betty saw in her erstwhile suitor the "sign of a rogue."
With the assistance of a seventeen-year-old servant, Betty helped
bring him to justice. A thief of many names, Elias variously called
himself "Thomas Stanbury," "Jarvis," and "William Mann." Audacious—and careless—for using multiple identities in the town of his
own residence, Elias rates as one of colonial Boston's least successful
and most hapless knaves. After his apprehension in 1701, he denied
the theft of the tankard and spoons and claimed he did not know
Betty Corbison.

According to Betty Corbison's version of events, Elias first noticed
her in 1697 when she was a servant in the household of Thomas

Palmer—a merchant gentleman on the rise in Boston. Perhaps having cased Palmer's home, or maybe just hoping to have an affair with the young woman, Elias introduced himself to Betty as "Thomas Stanbury" and told her that he was a cooper (a maker of wooden casks and barrels). Something resembling a courtship soon began. Betty later recalled that Thomas Stanbury showed a "pretense of love" and that he eventually expressed a desire to marry her. She was probably pleased with her new prospects. Marriage to a man with a practical trade would improve her station in life and might even release her from domestic employment.

At some point, Betty left the house of Thomas Palmer and worked for another Boston merchant, John Campbell. A Scotsman who later established what would become one of the town's most famous newspapers, the *Boston News-Letter,* Campbell was a respected member of the community who would serve as the province's postmaster general. At Campbell's house, located next door to the Anchor tavern, the courtship between "Thomas Stanbury" and Betty continued. Betty later stated that her suitor frequently "resorted unto her and had discourse with her by the side of the Townhouse" in an alley against Campbell's house. Here the couple met and presumably continued to whisper sweet nothings to each other. However, Betty must have thought "Thomas's" ever-changing appearance odd: sometimes he visited her in mariner's apparel; at other times he wore a wig or appeared bare-headed.

On the night of February 14, 1698, Elias, still calling himself Thomas Stanbury, was bold enough to try to enter the house of Betty's master. Arriving at Campbell's home about ten o'clock, he knocked on the door and for the first time was admitted to the house by Betty's fellow servant, Mary Dracut. Mary showed him downstairs to the cellar kitchen, where Betty soon joined them. The Campbells had retired for the evening—probably unaware the servants were entertaining a male guest downstairs. Here the women visited with Elias until midnight, when Mary excused herself to go to bed. Betty served her suitor a quart of beer in a large silver tankard. Taking advantage of Betty's hospitality, Elias asked for a pipe, which Betty promptly fetched. At about one o'clock in the morning—perhaps in an attempt to get Betty out of the room—Elias broke the fragile clay pipe against an andiron. Not satisfied that he had done enough smoking, he assured Betty he would have just "one pipe more and be gone." Betty went upstairs to find another pipe in the hall closet. But much to her surprise, when she returned to the cellar there were no signs of Elias. He had vanished—and so had Campbell's valuable silver tankard. Monogrammed with the initials I-C-S, the tankard was valued at almost £20.

Betty likely spent a restless night worrying about how she would explain the theft to her master in the morning. When she awoke, the robbery of the tankard was compounded by the unhappy discovery that two silver spoons were also missing from the kitchen table. Campbell's reaction to this turn of events can only be imagined. It would be reasonable to assume that if Betty were not fired the next day, she was for the remainder of her term of employment seen as an unreliable servant.

Betty later stated that she saw nothing more of "Thomas Stanbury" from February 1698 until April 1701, when he tracked her down at the home of her new employer, Edward Lyde. What inspired Elias to resume contact with Betty after such a long lapse remains a mystery, and it proved to be his undoing. Elias proceeded to Lyde's house, where on a Saturday night at ten o'clock he encountered Betty. The deposition of seventeen-year-old fellow servant Elizabeth Domini helps to flesh out the encounter:

> On a Saturday night past ten o'clock Elias Purrington came to my master Mr. Lyde's back gate and looked over the gate and called "Betty" and she asked "who is there?" and he bid her come and see, and she went to the gate and bid him to go round to the fore door she would speak with him there. So she went to the fore door and bid me sit up for her, and after he and she had been some time together there I heard a great noise and struggling and Betty Corbison called me to come and help her else, said she, "this rogue will ruin me" upon which I went to them and asked him if he was not ashamed upon Saturday night and at this time of it to make such a noise and a do there.

Enraged by the young servant's comments, Elias called her "a bold, impudent slut" and that "he was not born yesterday to be run down with a girl." If she did not go about her business, he would send her "about [her] business." With this, Elizabeth retreated upstairs to her bed, ignoring Betty's continuing pleas for help.

Turning his attentions to Betty, Elias asked if she wondered why he had been away so long. He explained that he had been on a voyage to the East Indies and out of the country since the night she saw him last, at John Campbell's house. An affronted Betty pretended that she did not know him. Elias, reciting the wrong alias, reintroduced himself as "Jarvis." Betty confronted him about stealing Campbell's tankard. He denied taking it and said that he abruptly left Campbell's house that night because a night watchman had come into the cellar and frightened him. Betty said that wasn't possible, as the cellar doors hadn't been open. She demanded that if he were truly innocent, he should go with her to Mr. Campbell's house and see himself cleared of the suspicion. He promised to comply with her request—and hastily disappeared again.

Shortly after this surprise visit, Betty told her former employer that the silver thief had reappeared. On her advice, Campbell and a constable visited a Mrs. Ireland, whose husband owned the vessel on which Elias had supposedly lately returned to Boston. After seizing a man they thought might be Elias, Betty stated that neither he nor two other men living in the Ireland household was the culprit. Elias later indicated that he was one of the men Betty Corbison vindicated on this occasion, implying perhaps that Betty was complicit in his scheme.

Elias was gone this time for only about three months. His decision to see Betty once again spelled the end of his career as an impostor in Boston. On the evening of Friday, July 4, 1701, he materialized again at the Lyde house looking for Betty. Fellow servant Elizabeth Domini recalled his arrival in her deposition:

> Friday night last past ten of the clock [he] came and knocked at my master's back gate upon which Elizabeth Corbison run to see who it was and she came back and told me it was the rogue that stole the tankard upon which I bid her go and talk to him and I asked if that

was a time of night to come and visit upon which [he] replied and
said whose negro was my master? I told him he was Demmeck and he
said "no, he was not" in French, saying "non il pas" and I see him
kneeling offering to come over the gate and so I whispered to Betty to
go and talk to him and that I would go and call Mr. Campbell.

Elias claimed to have been sick since they last saw each other in April. Betty asked why he had changed his name the last time she saw him, saying that this was a telltale "sign of a rogue." Elias then, in another remarkable lapse, gave her yet another new name, calling himself "William Mann." He asked Betty to come with him to the Boston Common. There he would "make satisfaction" by paying her with money for the wrongs he had subjected her to. When Betty refused, Elias said that he would give her his silver shoe buckles in token until he could bring her the money the following night.

At the moment Elias bent down to remove his shoe buckles, John Campbell and a constable approached Edward Lyde's porch to arrest him. The constable noted that Elias placed an arm "in a very loving manner" around Betty's waist as the constable demanded to know his name. Elias refused until they had "brought him away a good space off of the house" and then admitted to being Elias Purrington, a married man who lived in town. In his defense, Elias later claimed that he had never met Betty Corbison until the evening of his arrest. In his deposition Elias stated that as he was passing down the street on his way from the South Meeting House, an unfamiliar woman—Betty Corbison— offered him a beer. There, on Edward Lyde's porch, he was wrongfully apprehended for a crime he claimed not to have committed.

Whether motivated by love, lust, money, or all three, this episode concluded the clumsy imposture of Elias Purrington alias Thomas Stanbury alias Jarvis alias William Mann, the many-named con artist of colonial Boston. Elias Purrington returned to his wife, proceeded to have a family, and evidently remained free of notoriety for the remainder of his life. Betty Corbison, it appears, ultimately found a more appropriate suitor—in March 1719 a woman of the same name married John Thompson in Boston.

Chapter 9
In Prospect of a Fortune
1739

OFFERING A HANDSOME REWARD of twenty guineas, banker Sir
Richard Hoare's letter to *Boston News-Letter* publisher John Draper
purported to hunt for the missing heir to a fortune. The banker
sought the whereabouts of one Robert Palmer, a gentleman traveling somewhere in America who—if he could be located and
returned to England promptly—was entitled to a substantial inheritance from the estate of a wealthy gentleman. The letter arrived in
October 1739, and not long afterward Robert Palmer was found
entering Boston. The Englishman feigned surprise at this news and
claimed that the bequest came from his late brother-in-law, John
Nash, a bachelor who he said possessed a £300,000 fortune. During
his brief stay in town, Robert was coddled by Bostonians, who
"mightily caressed and generously entertained him," eager to ingratiate themselves with a gentleman of newfound means. However,
his unkempt appearance and strange story of his life and travels
soon aroused suspicions. In less than a week Robert's confidence
scheme collapsed. The banker's letter was determined a forgery
and Robert, suspected to be a "vile impostor," quietly slipped out
of town, leaving his victims furious and the town gaping with wonder at such brazen fraud.

Like other schemers who operated in Boston in the colonial period—
and generations of confidence men before and since—Robert Palmer
practiced the proverbial notion that the bigger the lie, the more likely

people are to believe it. At the root of his scheme was a meticulously counterfeited letter made to appear it was from a banker in London. If successful, Robert would obtain lines of credit in town. He might bask in the hospitality of polite society and even garner his getaway passage back to England. To make the letter convincing, Robert presented it as written by Sir Richard Hoare, a gentleman banker. Hoare was the grandson of a wealthy goldsmith of London who founded the family's banking house in 1672. In selecting Hoare, Robert played a masterstroke. Hoare's firm was the perfect one to represent the interests of someone like John Nash, his fictitious brother-in-law of immense wealth, for the bank served a highly elite clientele. Robert endeavored to get even the most minor details right, including Hoare's address, which he correctly presented as at the "Leather Bottle" on Fleet Street (so-called because a gilded leather bottle hung outside the shop).

Robert composed a letter from the banker that named him a major beneficiary of John Nash and called for his return to England with a request to all merchants, captains, and postmasters that he not only be provided passage home but be equipped with any "necessaries" befitting "his fortune." Sir Richard Hoare would meet all expenses on Robert's behalf. Robert decided to direct the letter to John Draper in Boston, who was likely to print it in his newspaper. It would then be only a matter of time before Robert, en route to Boston via Rhode Island, would be discovered and embraced as a creditworthy gentleman by the citizens of Boston.

Sometime in October 1739 Draper received the letter, which was delivered to his Newbury Street offices by Captain Fowle via Eastern-Branch, Maryland:

To: Mr. Draper, Printer in Boston, New England

WHEREAS, *Robert Palmer, an elderly gentleman commonly wearing a long gray beard, of a middle stature, a reddish nose, a small scar on the middle joint of his middle left finger, a wound on the arm above the elbow, bald headed, went a pilgrimage out of Great Britain about three years ago and took shipping in the Unity, out of some part of Scotland for America, in very mean apparel: whosoever can*

find the said gentleman, Robert Palmer, it will be worth any mer-
chant, captain, or postmasters while to see and persuade him to
come home there being left for him, by the will of John Nash, Esq.,
of Bath in Somersetshire, deceased, fifteen hundred pounds in cash,
and three hundred pounds per annum, in the county of Somerset in
Bathwick, who if he be not found, goes to his daughter, who by said
will has ten thousand pounds: there is twenty guineas reward for
any person who shall find or acquaint him herewith, so that he
returns to England; twenty guineas for his passage: and whosoever
shall equip the said gentleman with necessaries, according to his
fortune shall receive any sum or other charges paid, on sight of
himself or his receipt, by

Richard Hoar
Banker at the Leather Bottle, Fleet-Street.
London, March 3, 1738/9

Draper did not immediately run the full text of Hoare's communication in his newspaper but took a more cautious tack. First, he consulted
friends as to whether the document appeared to be authentic. Satisfied that it was, Draper ran an advertisement in the October 18–25
issue of the newspaper stating that he had received an account from a
London banker about a "very considerable" bequest of £1,500 in cash
and £300 per annum to one Robert Palmer. He requested the missing
beneficiary "repair to the printer for further information." The advertisement had one unexpected effect. It generated wishful thinking on
the part of several individuals in Boston named Palmer, some of
whom approached the printer, but none, Draper stated, were "of the
right Christian name."

In the meantime, Robert Palmer was following his own carefully laid
plans. At the time the advertisement was printed in Boston, he was
passing through Dedham en route to town. There he was quickly recognized as the missing beneficiary:

[Robert Palmer] heard the news first at Dedham, and the advertise-
ment being produced, it very much surprised him—he being there
declared to be the man to whom this fortune was left; the people on

the road to Boston were very ready to do good offices for him; and a
gentleman at Roxbury very ready to accommodate him with a horse,
and came with him to town, inviting him to return again and see
him; and if he should ever have occasion to ride into the country to
let him know of it, and a horse should be at his service at any time.

Arriving in Boston on a borrowed horse a short time later, Robert was escorted to the Royal Exchange tavern on King Street, where John Draper soon examined him "as to every particular" in Sir Richard Hoare's letter. We can imagine a crowd of curious Bostonians gathering around the newcomer in a smoke-filled tavern chamber as Draper's questioning began. Robert clinched the identification by naming John Nash as the source of the inheritance but Draper, pressing a little further, asked for the name of Nash's banker. Robert replied "twas Sir Richard Hoar," and as an added fillip, offered Hoare's address in London at the sign of the "Leather Bottle." Draper and others present reasonably concluded that Robert was "the very person" being sought by the London banker.

At this point, Robert began embellishing his story and awed the eager Bostonians with tales of a remarkable fortune. He volunteered that his late brother-in-law had been worth £300,000, and that £200,000 of that amount was on deposit with Sir Richard Hoare. During various difficulties, Nash had allowed Robert to draw on £50 at a time from Hoare, which "was always punctually paid." He offered this last comment, no doubt, for the benefit of prospective creditors in the audience willing to entertain similar transactions. Changing the subject slightly, Robert then wondered aloud why his own daughter, Nash's niece and "nearest relation in the world," would receive only £10,000 and, further, what had become of the rest of Nash's vast estate? Tears welled in his eyes as he said that no one else other than his "dear daughter" knew of the identifying mark on his finger mentioned in Sir Richard Hoare's letter.

Striking to those at the Royal Exchange must have been Robert's ungainly appearance. An ill-dressed man in his late fifties, of middle stature, bald, and possessing a long gray beard and a reddish nose, he hardly appeared the picture of a gentleman with such lofty associations.

When queried about his life since leaving Great Britain three and a half years earlier, Robert launched into a rambling, almost unbelievable narrative. Teary-eyed once more, he told a tale of having been a few years earlier "bound for a rogue" in England after a £1,000 business failure. To elude authorities, he grew a long beard, disguised himself in "mean apparel," and fled north to Scotland. From there he shipped out on the *Unity* to Maryland.

Once in America, Robert decided to pursue a new occupation. Being possessed of "a pretty good hand," he claimed to have opened a school in Talbot County. Misfortune soon struck him there in the form of a "clap of thunder," which he stated had rendered him deaf and "unfitted him" for the occupation of schoolmaster. From Maryland, Robert then made his way to Philadelphia, where he asserted that he had been cured of his deafness by Dr. Cadwallader Evans. Dr. Evans, according to Robert, was sympathetic to his plight and wrote the Englishman a certificate recommending him to the "charity of well-disposed persons." From Philadelphia, Robert pressed on to New York, where, after "relating his poor circumstances" to the mayor, he obtained charitable assistance to travel to Boston. Palmer then traveled east and at some point in his journey, he alleged, contemplated a change in plans. A veteran of "former wars," he considered taking to the seas with a company of privateers that he heard were being readied in Rhode Island. But this design was interrupted when he fell seriously ill at South Kingston. As reported in the newspaper:

> Hearing several vessels were fitting out at Rhode Island to go privateering after the Spaniards [and] having been a soldier in the former wars, he resolved to put in for some post as clerk or steward, but was prevented by being taken sick at South Kingston, of the slow fever, which lasted two months, where he was kindly treated [and] that upon his recovery hearing that a vessel was fitting out here, he said, he was resolved to see whether he could not get a berth in her.

Recovered and once again on his way to join the privateers, Robert stopped in Dedham, where, as his story went, he fortuitously heard about John Draper's advertisement for the missing heir. Having listened to this long-winded tale, onlookers at the Royal Exchange were puzzled by Robert's lack of enthusiasm about the news of his inheritance. While "many wished him joy" he attempted to "wave the discourse" by again launching into the history of his travels. This did not satisfy the crowd, and several asked him why he was not more pleased with the impressive legacy he was about to receive. As Draper reported:

> He answered, with a grave countenance, and a serious voice, that he was an infirm man, and above 55 years of age, and therefore could not expect a long continuance in this world, and ah! Why should he set his heart so much upon what he was so soon to leave; for his part, he said, he desired to improve the remainder of his time in preparing for another world.

This poignant explanation succeeded in eliciting the sympathies of several Bostonians, and, according to Draper, "many appeared as his friends, readily offering to take care of him." Offers were made to supply him in any way and even to "transport him handsomely home in the first ship for London." Robert's story was seen as a "wonderful providence" and remarkable for the coincidence that someone who had never been to Boston before should be in the vicinity—and not at sea as planned—just as the advertisement was published. Robert was given accommodation for the night and the next morning regaled with a breakfast "suitable for a gentleman in prospect of such a fortune." It was not the first hospitality the traveler had enjoyed since being discovered in Dedham, but it was almost the last.

Robert made his first major misstep early the next morning. Eager to set about town, he slipped into a tavern where, before ten o'clock in the morning, he ordered punch—in spite of having expressed an aversion to liquor the previous night. In the meantime, some of the men present at his interview began to wonder about the authenticity of the letter from Sir Richard Hoare and Robert's certificate from the mayor of New York. While Robert was busy imbibing at a local tavern, skeptics decided to show Hoare's letter to several merchants in town. All came to the conclusion that the banker's letter was "only a fiction; and sent by him or some friend of his along before, in order to answer his ends as soon as he got hither."

Robert's questioners did not wait long to strike. After Robert had gorged on a "plentiful" dinner that evening, Draper and others challenged him about his peculiar story. When they pointed out several inconsistencies and contradictions, the old man appeared "prodigiously shocked." A major problem with Sir Richard Hoare's letter was the unusual route taken in its delivery to Boston. "How a letter from London should be sent to Boston by the way of Maryland, the most indirect conveyance?" his questioners demanded. "How it should escape the charge of two post-offices in the way from Maryland, being entered first in Trenton Post-Office in the Jerseys?" Robert's response to these questions is not recorded.

The certificate from the mayor of New York was even more disquieting to the worthies of Boston. Apparently, it indicated that Robert intended to visit a relative in town at Michaelmas—a church festival held on September 29. He had failed to mention this during his interview the previous evening and, according to Draper, no "such relation [is] yet in town." Adding to the blunders was Robert's earlier statement that he "had no relations, as he knew of, in these parts."

As his scheme crumbled about him, Robert was pressed into admitting that the authenticity of the documents was questionable. Maintaining his innocence, however, Robert "solemnly declared he knew nothing at all of it till he came to Dedham; nor could he think who should do it." When a break came in his interrogation and his examiners left the room, Robert made a hasty exit, "leaving word he would come again when they were better satisfied." He clearly had no intention of facing his questioners again, for he was never seen again. Someone saw him fill his "pocket bottle" with rum early the next morning, and he was last seen heading toward Rhode Island. He said he was on his way to Virginia, and that it would "suit him better to take his passage" from Rhode Island. All trace of Robert Palmer disappeared as he headed south.

With the departed schemer the subject of much gossip in town, John Draper now decided to print an account of the entire incident in the

Boston News-Letter "to satisfy the inquisitive [and] caution those who may hereafter be in danger of being imposed upon." The story soon appeared in the newspaper and revealed a tale of duplicity and cunning that was to be unmatched in Boston for years to come.

Chapter 10
Dr. Seth Hudson:
The Greatest Villain of the Age
1761

NO SCOUNDREL WAS MORE REVILED in pre-Federal Boston than the notorious impostor Dr. Seth Hudson. Arriving in town by 1761 with a bold counterfeiting scheme in mind, Seth used his real name but lived extravagantly under the guise of being a wealthy traveler. He obscured his unsavory reputation at Fort Massachusetts in the late 1750s and insinuated himself into Boston society where, as a world-class con man, he successfully targeted some of the town's most prominent merchants as his victims in a treasury note scam. But before he could take flight with his ill-gotten gains, the doctor's fraud was detected and his criminal associations exposed. Seth's trial attracted unprecedented interest in town, and his subsequent punishment at the pillory and whipping post caused a major commotion with an immense crowd that, as one diarist put it, was frenzied into a state of "immoderate exultation." Engraver Nathaniel Hurd memorialized the scene in a humorous print. In July 1762, after serving only four months of a one-year prison term, Seth shipped out on the HMS *Launceston* bound for England, to the great relief of the townspeople of Boston.

The son of Seth Hudson Sr. and his wife, Mary Whipple, the future swindler was born on April 13, 1728, in Marlborough, Massachusetts. He was the eldest of eight children in what has been aptly described as "a roving family," one that lived primarily in Lexington and Marlborough but was frequently on the move. Details of Seth's education and medical training are sketchy, but he appears to have begun his practice at age twenty-one in 1749, when he served as a surgeon at Fort Massachusetts in the western part of the province. In 1751, he was listed on the original drawing of house lots at West Hoosac, where he was a miller.

Seth's military career evolved rapidly at the fort; he served first as a sentinel and surgeon and later as a commanding officer. His tenure there was punctuated by disputes with several officers, including most notably Colonel Ephraim Williams (after whom West Hoosac was renamed Williamstown in 1765).

Seth's difficulties at the fort came to a head by October 1757, when after an apparent incident of thievery he and his wife were turned out of the military camp by Ephraim Williams amid accusations of "truly odious and hateful" conduct. Four officers signed a deposition that recounted the disrepute into which Seth had fallen. The statement was written in response to the doctor's efforts to "cast many aspersions on the characters of Colonel Israel Williams, Colonel Ephraim Williams, Captain Wyman and others," whom he had endeavored to place "in an odious light." To counteract Seth's claims, the officers suggested that it "may not be improper that said Seth's general character should be known." The deposition branded Seth a liar and a thief:

> The character he has sustained among people intimately acquainted with him and under peculiar advantage of knowing his general conduct and the foundations of it is truly odious and hateful. A man that pays no regard to truth any farther than it serves his own secular interest and one that has been addicted to the hateful practice of stealing. Whether he was ever guilty of theft or not we can't absolutely say but that he with his wife were turned out of this fort by Colonel Ephraim Williams as he himself said upon a violent suspicion of theft, is what we give our attestation to.

Further damaging reports soon followed. A week later, Samuel Taylor and Benjamin Simonds were deposed, this time stating that Seth "frequently takes things in a clandestine manner, or in other words, is a thief." They noted that as a miller in West Hoosac, he "was universally complained of for taking unlawful toll."

After being expelled from Fort Massachusetts, Seth's activities were quiet, at least for a time. In January 1760 he was listed among the grantees of Pownal, New Hampshire, where his father, "Seth Hudson, Gentleman," was appointed moderator of the new town's first meeting. Probably at about this time Seth met his future accomplice, Joshua Howe of Westmoreland, New Hampshire, an experienced counterfeiter then in his mid-forties.

Seth did not tarry long in New Hampshire. Perhaps emboldened by his thefts at Fort Massachusetts, he was ready by 1761 to execute a more elaborate crime with higher stakes. He and Joshua Howe conceived a scheme of producing counterfeit Massachusetts treasury notes, mainly in £100 increments, which they would sell to unwitting Bostonians for cash. To produce the forgeries, the two men secured tools from Glazier Wheeler, a notorious counterfeiter living in New Hampshire. According to a study of colonial American counterfeiters, Seth and Joshua created their notes in a two-step process, first recreating the printed note and then forging the handwritten signature "by placing a true note over a counterfeit, tracing the writing with a sharp instrument, and then filling up with ink the impression on the false note." Among the signatures painstakingly reproduced were those of Harrison Gray, treasurer of the province. The counterfeiters correctly foresaw that people would be willing to pay cash for the "guaranteed" notes; offering 6 percent interest, they appeared to be attractive short-term investments. The scheme required much advance planning, the manufacture of flawless treasury instruments, and consummate acting skills on Seth's part. As the front man, he would be required to identify and court merchants of Boston, gain their trust, sell the bogus notes, and elude his victims before being detected in the deception.

According to one account, Seth arrived in Boston offering the unusual story of being a wealthy Dutchman "traveling for his own amusement." That he might have been able to impersonate a Dutch gentleman after encountering so many Dutch speakers at Fort Massachusetts is plausible, but that he would carry out such an impersonation while retaining his own decidedly un-Dutch name is a puzzling and unanswered aspect of the story. Given his rather flashy appearance in Boston (it was said he was dressed "very gaily," apparently favoring crimson velvet), Seth was "well watched" by the local citizenry. In spite of this caution, Seth's efforts to "push himself into genteel company" were effective enough to open doors. By the first few months of 1761, he had gained a foothold within the town's mercantile elite, and between March and July of that year he sold up to £800 in counterfeit treasury notes. His most prominent victim was Samuel Wells, a merchant and judge of the Court of Common Pleas, who in 1749 had been the target of a failed extortion scheme by James Williams and Mary Richards, recounted in Chapter 15. This time around, Wells did not escape unscathed. According to the Boston diarist John Boyle, even Yale-educated Samuel Wells "with all his sagacity" was taken for £100, although the actual amount was at least twice as much.

Having successfully netted hundreds of pounds, Seth and Joshua might have been wise to leave Boston after their last sting in July 1761. Instead, both men lingered in town. Before long, another counterfeiting operation in Boston was uncovered and on September 10 of that year Jeremiah Dexter, a counterfeiter from Walpole, was sentenced to stand at the pillory. A crowd soon gathered to watch the court's punishment meted out. Among the spirited bystanders appeared Dr. Seth Hudson. According to John Boyle, many in the throng "were very liberal in bestowing rotten eggs upon Mr. Dexter, particularly Dr. Seth Hudson." In light of his subsequent unmasking, this episode would later stand out as an act of supreme hypocrisy and become fodder for a satirist writing on the Hudson case. But the doctor did not have to wait long for his own comeuppance. Days later his treasury note scheme collapsed. Joshua was the first in the pair to be apprehended, and he hastily confessed that he was "a partner in villainy with Doctor Hudson" in selling fake notes. On October 8, both men were jailed to await a trial that would occur the following year.

No details of Seth's activities during his incarceration exist until February 8, 1762, when the *Boston Evening Post* reported that he had attempted a jailbreak: "On Thursday night last the noted Dr. Seth

Hudson, who has been for some months past confined in the gaol in this town on suspicion of counterfeiting the Province securities, had well nigh made his escape from thence, but being discovered he was prevented." By this time, Joshua Howe had already been convicted in a separate action of "procuring and keeping in his possession sundry tools for counterfeiting dollars." He had the disadvantage of a prior conviction for counterfeiting, and for this second offense, he would be committed to the house of correction and put to hard labor for a span of twenty years. The following month, Seth and Joshua, who both pleaded not guilty, were tried before the Superior Court. In spite of his imposture, Seth's social status in the eyes of his contemporaries had not diminished. He was styled "gentleman," not "doctor" or "surgeon," in the court records.

The case brought out so many onlookers that a change of venue was required. The *Boston Evening Post* on March 8 reported that the courthouse was "too small for the concourse of people that came out," and accordingly the trials were moved "to one of the largest Meeting Houses in this town, where the greatest number of people attended that was ever known at any trial in this place before." Before hundreds of spectators, perhaps the largest group assembled for a trial in Boston to that time, Seth was tried on four counts of counterfeiting and Joshua Howe on two. Within days, both men were convicted on all counts. The evidence was so strong that the jury did not even excuse itself to deliberate. The experience was said to be "a very mortifying thing to the Doctor—but excited the attention of the people greatly." Seth's punishment included being set in the pillory for one hour, receiving a whipping of twenty stripes, a fine of £100 for each conviction, and a one-year prison term. Joshua, who was convicted on both counts against him, received the same punishment with thirty-nine stripes.

If the scene during the trial was nearly chaos, then the circumstances surrounding Seth and Joshua's trip to the pillory and whipping post, probably located on State Street, resembled pandemonium. Engraver Nathaniel Hurd captured the colorful scene in a print entitled *H-ds-n's SPEECH from the Pillory*. Seth is depicted on the raised platform of the pillory with his arms locked upright. From below a man shouts up to him, "How does your physic work?" to which the doctor replies in double entendre, "Faith it has brought me to a stool," in reference not only to a stool used in public punishment but also, likely, the excrement that would shortly be pelted in his face. Dozens of men and a few women are shown milling about beneath the pillory and around the adjacent whipping post (where a half-naked Joshua stands awaiting his lashing). Two dogs wait near the pillory, perhaps brought as a ready source of feces to be thrown at the convicts. In the skies above Seth, the Devil is shown soaring past with a pitchfork in hand, crying, "This is the man for me." In the center of the engraving is a profile of Hudson showing his most pronounced features, an upturned nose and exaggerated, protruding jaw. The words "Dutch Tuck" appear on the blade of Seth's sword, perhaps a euphemism for "sly trick." Remarkable for his presence in the lower right-hand side of the engraving is at least one identifiable Bostonian: a peg-legged African American lemon-seller called "Black Jack" or "One Leg'd Jack," who died some years later at the almshouse. According to an early-nineteenth-century notation by a member of the Eliot family on a copy of this broadside owned by the Massachusetts Historical Society, the engraving contains "many persons in the crowd . . . well known to those who lived at that time." Sadly, today it is no longer possible to identify many of the characters Hurd included. Below this lively scene is Seth's "speech," thought to have been written by the noted wit Joseph Green:

> *WHAT mean these Crouds, this Noise and Roar!*
> *Did ye ne'er see a Rogue before?*
> *Are Villains then a Sight so rare,*
> *To make you press and gape and stare?*
> *Come forward all who look so fine,*
> *With Gain as illy got as mine:*
> *Step up—you'l soon reverse the Show;*
> *The Croud above, and few below.*
>
> *Well—for my Roguery here I stand,*
> *A Spectacle to all the Land:*
> *High elevated on this Stage,*
> *The greatest Villain of the Age.*
> *My Crimes hav been both great and many,*
> *Equal'd by very few, if any:*

And for the Mischiefs I have done
I put this wooden Neckcloth on.

There HOW his brawny Back is stripping,
Quite callous grown with often whipping.
In vain you wear your Whip-Cord out,
You'l ne'er reclaim that Rogue so stout.
To make him honest, take my Word,
You must apply a bigger Cord.

Now all ye who behold this Sight,
That ye may get some profit by't,
Keep always in your Mind, I pray,
These few Words that I have to say.
Follow my Steps and you may be
In Time, perhaps, advanc'd like me;
Or, like my fellow Lab'rer HOW,
You'l get at least a Post below.

Hurd's engraving was one of several works inspired by Seth Hudson. One, by an unknown author, also claimed to be *The Humble Confession of that* NOTORIOUS CHEAT, *Doctor* SETH HUDSON. The confession opens dramatically with Seth crying, "I come, I come," as terror sparkles in his eyes, and it proceeds to present him over ten stanzas as a repentant "rebel sinner." A more unusual publication was a comedy, also by an unknown author, published about the same time: *A Serious-Comical Dialogue Between the Famous Dr. Seth Hudson and the Noted Joshua How.* It features a humorous and at times risqué dialogue between Seth and Joshua, replete with puns and other witticisms. Among its passages are references to Seth's "distribution" of rotten eggs to the rabble gathered the prior year during Jeremiah Dexter's visit to the pillory. Seth's attire and physical appearance are also ridiculed, particularly his nose and chin. In one exchange, Joshua remarks, "Methinks your chin will be a convenient lodgement for some *matter in motion,* and your nose being somewhat turned up, will not refuse to bear its part in the labour of its brother *chin.*" Seth later says, "I do therefore affirm that it is inhumane to throw rotten eggs, or any other nastiness, at a defenceless man in the pillory; I would not serve a monkey so." The

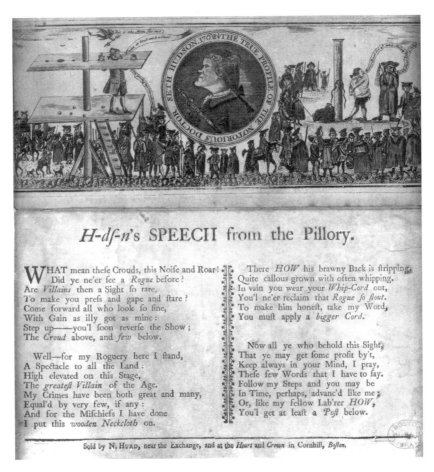

H-ds-n's Speech from the Pillory, *engraving by Nathaniel Hurd, 1762.*
Courtesy of the Boston Public Library.

comedy touches upon an array of topics and at one point even presents the memory of a meeting, presumably imaginary, between Seth Hudson and the greatest scoundrel of colonial America, Tom Bell. In this passage, Seth "recalls" the sobriety of his famous predecessor:

> *The famous* TOM BELL *once told me that he was never drunk in his life. He was so logical a thief, that he could steal, confess his theft to the very man he had injured, and yet be readily pardoned by that same man.*

In the meantime, the real Dr. Seth Hudson, after his humiliating public punishment, was returned to confinement. His imprisonment, however, was not lengthy. In a remarkable turn of events, Hudson's one-year prison sentence was cut short. After four months, he was permitted in mid-July to join the company of the HMS *Launceston*, a forty-four-gun English man-of-war bound for London by way of Gibraltar. In the ship's muster book, Seth was rated an "able seaman," implying he had prior seafaring experience.

Seth's departure from Boston undoubtedly came as good news to the town. And the story would end here were it not for the doctor's enterprising nature. Perhaps calling upon his earlier command experience, the versatile Seth made his short time aboard the *Launceston* a success. The following February he was elevated to the rank of Master of Arms, an unlikely promotion for a recently released convict.

Seth's career on the *Launceston* was short-lived, however. According to a Boston newspaper item, in December 1763 he returned to town briefly on a ship from Halifax. From Boston he traveled west, settling in the Albany area. Bostonians could not have been altogether displeased a few years later when they read of his demise. John Boyle noted the event in his journal on September 10, 1767: "Lately died of the smallpox in Albany. Dr. Seth Hudson, famous for the particular marks of distinction some years since conferred on him by the Superior Court of this Province for his ingenious practice." According to accounts, the doctor passed the contagion on to one of his former counterfeiting associates who was there on a visit. In life, Seth Hudson possessed a genius for fooling successful and learned men; in death he faced an adversary even he could not cheat.

The Humble Confession of that
NOTORIOUS CHEAT,

Doctor SETH HUDSON.

1762.

I Come, I come, the Villain cries,
  With Terror sparkling in his Eyes ;
While Fires from Hell his Soul inflame,
Distrest with Guilt -- and stab'd with Shame.

Ye murder'd Hours so gaily flown,
These present Pangs are all your own.
My tortur'd Soul reflects with Pain,
On all the thoughtless, guilty Train.

Forgive, My Country, O forgive ;
With deep Remorse I plead to live :
With Pity all my Crimes chastise,
And drink Repentance from these Eyes.

Hard'ned to Crimes -- prone to rebell,
I dar'd assault the Gates of Hell :
No Vice my callous Heart declin'd ;
No Ray of Grace illum'd my Mind.

Now all my Sins like Fiends arise,
And burning Tortures blast my Eyes :
Mercy from injur'd Heav'n implore,
Resolve by Grace to sin no more.

I come -- submit to all my Shame,
Nor dare my Injur'd Country blame :
Some Pity sure a Wretch may share,
Nor let me double Tortures bear.

Contempt I know is my Desert ;
But O let Pity reach the Heart :
And let these transient Pangs atone ;
Nor smile insulting while I groan.--

But ye whose Breasts are rib'd with Steel,
Whose marble Hearts disdain to feel,
Go lay your lurking Vices bare,
And judge with Rigour Follies there.-

And ye whose Souls relenting prove,
Those Twins of Virtue, *Pity, Love* ;
May righteous Heav'n at length bestow
That Mercy, you to other's show.

But O thou Power of Grace divine,
Thy Mercy grant -- for Mercy's thine ;
Tho' Man condemn -- do thou forgive,
And let a Rebel Sinner live.

The Humble Confession of that Notorious Cheat, Doctor Seth Hudson, *1762.*
Courtesy of the Historical Society of Pennsylvania.

Chapter 11
Madam Fitch's Treasure Scheme
1762

MIRIAM FITCH, the almost fifty-year-old wife of a respectable
Bedford miller, plotted to swindle—and possibly kill—three Boston
merchants in a scheme that could net her and her accomplice an
enormous windfall. The story of this unlikely con artist and her
noteworthy victims, Boston merchants Nathaniel Wheelwright
and Christopher Clarke, was recounted by diarist John Boyle in
his "Journal of Occurrences in Boston." In the fall of 1762 Miriam
came to Boston, where according to Boyle she met Clarke, perhaps
at his home or in his shop next door to the Heart and Crown tavern.
On November 9, Miriam made an intriguing proposal to Clarke. In
exchange for a sum of money, she would take him to a vault in Bedford where a large chest containing a fortune was hidden. Before
long, Clarke, Wheelwright, and a third unnamed Bostonian found
the offer irresistible and agreed to recover the treasure chest. The
scheme was in full swing but, by a twist of fate, Miriam's nefarious
plans were foiled and one of provincial Boston's most notorious
female "cheats" was brought to justice.

Born in Andover in September 1713, Miriam was the daughter of
Robert Gray and his wife, Miriam Lovejoy. Her marriage to Benjamin
Fitch occurred in her hometown in February 1732. The newlyweds
soon moved to Bedford, where Benjamin subsequently purchased a
saw and gristmill on the Shawshine River from the Bacon family. The
mill had been built by a member of the Bacon family in the prior

century and was, according to local tradition, burned by Indians during King Philip's War and rebuilt on the same spot. It was here on the banks of the Shawshine that Benjamin Fitch served the communities of Bedford and Billerica as a miller and farmer and where he and Miriam had at least nine children between 1733 and 1752. From this unremarkable rural setting a middle-aged female schemer inexplicably emerged.

The circumstances in which the miller's wife and her accomplice, Samuel Bacon, devised their scam, or the reasons behind it, are now unknown. The nature of Miriam's relationship with Bacon, a Bedford neighbor nearly ten years her junior, is also unknown. Their scheme was built upon the same miracle investment scam used by generations of con artists: a victim is approached with a "too-good-to-be-true" proposition that promises to yield great financial dividends. After receiving a payment, the perpetrators then vanish. In this case, Miriam was not planning her own disappearance but, rather, the detainment or elimination of her victim. That she would attempt such a blatant and dangerous deceit in Boston so soon after the Dr. Seth Hudson scandal had rocked the town shows incredible determination and naïveté.

Having developed a plan, Miriam left her husband and family and set out for Boston. She selected as her target Christopher Clarke, a merchant and caulker then in his mid-twenties. Clarke's newspaper advertisements for his Cornhill shop listed the latest imports of "English and India goods," including fine silks and fabrics of every description, spices, and other sundries, offered at wholesale and retail prices for cash, credit, or treasury notes. After ingratiating herself with the promising young merchant, Miriam revealed her proposition: for a sum, perhaps as high as £6,000, "she could show him a vault in Bedford where was concealed a large chest of money, which he might have if she could get it out and she would assist him in doing it." She explained that the chest contained a horde of gold coins, and since she was determined that neither her husband nor their children should ever have any part of the treasure, she was now offering him the chest and its contents for a premium if he would come with her and secretly remove it. John Boyle in his journal recorded that Clarke was "elated with the proposal, and thinking by the enterprise to make his fortune, agreed to go to Bedford with the woman, if he could raise the money."

Clarke confided the offer to a fellow merchant, Nathaniel Wheelwright, who he believed might be willing to share in the expense of Mrs. Fitch's premium. Few men in Boston were better connected among the mercantile elite than Nathaniel Wheelwright, then about forty years old and an active parishioner and benefactor of King's Chapel. He had solidified his position in Boston society seven years earlier by marrying heiress Ann Apthorp, daughter of the wealthy merchant Charles Apthorp. Wheelwright was also notable for his role in the 1750s for redeeming New Englanders held captive in Canada. On hearing of the remarkable opportunity, Wheelwright consented to supply the necessary funds as long as he was guaranteed a share of the proceeds. Clarke readily consented to this arrangement "rather than have the matter any further delayed." After the two merchants agreed to share in the treasure, "the money was brought out and tendered to Madam Fitch," but Wheelwright had mainly silver coins of small denomination on hand. Miriam balked at the sight of the weighty pile, saying "she could not carry it home conveniently, and desired she might have it in gold." Without enough gold in his house to accommodate Miriam, Wheelwright visited a neighbor (whose name is not known) to exchange the silver coins for gold ones. After Wheelwright let him in on the secret, the neighbor "cheerfully" agreed to muster up the gold if he, too, could be included in the transaction. The three men then paid Miriam, who quickly pocketed the funds and announced that she was ready to take them to the treasure site.

Without delay, the party mounted their horses and followed Miriam to Bedford. She conducted the men to a mill, probably the same one on the Shawshine owned by her husband, Benjamin. There Miriam opened a trap door. Pointing to a chest about ten feet under the mill, she told the men "if they would go down and get it to the head of the stairs, she with Mr. Bacon . . . would help them get it through the trap door." With the treasure chest in sight, Clarke, Wheelwright, and their unnamed partner proceeded down the stairs to retrieve it, but "no sooner were they at the bottom of the stairs, than she shut down the door upon them, and locked it upon the top, and run off." At this moment, the Bostonians knew they had been taken for fools or, as Boyle put it, "to their inexpressible grief, [they] found it was all a deception." While they stumbled about in the dark bowels of the mill, Miriam Fitch and Samuel Bacon raced away with the stolen money. According to Boyle, the trapped men were in imminent peril, for if they had "remained there but a few hours longer, they must inevitably have perished, as it was near the time the flood-gates were to be

Nathaniel Wheelwright, who was defrauded by Miriam Fitch. Portrait attributed to John Singleton Copley, ca. 1750; courtesy of the Massachusetts Historical Society.

hoisted, when the water would have been let in upon them." To their great good fortune, a passerby heard the men shouting and helped them escape the locked compartment. No doubt the merchants were embarrassed by their gullibility and profoundly grateful to be alive.

Miriam and Samuel did not get far. They were soon apprehended and confined to await a Superior Court trial that would occur in Charlestown the following January. When the case was heard, the evidence was overwhelming and both were found guilty. The court called the pair "persons of very ill fame, and dishonest conversation, and common deceivers and defrauders," and sentenced them to be set in the pillory in Boston for one hour with papers attached to their breasts that read "A CHEAT." In addition, they would serve a three-month prison term and suffer other penalties.

In the aftermath of the treasure scheme, both Clarke and Wheelwright returned to their commercial interests in Boston. Clarke remained active in business affairs, but about three years later Wheelwright suffered a spectacular business collapse and fled the country. He died in 1766 in Guadeloupe, a disgraced man. Miriam, by contrast, survived her failed treasure scheme by decades. Widowed in 1770, she lived until about 1802, when she died at an advanced age in meager circumstances. Her estate, valued at just under $39, included various worn, threadbare, and dilapidated items—all of this a far cry from the riches she attempted to cheat out of three Bostonians forty years earlier.

Part Three

A Miscellany of Miscreants

MURDER, KIDNAPPING, EXTORTION, thievery, dueling, prostitution—these and a multitude of other crimes took place in colonial Boston, and an eager public consumed accounts of them all. One of the town's most sensational criminal trials occurred shortly before the American Revolution. Levi Ames, a young man with an extensive criminal background, was sentenced to death for capital burglary in 1773. His execution created a major commotion and elicited the publication of more than ten broadsides, inexpensive "scandal sheets" purchased by people of all walks of life. But sometimes even relatively trivial matters captured the town's attention. In January 1768, for example, merchant John Rowe noted in his diary a "famous trial" of the day: Mrs. Kneeland stood accused of stealing a silver spoon from Dr Baker. (The defendant was found not guilty.) Murders aroused consideredable interest. Dr. John Greenleaf's children were murdered in 1750 and 1751, the first "serial" killing of its kind in Boston. By the late twentieth century the Greenleaf case had so completely faded from the annals of Boston history that some believed it to be an unseemly legend. A case that riveted Boston one day began a gradual slide into obscurity the next.

These forgotten crimes yield glimpses into the lives of seventeenth- and eighteenth-century Americans. Some crimes put the whole community on alarm. In the late 1730s and early 1740s a professional horse thief, Jabez Allen alias James Mead, threatened Boston and

Portrait of Captain John Bonner, burglary victim and engraver of a 1722 map of Boston.
Courtesy of the New England Historic Genealogical Society.

nearby towns. By February 1738, Allen had twice been convicted of the crime. On the second occasion he was sent to the gallows and whipped thirty stripes. The *Boston Evening Post* reported that he promised to leave the province after being set free but was "resolved not to go on foot," and "so, gentlemen," the newspaper warned, "look to your horses." Two years later the thief reappeared in Cambridge on a stolen horse—an incident quickly reported in the Boston press. When apprehending him, an officer asked Allen how he liked his horse. He purportedly replied that she was a "high Jade" and that he "feared some time or other she would throw him, and he should hang in the stirrup." Allen escaped hanging, by stirrup or gallows, and was instead impressed into naval service. By October 1742, he had deserted the *Augusta* in the West Indies and was rumored to have returned to Massachusetts in order to resume his old trade. Governor William Shirley promptly issued a proclamation to apprehend the province's most notorious horse thief.

Burglaries were a regular blight upon the safety and security of early Boston. Captain John Bonner, a wealthy mariner in his late sixties, was a victim of a major burglary, an incident that likely caused an uproar in town. When he returned from a voyage in early 1711, he found that not only had his wife Rebecca died shortly before, but their house had been robbed. Among the missing goods were piles of his dead wife's fashionable clothing and an assortment of other household items. The incident led Bonner to publish notice of a reward in the *Boston News-Letter* in February 1711:

> *Stolen or carried privately away out of the house of Capt. John Bonner in Cow-Lane near Fort Hill Boston, sometime before the late sickness of his late wife, or about the time of her decease, which was in the month of January last; the following particulars, viz. Of his wife's wearing apparel three silk gowns, one changeable colour, a second flowered and the third stript: three other gowns, one where of a double gown, one side silk-stuff, the other russell; a second double gown of silk-stuff and petticoat of the same, the third a black crape gown and petticoat of the same: four other petticoats, one changeable coloured silk, a second black flowered silk, a third plain black silk, the fourth a flowered sarge, one lutestring hood and scarf, three laced headdresses and one plain, three laced caps, two laced handkerchiefs, three under caps laced, three white aprons, three pair of laced sleeves, two white muslin hoods, one amber necklace, one muff, one new gilded Bible and several other books, some new garlick Holland, and dowlas, one flannel blanket, one pair of scales and a small set of troy weights, two copper pots, several pieces of plate, viz, one silver tankard containing about a quart, two silver cups with one handle, two silver porringers, one silver spoon, two gold rings,*

one pair of gold buttons, and sundry other things. Whoever shall restore or bring back again the above named goods unto said Bonner, or any part of them or give any true intelligence of the same so as that he may have them again shall be sufficiently rewarded, besides all necessary charges paid.

Whether Bonner ever recovered any of the valuables stolen in this curious incident remains unknown. In time, he married twice more and had several children, but the activity for which he is remembered today is his production of the first city plan engraved and printed in America. Bonner's 1722 map, which he advertised as a "curious ingraven map of the Town of Boston," shows the town as it appeared for much of its first two hundred years, "a small peninsula indented by deep coves that were separated by promontories surmounted by high hills." Reprinted and updated at various times in the eighteenth century, Bonner's map (reproduced on the endpapers) is one of the centerpieces of colonial Boston cartography. Captain Bonner died at age eighty-four, celebrated for his map of Boston and recalled as a "gentleman very skillful and ingenious in many arts and sciences."

Other crimes captured public attention. A number of duels were fought in early Boston, the most important of which took place in July 1728 between Henry Phillips and Benjamin Woodbridge. Several other skirmishes preceded it. On August 17, 1695, diarist Samuel Sewall noted that "a duel was fought this day upon the Common between Peggy and Captain Cole." "Peggy" seems to have been no stranger to trouble in town. He was almost certainly the Boston merchant Edward Peggy, who a number of years earlier had run into troubles in the Suffolk County Court for using "powders or other ways unlawful to engage the affections of women" and for fornication with Ruth Hemingway of Roxbury.

A second major duel recounted by Sewall and others occurred more than a decade later and this time attracted considerable public attention. On February 11, 1711/12, Thomas Lechmere wrote to his brother-in-law John Winthrop with news of the swordfight between two military officers, Lieutenants James Alexander and James Douglass, a few days earlier on the Common:

On Friday, the moon being in the dragon's taill (an ill omen), wee had something to do in Boston Common, — two of our sparks (officers), Messrs. Douglas & Alexander, had a mind to shew their manhood. Alexander (like the Great of old) gave the challenge. Douglas in honour could not refuse it, so very loveingly tooke theire departure from Boston into the Common; there they bravely gave the word draw; out they pulled spado, to it they went, & manfully engaged each other, & like two brave heroes gave each other a mortall wound. Douglas rece[ive]d his wound in the belly; Alexander through the shoulder & out the back, & 'tis doubtfull whither either will recover. This being the substance of the story or tragedy.

James Alexander lingered in agony for more than a week and died. His adversary, James Douglass, fled to Annapolis, Nova Scotia. The last word on Douglass came from Wait Winthrop, son of the Connecticut governor and grandson of the founder of the Massachusetts Bay Colony, the following month: "A vessel just now from Annapolis brings word that Douglass, the North Brittain that made his escape, is got thither, and like to be well of his wound."

One of the last duels fought on Boston Common in this period involved Captain Thomas Smart and John Boydell, who came to blows on December 16, 1718. At the time of the duel, Boydell had recently begun what would become a more than twenty-year tenure as register of probate in Boston; in due course he also became the publisher of one of provincial Boston's most important newspapers, the *Boston Gazette*. As with prior Boston duels, the root cause of the conflict remains a mystery. Apparently, both Smart and Boydell escaped from the fracas unscathed, but were fined £10 and jailed for twenty-four hours. This duel is cited as the catalyst for legislation the following June that prohibited dueling in Massachusetts and set penalties for violators, including fines of up to £100 and imprisonment of up to six months.

Violence with swords was not limited to dueling. In April 1749 a limeseller named Robert Hunt had an argument with a man and drew a sword on him. His would-be victim grabbed the weapon and broke it. As authorities approached Hunt's house, they found the deranged lime-seller firing a pistol out a window; he killed a boy on the street with a shot to the head. Subsequently taken to jail, Hunt hanged himself four days later by strapping a garter to the iron bars. When his body was transported to be buried near the gallows, a stake was driven through his lifeless body.

More macabre forms of mischief occurred when the town was seized by anxiety over smallpox epidemics, and particularly when embroiled in dissension over Dr. Zabdiel Boylston's experimental inoculations against the disease. Cotton Mather supported inoculations, a controversial stand. In the early morning hours of November 14, 1721, a homemade grenade—an iron ball with a lit fuse—was lobbed into Mather's house, landing in the bedroom the clergyman normally used. The "granado" nearly hit Mather's kinsman, Thomas Walter, a minister from Roxbury. When the device malfunctioned and was retrieved, Mather discovered a note attached to a long string on it. It read "COTTON MATHER, you dog, damn you: I'll inoculate you with this, with a pox to you." The following day Governor Samuel Shute offered a reward of £50 for further information on the incident, but the perpetrator of one of the town's most unusual murder attempts was never caught.

An equally strange incident occurred decades later, in 1764, during another smallpox outbreak. John Gray went into a house he was supposed to be guarding where a woman, Mrs. Adams, had just died of the infection. Entering the dead women's bedroom, Gray brushed past two nurses, claiming he was there on official business. He then scraped an arm of the corpse with rolled paper in an attempt to collect a specimen of infected skin. This suspicious activity was immediately reported to the selectmen of Boston, who apprehended Gray, placed him in the stone jail, and charged that he had engaged in a "malicious design to spread the infection of the small pox."

Colonial Boston also had its share of seedy scandals. Men who visited private houses or taverns occupied by persons of questionable morals were sometimes watched by their more virtuous neighbors. In September 1713 Cotton Mather noted in his diary that he had compiled a "catalogue of young men, who visit wicked houses," whom he intended to admonish. An earlier generation of men might have visited the house of one of the town's bawdiest women, Alice Thomas, a matron who has been called the "Massachusetts Bay Madam." By the time of her troubles in Boston, Alice had been widowed twice and was the mother of five adult children. She lived in Lynn with her first husband, but after he died Alice moved to Boston and married a widowed Welshman, vintner Evan Thomas. By 1671 Alice was once again a widow and was selling beer and maintaining a "house of entertainment" at the King's Arms Tavern in the North End. Being a tavern keeper was not Alice's only occupation. Her nights were filled with more illicit activities. In 1672 she was convicted of being an accessory in burgling warehouses and vessels at night, selling liquor without a license, and a miscellany of other colorful crimes. Her chief offense, however, was in turning her tavern into a bordello by giving "frequent, secret, and unseasonable entertainment in her house to lewd, lascivious, and notorious persons of both sexes, giving them opportunity to commit carnal wickedness, and by common fame, she is a common baud."

In a deliberately painful and humiliating punishment, Alice was made to strip to the waist and walk behind a cart to which she was tied while being "whipped through the street to the prison." In addition, she was to stand at the gallows with a rope around her neck, pay fines, and serve a prison sentence. In time, she was permitted to leave the prison during the day in an arrangement one scholar has referred to as a Puritan-era "day work program." After her incarceration, Alice returned to her business interests in Boston but apparently never again operated a brothel.

Alice Thomas was not the only convicted "madam" in the town's history. In May 1753 one of Boston's most infamous whorehouses was shut down. Hannah Dilley, the wife of a local felt maker, was tried for operating a house on Cold Lane—not far from Faneuil Hall—where men were entertained for the purposes of "lechery" and "fornication." Hannah enticed men to the house in order "to carnally lie with whores" she procured. For her crime, Hannah was sentenced to stand for one hour on a five-foot-tall stool in front of the courthouse on King Street. As was customary in public punishments, a paper stating her crime was affixed to her breast for all to see. In addition, she was fined £10. After successfully pleading dire poverty to the court, Hannah's fine was reduced to £5.

A rare firsthand account of men visiting a pair of prostitutes survives from 1683 when several Bostonians, including barber and surgeon Samuel Checkley and bookseller Samuel Phillips, called upon two sisters living at "the Printer's house" for the purpose of having sex. According to Checkley's deposition, Phillips told him and Thomas Saffin that "the other night he had done a thing that he would not do again for a £1000 because he had a wife which he loved well and he should wrong her if he did." Saffin pressed to know what he had been up to, and Phillips answered

> *that for two pints of wine he would tell us both where we might have two wholesome young women at our command and that he would go with us and show us the house which accordingly he did at eleven o'clock at night and told us that the yard door was open. Where we might go right upstairs and knock at the door on the left hand, going upstairs without disturbing the people which lived underneath.*

Phillips assured his cohorts that he would not be recognized by the young women because he had, on his prior visit, "changed his name and there was no light in the chamber." Phillips had been accompanied by Samuel Bill. Negotiations between one of the men, probably Phillips, and one of the young women had broken down and she "consented that he should lie with her for nothing." At this point, he was unable to perform sexually: "his prick would not stand . . . he could not make it stand for his life, which made him so mad that he gave her two or three damned slaps upon her naked thighs and let her go." In the aftermath of these visits, Hannah Hounsell became pregnant and named Thomas Saffin as the father. Depositions were taken in November 1683 and Samuel Phillips, eager to see his reputation remain untarnished, offered Saffin £12 to help ensure his name would not be mentioned in the proceedings. Saffin wanted an additional £3, which Checkley was willing to pay "rather than such a piece of debauchery should come into court." In spite of these bribery attempts, Samuel Checkley was deposed and the imbroglio became public knowledge.

Samuel Phillips and his cohorts were not the most eminent Bostonians who became mixed up with women of ill repute. Decades later, John Hancock, the patriot, was known to be involved with a woman, said to be a prostitute, whom he kept as his mistress prior to marrying Dorothy Quincy. Shopkeeper Dorcas Pringle Griffiths was, according to Thomas Flucker, "a common prostitute and bred up her daughter in the same way, she was kept by the famous Hancock, and when he turned her off, she lived with Capt. Johnson." Unlike Hancock, Dorcas was a Loyalist and later took refuge in England, where she petitioned the British government to restore assets lost to her after American independence.

MURDER AND ATTEMPTED MURDER were the most serious crimes in colonial Boston, but they were relatively uncommon by today's standards. Several episodes of murder in early Boston were the result of sudden violent rows between men, such as an August 1713 clash between mariners. In this incident, David Wallis fatally stabbed Benjamin Stolwood in a dockside quarrel. Found guilty, Wallis was executed the following month.

The town responded with particular repugnance to the murder of an infant or child. One of the earliest murders in the colony occurred in 1644 when William Franklin of Roxbury tortured a young apprentice, Nathaniel Sewall. Franklin allowed Nathaniel to become malnourished, and in one bizarre episode "hoisted the boy up into a chimney and left him suspended there for a long time." After these and other instances of inhumane treatment at the hands of his master, Nathaniel finally expired. William Franklin was found guilty of willful murder by the Court of Assistants and hanged in June 1644.

Because of the strict taboo against out-of-wedlock pregnancy, infanticide was another violent crime seen in colonial Boston. Two of Boston's most notable infanticide cases occurred in 1698 and 1733. In both cases, the women involved were from decent but humble Boston families. Both fell into promiscuous behavior that resulted in pregnancy, which led them, in desperation, to commit murder. Both were publicly executed amid "evangelical fanfare." Sarah, the seventh child of mason Bartholomew Threeneedles and his wife Damaris Hawkins, had already given birth to one illegitimate child when she became pregnant again at the age of nineteen. She confessed that she was subject to "rash wishes" and "mad passions." Her parents were forgiving but feared the worst for their wayward daughter. On September 26, 1698, Sarah gave birth to her second child, a boy, whom she abandoned in a pasture shortly after his birth. His tiny body, when recovered, was found to be bruised.

During her trial the following month, Sarah identified the father of her dead son. Before a large concourse of onlookers, she claimed that Thomas Savage, a prominent shopkeeper of Boston, had "ruin'd" her by impregnating her. Savage, the thirty-year-old son of merchant Thomas Savage and his wife, Ann Scottow, had followed his well-known father in both mercantile and military occupations. Savage vigorously denied Sarah's claims. Samuel Sewall observed and recorded the courtroom encounter between Sarah and Thomas Savage:

> Thomas Savage junior, shopkeeper, and Sarah Threeneedle were brought face to face in a very great Audience: She vehemently accused him, and he asserted his innocency with vehement Asseverations. She said he had ruin'd her; if he would have promis'd her any thing, it had not come to this. Said She forgave him, Judgment of God hung over him if did not repent.

Sarah's charges against a leading Bostonian did not help her case, and her reluctance to admit regret for her actions undoubtedly worked to her disadvantage. Found guilty by the court, she was sentenced to death. Cotton Mather treated Sarah's story in *Pillars of Salt,* his 1699 treatise on executed criminals in New England. Mather revealed that prior to her condemnation, Sarah was caught in further "crimes of unchastity," namely, having sexual relations with a fellow prisoner, an incident providing surplus evidence of her wantonness. On a serene day in November 1698, Sarah Threeneedles was brought to the South Meetinghouse, where Mather preached on her crimes before a crowd so large it not only filled the main chamber but spilled out onto the street. After being subjected to a lecture on the subject of murdering her "base born" child, Sarah was taken to the execution place and hanged before the masses. Sarah Threeneedles's accusations against Thomas Savage evidently had little lasting effect on his reputation in town; within three years he began to serve in a variety of public offices in Boston, including those of constable and selectman.

The case of Rebecca Chamblit occurred more than thirty years later. The youngest daughter of Henry and Elizabeth Chamblit (or Chamlet) of Boston, Rebecca was a twenty-seven-year-old domestic servant in town when she committed her crime. In a final confession—*The Declaration, Dying Warning and Advice of Rebekah Chamblit*—read at her execution and later published, Rebecca recalled the events that led to her downfall. She remembered her "tender" upbringing in her father's house, where she stated she had been well reared. At about sixteen she was baptized and, for a time, lived in a righteous manner, but after two or three years fell into "unclean, sinful" patterns that marked the beginning of her "ruin for this world." Rebecca claimed that after this lapse she managed to return to a respectable life until the events that led to her conviction in 1733.

In the fall of 1732 Rebecca found herself pregnant by a man she later chose not to name. It appears that she disguised her pregnancy. On Saturday, May 5, 1733, while performing household chores for her employers, Rebecca recalled having a "considerable hurt," which continued for three days. During this time she could not detect any movement or signs of life in the baby she was carrying. Her discomfort continued until she quietly delivered a male infant the following Tuesday. The infant showed no obvious signs of life, but not knowing for certain whether it was dead or alive, Rebecca a few minutes later threw it into the "vault." Or, as the diarist Benjamin Walker Jr. put it when the story circulated in Boston, Rebecca discarded her son "into a house of offal or shithouse." Rebecca later acknowledged that the baby may indeed have been alive at its birth: "I confess its probable there was Life in it, and some Circumstances seem to confirm it."

Rebecca's printed confession was not only meant to tell her story but to be a warning to others, especially young women. Rebecca acknowledged the presence of houses of ill repute in Boston, stating,

"I am sensible there are many Houses in this Town, that may be called Houses of Uncleanness, and Places of dreadful Temptations to this and all other Sins. O shun them, for they lead down to the Chambers of Death and Eternal Misery." After the detection of her discarded infant, Rebecca was tried and convicted by the Superior Court of "concealing the birth of her spurious male infant ... afterwards found dead."

Diarist John Rowe, who recorded the punishment of John and Ann Richardson as well as events mentioned in other chapters. From Letters and Diary of John Rowe, Boston Merchant.

Rebecca was present when on September 23, 1733, the Reverend Thomas Foxcroft delivered a sermon based on her crime entitled "Lessons of Caution to Young Sinners." Four days later, before throngs of onlookers in Boston, she was hanged.

One of the most atrocious examples of attempted infanticide in provincial Boston occurred in 1764 when John and Ann Richardson endeavored to kill a baby by starvation, abuse, and exposure. On July 9, 1763, Ann Everton, an unmarried woman, gave birth to a female baby. A few months later, Ann married Boston laborer John Richardson, probably the infant's father, in a ceremony at Christ Church. Shortly after their marriage, John and Ann began to set about to destroy the baby's life. Over almost five months they beat, bruised, and wounded the girl, deprived her almost entirely of nourishment of any kind, and left her insufficiently clothed in a small, cold, wet room. The room was partially exposed to the elements, and snow and rain frequently blew into it. Remarkably, the baby did not die.

How authorities discovered the infant is not known, but her appearance when found was almost unbelievable. Wasted away and presenting "a ghastly spectacle terrible to behold," the little girl was removed from the house. The Richardsons were arrested and tried for attempted murder, a charge to which they pleaded not guilty. Having heard the evidence, the jury found them guilty and the couple was sentenced to be set upon the gallows for the space of one hour with ropes around their necks. Almost exactly a year after their marriage, John and Ann were sent for punishment at Boston Neck. The case aroused considerable public interest and scores of Bostonians were on hand to see the punishment meted out to a couple considered to be "devoid of humanity." Diarist John Rowe was a witness and recorded that the angry crowd "pelted him which was what he deserved."

Like so many incidents before and after, the Richardson case was sensational enough to merit the publication of broadside verse, *Inhuman Cruelty: Or Villainy Detected.* Since the baby survived, John and Ann Richardson were spared the capital punishment meted out to Sarah Threeneedles and Rebecca Chamblit.

The people of colonial Boston were regularly swept up in the drama of these crimes and scores of others like them. Ranging from lurid to laughable, trivial to tragic, tales of the town's most infamous miscreants captured wide public attention. For ministers and printers, the most serious misdeeds provided opportunities to publish moralizing sermons or didactic broadsides. For others, these incidents and their consequences offered not only cautionary tales or venues for biblical invective, but also sparked gossip, provided entertainment, and, perhaps most of all, reaffirmed the social order.

Chapter 12

Carrying the King Away:
A Bostonian's Brush with Treason
1667

A MAN KNOWN FOR speaking his mind, Arthur Mason made a
rash outburst that could have cost him his life. A biscuit baker by profession, he also served as a constable. One night in mid-January 1667
Arthur was on the lookout for a group of men who had caused a dis-
turbance the previous evening. He suspected they were flouting the
law of the Puritan community by congregating at a tavern on a Saturday night. The men in question were not typical troublemakers; they
were the King's commissioners—a group appointed in 1664 to
enforce the policies of Charles II. Among them were Sir Robert Carr,
Colonel George Cartwright, Colonel Richard Nichols, and Samuel
Maverick. Within moments, Arthur impulsively used language that
resulted in cries of "treason!" and threats that he would be hanged.

Arthur had expected the commissioners to be at John Viall's Ship
Tavern near Scarlett's Wharf, but instead found them across the street
at the house of merchant Thomas Kellond. Brandishing a staff on his
arrival, Arthur told the men he was glad to see them there, "for if he
had found them on the other side of the street he would have carried
them all away." Arthur engaged in a heated exchange with Sir Robert
Carr, who admitted it was he who had beaten a constable the previous night and that he would "do it again." Affronted by their conduct
the previous evening, Arthur rebuked the commissioners for being
"so uncivil as to beat a constable and abuse authority." This comment
agitated Sir Robert Carr. A formidable man with whom to spar, Carr

had been created a Knight of the Royal Oak by Charles II seven years earlier. In spite of such exalted connections, Carr was reputed to be of "very weak understanding." Arthur became provoked and made a slip that would have serious consequences:

> Mason replied, that he thought his Majesty's commissioners would not have beaten his Majesty's officers, and that it was well for them that he was not the constable who found them there, for he would have carried them before authority. Sir Robert asked, if he dare meddle with the King's commissioners? Yes, says Mason, and if the King himself had been there I would have carried him away; upon which Maverick cried out, treason! Mason, thou shalt be hanged within a twelve-month.

Having blurted out that he would have arrested and carried away "the King himself," Arthur put himself in considerable jeopardy. An astounded Sir Robert Carr asked Sir Thomas Temple, the governor of Acadia, and others in the assembly at Kellond's house "to take notice of what passed." The following morning, Samuel Maverick contacted Governor Richard Bellingham. In his note, he charged Arthur with "high treason for the words spoken" and requested that the governor have him apprehended. Bellingham decided that the matter was of "too high a nature for him to interpose in" and so required Arthur to appear before the Court of Assistants.

Sir Robert Carr refused to present himself before the Court of Assistants, but another witness, Nicholas Paige, provided a deposition against Arthur. Arthur prepared a strong defense, claiming that the witnesses' depositions were inconsistent and contradicted each other. He attempted to discredit Paige's account in particular by stating that he was "a known ill willer to me, on a former grudge of long standing." His comments about the king could not be treason, he explained, because he knew that the king was not there: it "could not rationally be supposed that his Majesty would or could be there, I knowing he was not and that it was impossible for him to be there." He pleaded that his words were uttered only in the "heat of discourse" as he executed his office as constable. By May 1667, the case was turned over to the General Court. Arthur's scandalous

The children of the outspoken Arthur Mason: left to right, David, Joanna, and Abigail.
Portrait by an unknown artist, 1670. Courtesy of the Fine Arts Museums of San Francisco;
gift of Mr. and Mrs. John D. Rockefeller 3rd.

words, it determined in the end, were "rash, insolent, and highly offensive" but they had not reflected "any overt act, or evil intended against the King." Spared conviction as a capital offender, the General Court sentenced Arthur to be admonished "in solemn manner" by Governor Bellingham.

The treason incident was not Arthur Mason's last dust-up in Boston over his outspoken manner. In 1670, he was disenfranchised as a freeman of the colony in an incident that occurred at the old meetinghouse of the First Church. Arthur, who was not a member of the congregation, was asked by the elders to leave a meeting of the church. When he balked at the request, John Leverett instructed him to leave, an order that inspired Arthur to become defiant and loudly stomp out with his wife, a member of the church:

> I spoke unto him that he would depart and not disturb the Church in their occasions; he replied that if he did depart he would have his wife away with him, it was returned to him that she was one of the Church and ought to be there, he said he would not go without her, so he went out of the place where he was, went through an alley to the pew where his wife was sitting and in a presumptuous and daring manner and saying he would have her away, took her by the hand and held her and so took her away from out of the meeting house.

As Arthur and his wife, Joanna, departed, John Leverett called out for a constable to arrest Arthur for his egregious conduct and bring him to prison. In due course, the case was tried and, having been found guilty, Mason was disenfranchised—an act that essentially deprived him of the right to vote—for his use of "sinful, passionate, and unadvised words and behavior" before the First Church of Boston. The following year, Arthur acknowledged his transgression and successfully petitioned the Court of Assistants to reinstate him as a freeman.

In spite of these clashes, Arthur made his mark in Boston as a prosperous biscuit baker. His business proved successful enough for him to build a mansion on School Street adjacent to the Boston Common. As a further sign of his affluence, in 1670, the same year as his contretemps with the church elders, he commissioned portraits of his family by an unidentified artist. In one of the surviving portraits, three of Arthur's children, David, Joanna, and Abigail, appear together—richly attired and carefully posed in a style reminiscent of Tudor or Jacobean works. Alice holds a flower and her elder sister, Joanna, holds a fan, an indication of a "highborn lady." Years later, Joanna Mason's virtues were extolled by English bookseller John Dunton, who called her "the flower of Boston."

In subsequent years, Arthur Mason's penchant for directness continued. "Another of my fellow-ramblers is Mr. Mason, a grave, sober merchant, a good man, and well respected," recounted John Dunton, "amongst honest men downright honest, but very blunt: one that would speak his mind, however men took it." Dunton recalled an incident in which Arthur offended a local gentlewoman by his brusque acknowledgment of her lack of housekeeping:

> I remember once, that when he went to visit a Bostonian gentle-woman, she told him she was glad to see him, but sorry that he came at such a time when her house lay so dirty, and so much out of order. To which Mr. Mason only returned, Why, prithee, when wasn't other-wise? Which blunt expression (which perhaps carried too much truth in it) the gentlewoman took as an affront. But 'twas all one to him, for he would make no retraction.

One of Boston's earliest free speakers, Arthur Mason survived a trial for treason, a skirmish with the First Church of Boston, and the judgment of neighbors who found his curt manner offensive.

Chapter 13

Death on the Common:
The Duel of Benjamin Woodbridge
and Henry Phillips
1728

"HONORED MADAM," wrote an anxious and cash-starved Henry
Phillips from La Rochelle, France, to his widowed mother, Hannah
Phillips, in Boston, in March 1729. "According to your desire I am
come into France, but find it as all other places extremely chargeable,
especially to me who have so small a stock. Whether I am like to get
my pardon, only God knows." Henry, the twenty-five-year-old scion
of a Boston publishing and bookselling family and a 1724 graduate of
Harvard College, was an unlikely fugitive from the law. He escaped to
France with the aid of Boston merchant Peter Faneuil after fighting a
duel on the Boston Common on July 3, 1728, that resulted in the
death of another prominent young man, nineteen-year-old Benjamin
Woodbridge. Indicted for murder, seriously ill, and running out of
money, Henry was desperate for a pardon that might have cleared
the way for his return to Boston. While much of proper Boston supported Henry's cause, time was not on his side.

During the late seventeenth and early eighteenth centuries, dueling on
the Boston Common was a rare, but not unheard-of, event. In his diary
Samuel Sewall recorded three such conflicts prior to the Woodbridge–
Phillips duel, an event that many chroniclers have erroneously stated
was the first duel, or first fatal duel, to take place on the Common.

The 1728 victim was Benjamin Woodbridge, a young man who had
been sent to live in Boston by his father in 1716 at the tender age of

six or seven, possibly to the home of the Reverend Benjamin Colman. Benjamin's father, Dudley Woodbridge, was a jurist and merchant who lived in the Caribbean and England, and a member of a family with enviable credentials in the highest circles of Boston society. By 1721 an orphaned Benjamin appears to have been a part of the household of ship chandler Samuel Sewall (nephew of the diarist of the same name). Benjamin's association with the Sewall family continued some years later when he entered into business with Samuel's brother, Jonathan Sewall, also a ship chandler.

Like his eventual adversary Benjamin Woodbridge, Henry Phillips was also born to a well-known and affluent family. The Phillipses were notable for their mercantile successes. Henry was the last-born of some eight children of the Boston bookseller, stationer, and merchant Samuel Phillips and his wife, Hannah Gillam.

Shortly after his father's death, Henry enrolled at Harvard College, where he was known as "Blubber Phillips." At some point during his studies he was fined ten shillings for entering into a minor but apparently good-humored infraction with two classmates. Henry subsequently took over his late father's business. A fashionable bachelor, he owned houses in both Cornhill and Merchant's Row that were richly furnished with desks, looking glasses, leather and Turkey-work chairs, various paintings and prints, and even a gilt cabinet. His elegant clothing and furnishings included a scarlet waistcoat and breeches, flowered waistcoats, silk stockings and handkerchiefs, a wig, two sword belts, riding boots and spurs, a pocket pistol, powder horns, a flute, a diamond ring, a gold watch, and gold buttons.

The Phillips family solidified its place in the mercantile elite of Boston when in 1725 Henry's brother Gillam made a match that brought together two important families of the province. His bride was Mary Faneuil, sister of merchant Peter Faneuil—famous for his gift of a hall to the town in 1740. This relationship later proved crucial.

When and where Henry Phillips and Benjamin Woodbridge first encountered each other in Boston is not known, but their friendship was a troubled one and, in the end, deadly. On July 3, 1728, the two young men clashed on the Boston Common somewhere near the Great Elm, leaving Benjamin the victim of severe sword wounds and Henry a man on the run.

Henry had a reputation for enjoying a good time at local taverns. Possibly the two young men argued after an evening of gaming and drinking. According to Henry, troubles between the two had been brewing for some time, and he claimed that limner Peter Pelham, later the stepfather of artist John Singleton Copley, said that a mutual acquaintance had been urging Benjamin Woodbridge into a duel. Robert Handy, Benjamin reported, had been pressing him "for three weeks or a month to challenge [Henry], which he said he would never do, till at last to be sure over-persuaded by that vile fellow."

Robert Handy, the so-called vile fellow, was involved with a local military company to which Benjamin belonged, and Handy appears to have had custody of some of its weapons. Far from identifying himself as an instigator of the swordfight, Handy later characterized his involvement in the dispute as that of peacemaker. Events unfolded

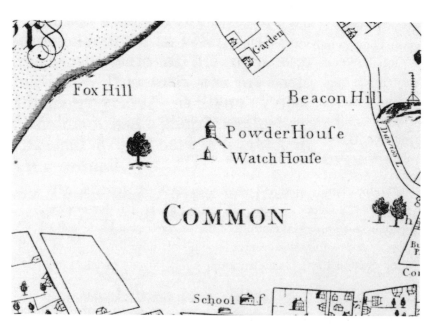

Detail of Bonner's 1722 Boston map, showing the area of the powderhouse on the Boston Common where the duel between Benjamin Woodridge and Henry Phillips took place.

sometime before nightfall on July 3, when Benjamin came to Robert Handy at the White Horse tavern and requested a sword. Asked why, Benjamin said he had been called into the country on business. Handy doubted the answer and pressed for more information, likely intuiting that the weapon might be used against Henry. Benjamin persisted, and Handy reluctantly turned over to him a sword and belt. Suspicious, Handy and another man quietly followed Benjamin to the Common. Approaching him near the powderhouse, Handy again questioned the young man about his intentions. Benjamin remained silent. Moments later, to no one's surprise, Henry Phillips appeared on the scene, "walking towards us, with his sword on his side and cloak on." Handy voiced his concern that a swordfight was about to take place, but both young men denied it. Henry barked that he had private business with Benjamin and asked Handy to go about his own business. Handy, still fearing a quarrel, insisted on knowing the nature of the business, a demand that served only to agitate Henry. Handy walked up the Common and the two men walked down it. It was then about eight o'clock.

According to his version of events, Handy did not stray far. A short time later he returned to the vicinity of the powderhouse, where he spotted Benjamin "holding his left hand below his right breast." Within seconds it was clear that the young man had been severely wounded:

> I discovered blood on his coat, asked the meaning of it. He told me Mr. Phillips had wounded him. Having no sword I enquired where it was. He said Mr. Phillips had it. Mr. Phillips immediately came up with Woodbridge's sword in his hand naked, his own by his side. I told them I was surprised they should quarrel to this degree. I told Mr. Phillips he had wounded Mr. Woodbridge. He replied yes so he had and Mr. Woodbridge had also wounded me, but in the fleshy part only, shewing me his cut fingers. Mr. Phillips took Mr. Woodbridge's scabbard, sheathed the sword, and either laid it down by him, or gave it to him.

Feeling faint, Benjamin asked Handy to summon a doctor. Handy started off but Henry begged him to stay with the wounded man until he could return with a surgeon. Handy "prayed him to hasten, but did not care to return" to Benjamin's side and hastily departed the scene. Back at the White Horse tavern minutes later, Handy told Thomas Barton and George Reason of the bloody clash that had just occurred and allegedly asked Barton to go back and check on Benjamin. But, hearing that Henry had gone to get a surgeon, Barton instead joined Handy in departing for a dinner party without checking on Benjamin's condition.

In the meantime, Henry had bolted from the Common in search of medical assistance. At some point he arrived at the Sun Tavern near Dock Square, where he located Dr. George Pemberton. Henry asked Pemberton, a surgeon and innkeeper, to look at his wounds. As he was being examined, Henry admitted that he had injured Benjamin Woodbridge and that he "feared [the wounds] would prove mortal." He asked Pemberton to return with him to the Common. Pemberton called for the assistance of another Boston physician, Dr. John Cutler, and shortly with Henry Phillips they made their way to the area of the powderhouse in search of the fallen duelist. Oddly, they couldn't find Benjamin there, and Henry swiftly departed. Cutler and Pemberton then went to Benjamin's lodgings but couldn't find him there, either. Going to Cutler's home, they found Henry, who "was very greatly concerned; fearing he had killed Mr. Woodbridge."

Henry had some minor injuries on his belly, leg, and hands. As Cutler dressed the wounds on his belly and hands, Henry worried aloud that he might have killed Benjamin Woodbridge. The doctor "endeavored to appease him & hope better things."

Next, Henry probably headed to the mansion of Gillam Phillips's brother-in-law, Peter Faneuil. It was most likely there that the young man realized that Benjamin might be dead and, if so, that he would almost certainly be charged with murder. A plan for his escape from Boston was hatched: Captain John Winslow of the pink *Molly* would need to transport Henry to the man-of-war *Sheerness* waiting farther out in Boston Harbor. This vessel would carry him to France and beyond the reach of provincial authorities. Fickle weather nearly foiled the clever getaway plan.

At about eleven o'clock, Gillam Phillips located Captain Winslow and asked the mariner to "carry off his brother Henry, who had wounded or killed a man." They then set a time to meet again at tavern owner Luke Vardy's house. From Vardy's house they moved to the house of Colonel Estis, where, in the yard, Gillam and Captain Winslow were soon joined by Henry Phillips, Peter Faneuil, and Adam Tuck. The men then split into two groups: Faneuil and Tuck spirited Henry off by dark of night to Gibb's Wharf, while Gillam accompanied Captain Winslow to the *Molly,* where they picked up four crewmen and stealthily rowed to Gibb's Wharf to collect Henry. By midnight Henry Phillips was on his way to the *Sheerness.*

John Underwood, a crewman from the *Molly,* later reported that the plan to reach the *Sheerness* was nearly thwarted when the small boat ran aground at Dorchester Neck in the "fogg or thick weather." The party sought shelter at a nearby house for an hour, then continued their quest for the man-of-war, which lay somewhere between Castle and Spectacle islands. Eventually they located the *Sheerness,* where Gillam and Tuck stayed for an hour and a half before making their final farewells. As the *Sheerness* slipped out of the harbor, Henry Phillips began his voyage to France, where Peter Faneuil arranged for him to be sheltered in La Rochelle by his uncle, Jean Faneuil. Lucius Manlius Sargent described the departure of the *Sheerness:* "Over the waters she went, heavily laden, with as much misery, as could be pent up, in the bosom of a single individual. He was stricken with that malady, which knows no remedy from man—a mind diseased. In one brief hour, he had disenfranchised himself forever, and become a miserable exile."

As Henry Phillips was being bustled out of Boston, Benjamin Woodbridge lay dead, or close to it, on the Boston Common. What happened after he was last seen alive, sometime after eight o'clock according to Robert Handy, remains mysterious. One possibility is that when it began raining, Benjamin, in a last expenditure of energy, struggled to find shelter beneath a tree, perhaps the Great Elm itself, and collapsed there, undetectable to his would-be rescuers. It is strange that three men, presumably carrying lanterns, could not locate Benjamin in this vicinity, which suggests that he was somehow obscured. Further search parties were dispatched to the Common, and at some point after three in the morning his lifeless body was finally discovered. According to diarist Benjamin Walker Jr., it was found "beyond the powder house [having been] all night in the rain." From there Benjamin's body was taken to the house of his partner, Jonathan Sewall, for inspection by authorities during the inquest.

The next morning, as news of the fatal duel spread through town, the sensation was nearly unprecedented. Samuel Sewall, on hearing of the death of his nephew's partner, wrote in his almanac: "Poor Mr. Benjam[in] Woodbridge is found dead in the Common this morning, below the Powder-house, with a sword thrust through him, and his own sword undrawn. Henry Phillips is suspected. The town is amazed!" In the morning the council made an immediate but unsuccessful effort to find the vessel carrying Henry Phillips among the harbor islands or at the Boston lighthouse and return the fugitive to town. Acting Governor William Dummer issued a proclamation in the morning that was carried in the *Boston News-Letter* four days later:

> *Whereas a barbarous murder was last night committed, on the body of Benjamin Woodbridge, a young gentleman, resident in the town of Boston; and Henry Phillips, of said town is suspected to be the author of said murder, and is now fled from justice; I have therefore thought proper to issue this proclamation, hereby commanding all justices, sheriffs, constables, and all other officers, within this Province, and requiring all others, in his Majesty's name, to use their utmost endeavors, that the said Henry Phillips may be apprehended and brought to justice; and all persons, whosoever, are commanded, at their utmost peril, not to harbor or conceal him. The said Henry Phillips is a fair young man, about the age of twenty-two years, well set, and well dressed; and has a wound in one of his hands.*

In the meantime, Benjamin Woodbridge was soon buried "decently and handsomely" at the edge of the Granary Burying Ground in a service attended by "most of the merchants and gentlemen of the town." His headstone, located hard against the wrought-iron fence facing Tremont Street, remains visible to this day.

In the following weeks, a peculiar public sympathy for Henry Phillips began to emerge. These sentiments culminated on July 29 in a paper signed by ninety-two gentlemen of Boston in support of the young man's character. Henry, the paper alleged, was "a youth of a very affable, courteous, and peaceable behavior and disposition" who did not quarrel, was slow to show anger, and was "living chiefly an academical life." Signifying their support of this position were some of the most prominent members of the community and leading citizens of New England, including governors, merchants, and churchmen. The province's new governor, William Burnet, later added his signature to the document. Andrew, Peter, and Benjamin Faneuil were signatories, but the Sewalls, who were so closely associated with Benjamin Woodbridge, did not participate in the affidavit. In spite of this remarkable document, on August 2, 1728, at the Court of Assize in Boston, Henry Phillips, "the fair young man," was indicted for murder in absentia.

On his arrival in France, Henry Phillips was taken in by Peter Faneuil's uncle Jean. During his lonely months in La Rochelle, Henry hoped to prepare the case for a pardon from George II that might allow him

Benjamin Woodbridge's gravestone. From Faneuil Hall and Market *by Abram English Brown.*

Henry Phillips's helper, Peter Faneuil, in a portrait by John Smibert, ca. 1739. Courtesy of the Massachusetts Historical Society.

to return to Boston. In his March 1729 letter to his mother he complained about his circumstances. While the outcome of his quest for a pardon was unsure, he was painfully aware that he was running out of money, and "so must desire something may be done for me, not to let me spend the last farthing." As to his state of mind, Henry confessed that "I have not had one moment's pleasure since I left you, nor do I expect any in this world." Hannah Phillips knew where she was needed and hastily departed for London, presumably to investigate the business of the pardon, and then to see her son in France. The reunion was not to take place. Henry had a lingering illness that kept him almost incapacitated. As he lay dying, Henry balked at signing a will, an action that would have great consequences in his family for years to come. On May 29, 1729, the "fair young man," now an exile wanted for murder, died at La Rochelle. The Faneuils recounted his final hours for his family in Boston:

> [A]bout three o'clock in the morning a cold sweat took him—he then asked for a clean shirt, and told the English nurse this will be the last you will give me, half an hour after having taken some dyet drink laid himself on his pillow and he departed without any struggling.

In an interesting postscript to the intestate death of Henry Phillips, the settlement of his sizable estate—valued at more than £4,000—was bitterly contested by his family in New England. Gillam Phillips felt entitled by English common law to the entire estate and instigated the noted case of *Phillips* v. *Savage* in England against his elder sister, Faith Phillips Savage. Under Massachusetts law, she was among the heirs. In the end, the Massachusetts statute prevailed, splitting the estate between several heirs in the family.

In the aftermath of the Woodbridge–Phillips duel, the council enacted new legislation on the subject of duels. On July 24, 1728, a new, more stringent law was passed against anyone being "so hardy and wicked as to fight a duel, or for private malice, displeasure, fury or revenge, voluntarily engage in a rencountier, with a rapier or small sword, back sword, pistol or any other dangerous weapon." The penalties were stiffened to include being carried in a cart to the gallows with a rope around one's neck, and being set upon the gallows for an hour, followed by up to a year of jail time. In spite of this legislation, the practice did not end completely. One of the last known duels in pre-Federal Boston occurred on the Common in 1742 between Caesar and Tom, black servants of Boston, and their seconds.

Chapter 14
Heiresses Abducted:
The Kidnapping of the Misses Mackintosh
1736

THE CHATELAINE OF A GRAND HOUSEHOLD and the wife
of a wealthy and important man, Elizabeth Mackintosh Royall was an
exemplar of elegant living in pre-Revolutionary Massachusetts. Her
portrait by John Singleton Copley, painted near the end of her life,
offers no hint that in her youth she was, as one author put it, a young
lady well acquainted with sorrow and—in one instance—terror. In
September 1736 Elizabeth and her younger sister Mary, a pair of
teenaged orphaned heiresses living in Boston, were kidnapped by
an uncle from Scotland who attempted to transport them overseas,
where they could be united with a family they had never known. In
an effort to control their fortune and marry the girls off to men of
his choice, Shaw Mackintosh masterminded one of provincial Boston's
most remarkable crimes and nearly got away with it. Thanks to a
speedy response by Governor Jonathan Belcher and adverse weather
conditions encountered by the getaway vessel, the kidnapping was
swiftly foiled at sea off the coast of Massachusetts. Shaw Mackintosh
was arrested and the badly shaken girls were restored to their guardian,
merchant Job Lewis. The tale of their kidnapping and rescue—today
a long-forgotten scandal of Boston's distant past—created a sensation
in the fall of 1736.

Born in New England to a Highland family of great prominence in Scotland, Elizabeth and Mary Mackintosh were descended by both of their
parents from the hereditary leaders of the Clan Chattan, a federation of

Elizabeth Mackintosh Royall, who was kidnapped with her sister, Mary, by her uncle in 1736.
Portrait by John Singleton Copley, ca. 1769. Courtesy of the Virginia Museum of Fine Arts.

several Scottish families. Through their father, Lachlan Mackintosh, the girls were co-heiresses to the estates of the Mackintoshes of Borlum in Inverness. Their paternal grandfather, Brigadier William Mackintosh of Borlum, had fought on the losing side of an attempted overthrow and ended his years as a state prisoner in Edinburgh Castle, where he died in 1743, never having met his granddaughters in New England.

Elizabeth and Mary Mackintosh were also descended from a second strand of the same family. Their maternal grandfather was Colonel Henry "Harie" Mackintosh, a trader who left Scotland for more distant shores and eventually settled in Bristol, Massachusetts (a part of Rhode Island from 1747). In addition to business interests in England and Holland, he acquired land as far afield as a plantation in the Dutch colony of Surinam in South America, which he owned together with a Mackintosh nephew. Some time after settling in Bristol, Henry Mackintosh was joined there by a great-nephew, Lachlan Mackintosh. Lachlan was the heir of the family's valuable Badenoch estates in Scotland through the will of his grandfather, but instead of remaining among his ancestral stomping grounds, he decided to begin a new life—albeit a short one—with his great-uncle Henry in New England.

After arriving in Massachusetts, Lachlan did not wait long before marrying a near kinswoman. In a match that undoubtedly gratified the Mackintosh clan but added to the complexity of family relations, he wed his great-uncle Henry's daughter, Elizabeth Mackintosh, at Bristol in 1721. The couple's first daughter, Elizabeth, was born there in September 1722, but the family's bright prospects were cut short the following June when Lachlan was lost at sea. Elizabeth was pregnant at the time of the tragedy and gave birth to a second daughter, Mary, two months after her husband's death.

After an appropriate interval in mourning, Elizabeth married again, this time to the merchant Francis Borland of Boston. Elizabeth moved to Boston and likely left her infant daughters behind in Bristol in the care of her mother, Elizabeth Byfield Mackintosh. In 1725, after being "very infirm," Colonel Henry Mackintosh died. In his will he directed that his granddaughters should remain with their grandmother and be brought up in a manner appropriate to young ladies of their station in life. His entire estate, including properties in New England, England, Holland, Surinam, and elsewhere, would eventually devolve upon Elizabeth and Mary Mackintosh. Colonel Mackintosh could not have envisioned that his young granddaughters would soon be left orphans and ultimately be the subjects of an elaborate kidnapping plot by a scheming relative.

The death of Henry Mackintosh marked only the midpoint in the sad events that would dominate Elizabeth and Mary's young lives. Within a year of their grandfather's death, their mother died in Boston, and in 1728 their grandmother, who had since married Simon Davis of Bristol, was officially appointed their guardian. Mrs. Davis's custody was abbreviated in the spring of 1730 by her own death—the passing of Elizabeth and Mary's last living relative in America.

Interestingly, Elizabeth Davis did not propose the girls' stepfather, Francis Borland, as their guardian, but rather appealed to her friend Nathaniel Kay of Newport to fulfill the role. She requested that Kay endeavor to see that the girls have "an education suitable for their condition and quality" and that her choicest plate, gold, silver, jewels, and linen be presented to them upon reaching eighteen or marrying. By 1734 another change was in store for the girls. Job Lewis, a Boston merchant and a founder of Trinity Church four years earlier, was appointed guardian through the efforts of Governor Jonathan Belcher. The girls supposedly had a strongly unfavorable reaction to this appointment and ran away to the house of William Munroe, an executor of their grandmother's estate. In spite of their objections, Elizabeth and Mary were sent to the Lewis household in Boston, where they apparently found happiness in time. Mary even met her future husband there.

What contact, if any, Elizabeth and Mary had with their remote Scottish relatives after their father's death is unknown. An uncle, Shaw Mackintosh, assumed his position as head of the family and appeared in Boston in June 1736 to meet his American nieces. Although the girls accepted him as their kinsman, others, according to a later newspaper account, harbored suspicions about the visitor. Shaw soon made his intentions known: he wished Elizabeth and Mary to appoint him their guardian, quit Boston, and embark for Great Britain, where he could supervise a "better" education for them. He also offered that they would make more suitable marriages overseas than they could in the province—diplomatically adding for his hosts that he intended no offense by the comment. Shaw failed utterly to convince Elizabeth and Mary of the virtues of his proposal.

When the girls rejected his offer, it did not take Shaw long to realize that he would have to turn to more underhanded methods to gain control of his nieces and their fortune. Shaw, who was characterized by a Mackintosh family historian as a frivolous and selfish man, may have wished to press a claim on the Badenoch estates to which Elizabeth and Mary were entitled after their father's death. Colonel Henry Mackintosh's plentiful estate presented a further temptation. Finally, it is entirely possible that Shaw's subsequent actions may have been the result of misguided gallantry—a bungled effort to restore his American nieces to their proud Scottish family. Abductions and forced marriages of heiresses were not unheard-of practices among the Highland Scots. In *Manners, Customs, and History of the Highlanders of Scotland,* Sir Walter Scott asserted that "Scottish law-books are crowded with instances of this sort of *raptus,* or, as it is called in their law, 'forcible abduction of women.'" Scott alleged that "in some circumstances, no absolute infamy" came from these brutal acts and that some even claimed they resulted in the "happiest matches."

In spite of Shaw's entreaties to join him, the young ladies, particularly Elizabeth, were unmoved. Perhaps by this time they had become genuinely fond of Job and Sarah Lewis and could not envision leaving the only land they had ever known. Their refusal sparked more desperate action by Shaw, who quietly set about making the arrangements for an abduction that would appear to have been committed by drunken sailors. His plan involved spiriting the girls to Nantasket, where they would be transferred to a vessel bound for England. Only then would Shaw have secured his nieces for their family in Scotland.

On an otherwise unremarkable Saturday evening in September 1736, Shaw's scheme unfolded. It began with an innocent social occasion. He invited Job and Sarah Lewis and his nieces to dinner at his lodgings. After dining and enjoying a suitable interlude of hospitality, Job Lewis departed, leaving his wife and wards to linger a little longer with their host. The girls tarried with their uncle and Sarah Lewis until some time between nine and ten o'clock. Shaw and a black servant carrying a lantern escorted them home along the dark streets of town. Approaching the Lewis house, the party suddenly encountered a group of rowdy mariners. The men appeared to be drunk and one of them smashed the servant's lantern. Seconds later the girls were, as the newspaper later put it, "seized and taken up in the arms of men, waiting there for that purpose." Screaming and crying and undoubtedly frightened out of their wits, Elizabeth and Mary were carried by the strangers to Richard Hood's wharf, where a small boat waited to row them away "with great dispatch." Shaw Mackintosh may have made his escape from the vicinity of Job Lewis's house by pretending to chase the drunken mariners to the edge of the wharf.

From Hood's Wharf, the hysterical girls and their duplicitous uncle were rowed to Nantasket, where the *Sea Nymph*, under the command of Stephen Dunston, awaited their arrival. In the meantime, word of Elizabeth and Mary's kidnapping spread like wildfire through Boston. Upon hearing the news, Governor Belcher directed the commanding officer at Castle William to send the ship *Squirrel* to pursue the *Sea Nymph* and "fetch up" the villain and his abductees. Fortunately for Elizabeth and Mary, the getaway was thwarted by an adverse condition their uncle could not have foreseen. The wind, "not favoring the design of Mr. Mackintosh," kept the *Sea Nymph* from sailing very far out to sea that night. In spite of a significant head start, Captain Dunston's slow-moving vessel was intercepted by the *Squirrel* early Sunday morning. Shaw was immediately taken into custody by the *Squirrel's* men and by nine in the morning, Elizabeth and Mary were, to the great relief of the townspeople of Boston, safely restored to the care of their guardian.

Shaw was brought before a group of justices of the peace hastily gathered to examine him. He defended his actions and publicly admitted the "attempt" and "boldly justified himself in it." In a matter of such importance, Shaw stated that he was prepared to take his nieces from Job Lewis's house by force if it had been necessary in order to "carry them home." Shaw was interviewed for several hours and then ordered to prison. At the courthouse in Boston the next morning, Shaw was further examined before the justices and, given the astounding nature of the events, a "vast number" of Bostonians turned out to witness the event. In the meantime, Job Lewis offered a reward of £10 for every accomplice of Shaw's who was turned in and convicted.

The family of Isaac Royall Jr., 1741, in a portrait by Robert Feke.
Left to right: Penelope Royall, Mary Mackintosh Palmer, Elizabeth Royall (infant),
Elizabeth Mackintosh Royall, Isaac Royall Jr. Courtesy of the Harvard Law School.

Boston newspapers published lengthy accounts of Shaw's "very uncommon, bold and violent attempt" against his nieces, who, the paper continued, were "heiresses to a very considerable estate."

Shaw's case was placed before the Superior Court of Judicature, then sitting at Worcester. On September 24, 1736, Boston diarist Benjamin Walker Jr. witnessed Sheriff Winslow and Deputy Bradford transporting the Scot from the Boston jail and up Queen Street in "a chair" en route to Worcester for his hearing, a procession that undoubtedly attracted numerous onlookers. At Worcester, the court set bail at £8,000 and required that Shaw appear the following month at the court's session in Salem. At that session, Shaw was given the choice of either remaining in Boston for a hearing at the Court of Assize the following February or being set at "liberty to depart" New England for Europe. A single-minded man, Shaw made at least one more effort to justify his transportation of Elizabeth and Mary. In a hearing before Governor Belcher in early December, Shaw's last-ditch efforts proved unsuccessful. Having failed to procure his nieces or their estate, a defeated Shaw embarked for London in early December 1736.

For Elizabeth and Mary, their uncle's departure must have marked a return to some level of normalcy and happiness. Elizabeth was the first of the sisters to wed. In March 1738, she married Isaac Royall Jr. of Medford, a well-connected gentleman, later a member of the General Court, a benefactor of Harvard College, and a noted Massachusetts Loyalist. In 1739, Mary Mackintosh selected Thomas Palmer Jr., a Boston merchant and the brother-in-law of Job Lewis, as her husband. The *Boston Gazette* in 1739 announced the nuptials of "a young lady of great merit and fortune" in an event at King's Chapel, followed two days later by a ball and "handsome collation" at Mrs. Austin's Long Room. Elizabeth and Mary remained close, and when Robert Feke painted the Isaac Royall family in 1741, Mary was asked to join her sister and in-laws in the portrait. For the young women who survived great losses, not to mention a foiled kidnapping, the meaning of family must have assumed a special significance.

Chapter 15
Villainous Papers:
An Extortion Plot Against
Two Gentlemen of Substance
1749

AUDACIOUS IN THEIR ATTEMPTS to extort large sums of money from "gentlemen of substance," James Williams, a mariner, and Mary Richards, the wife of a local baker, in 1749 targeted two of Boston's most prominent men. Their intended victims were Samuel Wells, a merchant and legislator, and William Shirley, the governor of Massachusetts and commander-in-chief of British forces in New England. Williams and Richards wrote at least two anonymous letters demanding money and threatening violence. The first directed Wells to place £300 between stones atop Beacon Hill or risk suffering great damages. Later, after the letter was made public in a proclamation by William Shirley, the conspirators turned their attentions to the governor and demanded that he drop £500 beneath the root of a tree on Boston Neck. In both cases, the writers swore that if the recipients failed to comply with their wishes, they would ensure their "utter destruction" by burning their houses, warehouses, and vessels, and possibly kill one of them. These foolhardy letters, according to Governor Shirley, represented the first instance of such "execrable villainy" attempted in the province of Massachusetts.

The reasons behind this brazen attempt at extortion are uncertain, but the letters present two possible scenarios. In the first, the extortionists portrayed themselves as struggling merchants in dire straits. The second letter claimed that they were past members of Shirley's regiments, had served with him in various locations, and that half of them had never received adequate pay. This premise may have had some truth—the Massachusetts government was then investigating incidents regarding "soldiers who had not been equably compensated for their services." Or it may have simply been plucked from the newspaper accounts of a controversy then brewing. Motivations aside, the letters did not constitute a traditional blackmail attempt. With no threat of exposure, the letters appear to have been an effort, however misguided, to overwhelm Wells and Shirley with the fear of financial ruin or even murder. Neither man capitulated to the demands and, in all likelihood, Wells and Shirley considered the letters to be the preposterous products of crooked amateurs.

In mid-April 1749, James Williams and Mary Richards composed their first letter, replete with poor spellings and meager punctuation. The selection of Samuel Wells as its recipient may have been based on public perceptions about his wealth. A native of Wethersfield, Connecticut, and a 1707 graduate of Yale College, Wells was an ordained minister who had given up his pastoral charge in 1722 in order to pursue business interests in Boston. As the husband of a local heiress, Hannah Arnold, and the owner of a thriving market, Wells was later reputed to be one of the richest merchants in town.

The letter was delivered to Wells's home near what was then the south end of town. Opening the strange epistle, he must have been astounded by its contents. "We are three gentlemen in want of money to carry on our business," it read. Describing their circumstances as "very hard at this time," the letter requested that Wells help the unnamed correspondents with a "loan" of £300, which they claimed they would repay within a year. The authors then specified how the cash was to be delivered. First, Wells was not to mark the bills in any way for later detection or give them any defective or forged currency: "Put no private mark on any of them . . . nor none that is counterfeit nor bad, for if you do it will be the worse for you." They then demanded that once Wells had the money ready, he "must carry the same to the top of Beacon Hill and hide it right under the mast between them ton stones." The drop-off must take place at ten o'clock at night and, after hiding the money between the stones, Wells should proceed directly home and "never let your dearest friend know the secret." If Wells revealed the transaction, then the authors promised that "you shall shortly lose your dear house and life in the fray." The ensuing fray, as they described it, would include the torching of "every house, barn, warehouse, wharf belonging to you in Boston or elsewhere, and all your goods . . . that we can find in the term of the year and your person if possible." Further, if forced to borrow money elsewhere, the writers would come to Wells's house "sufficiently armed to defend ourselves and destroy you." In closing, they directed him to

Governor William Shirley, targeted by extortionists James Williams and Mary Richards, in a 1747 engraving by Peter Pelham. Courtesy of the New England Historic Genealogical Society.

obliterate the evidence of their extortion: "None of this paper nor writing ever must be seen but burnt directly upon peril of your life." Wells promptly showed the letter to Governor William Shirley.

Within a few days Governor Shirley reported the matter of the "villainous paper" received by Wells, a member of his council, to the General Court and suggested further action:

> Gentlemen, this being the first instance of this kind of execrable villainy attempted in this Province, it highly imports this Legislature to make provision for preventing and punishing the same attempts for the future.

Shortly thereafter Shirley issued a proclamation offering a reward of £200 in which it was recommended that "verbatim extracts from the impious, insolent, and inhuman language" used in the letter be included so as to stir up the public in identifying the "profligate and abandoned wretches" who had perpetrated the crime. But before Boston's townspeople had been sufficiently stimulated to help name the culprits, Governor Shirley in the following month became the focus of the extortion plot. James's first letter probably went astray before reaching Shirley, but the governor did not have to wait long before another extortion attempt was made. James, again writing anonymously, opened his second communication with the governor by letting him know that his new mansion in Roxbury had been in jeopardy of being torched:

> Your not complying with ours of May 20th 1749 Saturday, which we left in your yard next [to] the bookbinder's shop, which we believe you have seen which has made some dispute among us for some was for going and firing your fine country house without any more delay but some of us thought maybe you had not found it.

Without further ado, James got down to his ugly business. He ordered the governor to take £500 on Tuesday night, May 30, 1749, and place it beneath a tree that stood halfway out on Boston Neck. At that location, he was instructed "to hide the same close under the root of the tree and cover it over with dirt so that . . . we may get it when we please and without danger." If Shirley did not comply with this plan, James threatened that he and his party "will surely burn all your fine country seat . . . and other places which will be a disadvantage to you and country, too, for we will not be bobbled no more by your Excellency than we will by Esquire Wells." James ridiculed the governor's "good counsel" to Samuel Wells and the proclamation he issued, sneering that "we should mind it no more than the dust under our feet." In addition to threatening the governor, James said he would kill Samuel Wells by "burning his house and him" if he did not deliver money on their "next summons." Further, the extortionist told Shirley that posting a watch around the Province House, the mansion in town used by governors, or his estate in Roxbury, would be fruitless because his group was composed of former soldiers and could infiltrate such a guard:

> If your Excellency should set a watch round your house in the country
> or town of any quantity of men, some of us shall be there for we have
> all served under your Excellency's regiment in one place or another
> and some have been disbanded and never half of us half paid, and
> we shall be ready forever round your elbow to watch your motions.

James closed by stating that he and his cohorts had taken a "solid and firm oath to stand by each other in life and death forever and ever, amen." Shirley's immediate reaction to this brazen letter is unrecorded, but by August of the same year he brought to the General Court notice of a third extortion attempt, "the same kind of villainy that was twice lately practiced in this Province for extorting money by threatening gentlemen of substance with the destruction of their estates and persons in case of refusal to comply with the demands of these miscreants." In that month the legislature finally took action on a bill to prevent and punish "such pernicious practices in the future." In September, Shirley sailed from Boston on an extended overseas trip, leaving behind forever the annoyances of the peculiar plot against him and Wells.

Just how James Williams was identified as the author of the extortion letters is not known, but by the end of December 1749 he was apprehended and bound over by the Superior Court of Judicature until its next term. It is possible that he was fingered as the prime suspect

by Thomas Greene, a prisoner who was brought from jail to give testimony in the case. Among those posting surety for James was Samuel
Richards. In the following months, Richards and his wife became
embroiled in the affair and eventually were indicted along with James.
In May 1750, James Williams and Mary Richards were found guilty of
writing the "incendiary" letter to Samuel Wells. James was sentenced
to be set upon the pillory for two hours, receive thirty stripes on his
naked back, and be jailed for one year. In addition, he was bound to
sureties in the amount of £100 to keep the peace for three years.
Mary Richards, for her part in the crime, was sentenced to be set
upon the pillory for two hours, pay a fine of £50, and also obtain
sureties for good behavior. Interestingly, her husband was adjudged
not guilty and later successfully petitioned the court to moderate the
fine imposed upon his wife to £30. The absence of records for James
and the Richardses suggest that they either did not remain long in
Boston or simply drifted into quiet obscurity. Having avoided the
fiery death threatened by James and Mary, Samuel Wells continued to
reside in Boston, serving in various posts of responsibility. In 1762 he
was again the target of a criminal scam by the notorious imposter Dr.
Seth Hudson (described in Chapter 10). Samuel Wells died the age of
eighty in 1770, the veteran of two of Boston's most colorful criminal
conspiracies.

Chapter 16

Murder by Arsenic:
The Ill-Fated Greenleaf Children
and Their Portraits
1750–1751

"MY DEAR MRS. ROCKEFELLER," wrote antiques dealer Katrina Kipper on her Queen Anne Cottage stationery to American folk art collector Abby Aldrich Rockefeller in 1943. "You may remember several years ago you purchased of me an early portrait of a child in a pink dress. Not exactly a primitive but an early eighteenth century one. There were a pair," Mrs. Kipper continued, "one a little child in blue which you did not take, as you did not like it as well as the pink clad one. Since then I have found out the history which I think will be of interest to you." Little did Mrs. Kipper realize what a strange and clouded history she was revealing to Mrs. Rockefeller. But so began a letter, not unlike scores of others that would eventually be exchanged among scholars, collectors, and museum curators, regarding portraits of the children of Boston apothecary Dr. John Greenleaf and his wife and the mystery that swirled around their three children. In time, the haze obscuring what really happened would clear and evidence of two or three murders would emerge. Remarkably, some scholars in the twentieth century saw this case—one of the most astounding murders in provincial Boston—as apocryphal.

In 1743 Priscilla Brown, a beautiful, strikingly pale-skinned daughter of Robert Brown of Plymouth, married Dr. John Greenleaf, a Boston apothecary. The success of their union appears to have commended itself to Priscilla's younger sister Mary, who a few years later followed in Priscilla's footsteps by marrying Dr. Greenleaf's younger brother William, creating the sort of intertwined family tree once so common in New England clans.

John Greenleaf was a druggist but not, according to the family, a full-fledged physician. He operated an apothecary shop in Boston, likely the same one established by his mother years earlier, and over time he became both influential and prosperous. He was, like many of his contemporaries, an active parishioner of the fashionable Brattle Street Church, an institution he had helped to found. Among Dr. Greenleaf's most select properties was a store in Dock Square in Boston, long the oldest building standing in town, which featured the date 1680 in its front gable. (This famous building, known as the "Old Feather Store" or the "Old Cocked Hat," was demolished in 1860.) Dr. Greenleaf's brother William, an "ardent Whig," merchant, and sheriff of Suffolk County in the late 1770s, was an even more important man in town. The Boston branch of the family was on the rise. If the term "Boston Brahmin" pertains to families of prestige and wealth in the post-Revolutionary period, then the Greenleafs qualified as junior members of the pre-Brahmin era gentry. Newcomers to this elite and willing to display their success, the Greenleaf brothers, their wives, and children sat frequently for portraits by local or visiting artists, including John Singleton Copley, Joseph Badger, Joseph Blackburn, and John Greenwood. Richly attired and well respected, the Greenleaf brothers possessed an air of cultivation. William Greenleaf, for example, was later recalled as a tall, slim gentleman who walked about the streets of Boston wearing single-breasted coats with ruffles at his neck and wrists, carrying a gold-headed cane, and sporting "a cocked hat on his head, after the fashion of the colonial times." But beneath the displays of grandeur and success, a darker, unhappier story waited to be told.

Early in their marriage, John and Priscilla Greenleaf had at least two children, probably male twins, who died in infancy. This misfortune was followed by much brighter circumstances. Between 1746 and 1750 the couple enjoyed the birth of two girls, Priscilla (Junior) and Elizabeth, and a boy, John (Junior), all of whom survived and were, by every indication, treasured by their parents. Folk artist Joseph Badger painted the two girls, if not all three children. Priscilla's portrait, the object Mrs. Rockefeller later passed up to her everlasting regret, has been noted for its "quaintness and a naïve and piquant charm which is most appealing." In it, she is shown seated wearing a white cap with muslin ruffles, a low-necked blue-green gown, and a white stomacher with a scalloped edge. On her lap is a cherished dog, probably a cavalier King Charles spaniel. Elizabeth's portrait depicts her with a "cupid's bow mouth" and a white mobcap with "pansies and [other] flowers decorating it." In her hands, she clutches a pear. Portraits of all three children were later painted by a superior artist, John Singleton Copley. The gentleness of Copley's work is exceptional: John Greenleaf Jr. wears a plumed cap (an item apparently copied from an earlier English mezzotint source) and caresses a doting lamb; Elizabeth balances a nosegay of plump roses on her lap; Priscilla, as in her portrait by Badger, rests a hand on a small lapdog. The fine clothing and exquisite deportment of the children befit the offspring of the most successful apothecary of mid-eighteenth-century Boston.

It was a tragedy when these beautiful children began dying under strange circumstances. By January 17, 1751, all three had perished. In the early-morning hours of that day the last-surviving child, eleven- or twelve-month-old John, died after suffering "in great misery" for many hours. The newspapers reported the shocking cause of death: poisoning by arsenic. By modern standards, the papers were extremely discreet, omitting even Dr. Greenleaf's name from reports. Perhaps details of the maudlin story were considered outside the bounds of good taste to print, or maybe respect for the Greenleaf family influenced local coverage. As a result of this scant coverage, just how the murder culprit was identified is not known. As young John lay dying on January 16, suspicion landed on Phyllis, a slave about sixteen or seventeen years old. As a renowned apothecary, Dr. Greenleaf certainly would have been adept at detecting the signs of poisoning, and through the practice of his profession many medicines and lethal compounds could have been available for this purpose. When their last child died, the Greenleafs realized that something was afoul. Phyllis, they discovered, had drugged her infant charge. She was arrested that morning on suspicion of "putting ratsbane several times into what it drank." According to the *Boston News-Letter*, Phyllis, a "wretched creature," soon "acknowledged not only the poisoning of this child, but also another of the same family that died very

*Priscilla Brown Greenleaf, mother of three ill-fated children, in a portrait by
Joseph Blackburn. Courtesy of the Museum of Fine Arts, Houston;
the Bayou Bend Collection, gift of Miss Ima Hogg.*

suddenly some months ago." According to the *Boston Evening-Post*, her
prior victim was "about fifteen months old," which, if correct, means
that Elizabeth Greenleaf was the child killed in a similar grisly style.
The oldest child's manner of death is not stated, but according to the
family, Phyllis killed Priscilla, too.

The three murdered Greenleaf children, in oil portraits by John Singleton Copley: clockwise from top left, Elizabeth (The Metropolitan Museum of Art), Priscilla (private collection), and John (The Metropolitan Museum of Art). Used by permission.

Phyllis's motive for killing the Greenleaf children remains a matter for speculation. Possibly the crimes were carried out in retaliation against a family that mistreated her; perhaps she was mentally deficient. One erroneous tradition states that she murdered the children all at one time so that she could see a military display on the Boston Common. Found on a piece of paper attached to the back of Elizabeth's portrait by John Singleton Copley, this story alleges that "[Phyllis] wishing to go to the Boston Common and watch the 'Redcoats' drill, gave them all laudanum to put them to sleep. All three were dead in the morning. The nurse confessed, and was hung, quartered, and burned on the Boston Common."

In the spring of 1751 Phyllis pleaded guilty before the Superior Court of Judicature and was convicted for the murder of John Greenleaf Jr. No mention of the deaths of Priscilla or Elizabeth is found in the records of the trial, but conviction for just one instance of murder was sufficient to execute the perpetrator. Phyllis had, as suspected, killed the boy by plying him with arsenic-spiked milk. The tragedy continued with another, unexpected victim. About a week after Phyllis was sentenced to death in April 1751, Phyllis's own mother died suddenly—as reported in the newspapers, from an "excess of grief." On May 16, 1751, Phyllis was brought from jail to hear the Reverend Mather Byles preach his execution sermon *Before the Execution of a Young Negro Servant, for Poisoning an Infant*. A short time later, before hundreds of onlookers on Boston Common, the unrepentant teenaged convict was hanged.

The death date of the children's mother, Priscilla Brown Greenleaf, is unrecorded; it is possible that she died after the murder of her children. She was certainly dead by 1759, when her husband remarried. In 1788, Dr. John Greenleaf himself died in Boston, having outlived his first two wives, at least six sons, and two daughters. Painfully fresh toward the end of his life was the death of his teenaged son, another boy named John, who was at the time a student at Harvard College.

The children's portraits led to a curious epilogue to the story, in which the murders were slowly erased from the pages of Boston history. Some of the Greenleaf portraits descended through the family; others were sold and acquired by collectors or museums. By the time Abby Aldrich Rockefeller purchased Joseph Badger's portrait of Elizabeth Greenleaf in 1937, art historians were beginning to grapple with the strange stories surrounding the children. A Greenleaf family history published in 1854 stated simply that the children had "died young," but another genealogy published some forty years later said that they had been "poisoned by a slave nurse." It is likely that Mrs. Kipper, the antiques dealer, had by the time of her correspondence with Mrs. Rockefeller found an article on the artist Joseph Badger saying that the girls had been "poisoned with laudanum administered by a negro nurse." Original court records having gone undetected, the murder story continued to be shrouded in mystery in art circles until 1975, when an art historian attempted to debunk it. Having doubted the story as a "lurid, dramatic tale that people repeat unthinkingly" for some time, Alfred Frankenstein turned to Boston scholars to authenticate the story. "A careful check of the records by the Boston historian Walter Muir Whitehill, and his associates at the Boston Athenæum," Frankenstein disclosed, "has failed to turn up anything to substantiate this story." Not content to let the story remain a colorful, if unlikely, family legend, Frankenstein decided to make it an example. Art history, he argued, has no time for such unseemly concoctions as the Greenleaf murder story:

> It is a complete fiction, typical of the folklore that clings, especially in family traditions, to many paintings and makes popular art history more interesting but considerably less reliable than the truth. Nevertheless, the realities of art history can be enormously interesting, if on a different level from the blood-and-guts of the Greenleaf story.

From that time and through the 1990's, art catalogues and other publications have been tentative in the matter of the Greenleaf children and the cause of their demise. Sadly, the murder story is neither a lurid fantasy nor an unsubstantiated folk tale. Rather, it was in all likelihood the first multiple-murder case of its kind in Boston.

Chapter 17

An Impudent Woman
1772

THE SCANDAL SURROUNDING THE EXPLOITS of Elizabeth
"Betty" Smith found an unlikely chronicler in the person of twelve-
year-old diarist Anna Green Winslow, a well-bred young lady board-
ing with relatives in town. On February 25, 1772, after returning
home from Samuel Holbrook's writing school on the Boston Common, Anna sat down at noon and wrote to her mother in Nova Scotia
to tell her the latest news: "Dear Mamma, I suppose that you would
be glad to hear that Betty Smith who has given you so much trouble,
is well and behaves herself well and I should be glad if I could write
you so." However, such good news was not possible, and Anna began
to tell the tale of a woman who had fallen into a spiral of criminal
activities in town. Betty's thievery, committed against the backdrop of
a town recently shaken by the Boston Massacre, would land her in the
workhouse, take her to the whipping post and gallows, and bring her
the possibility of ten years' forced servitude to repay one of her victims. Anna Winslow's diary, court records, and a broadside printed to
commemorate Betty Smith's trip to the gallows help reconstruct an
account of one of pre-Revolutionary Boston's most notorious female
thieves.

Anna Green Winslow was born to a family that had lived in Boston
for several generations. At the time of her education, however, her
parents, Joshua Winslow and Anna Green, were living in Cumber-
land, Nova Scotia, where her father was commissary-general of the

British forces. Parishioners of the Old South Church, the Winslows were well connected to some of the leading pre-Brahmin era families of the day, and the family numbered among its hallowed ancestors John Winslow and his wife, *Mayflower* passenger Mary Chilton. Sending their daughter to be "finished" in Boston was an appropriate rite of passage for a young lady in polite society. In 1770, Anna was placed in the care of her aunt Sarah Winslow Deming at her house at Central Court, near the location of Washington and Summer streets today. Her charming diary and letters recount the education, social life, gossip, and fashions entertaining to a young lady of the period.

A portrait miniature of Anna Green Winslow, the twelve-year-old girl whose diary told the story of Betty Smith. From The Diary of Anna Green Winslow.

The circumstances that brought Betty Smith together with the Winslows are not known, but possibly Betty was at some point in domestic service to the family and perhaps in that capacity caused Mrs. Winslow "so much trouble." It is also possible that Betty was the woman named Elizabeth Smith who was received in 1769 into Boston's almshouse, a facility for the indigent or ill, located on the northeast corner of Beacon Street near the Boston Common. Described as sick and without the wherewithal to support herself, Elizabeth Smith was identified by the almshouse as a stranger to the province. Whatever the relationship between Betty Smith and the Winslows, Anna knew that her mother would be interested in news of the unfortunate woman. Some of the gossip about Betty may have been communicated to Anna by "Jemima," apparently a servant at the home of Boston schoolmaster James Lovell.

In her letter, Anna gave a full chronology of Betty's misadventures over the last year, starting with her involvement with the 29th Worcestershire Regiment, infamous for its involvement in the Boston Massacre on March 5, 1770. According to Anna, "no sooner was the 29th Regiment encamped upon the Common but Miss Betty took herself among them (as the Irish say) and there she stayed with Bill Pinchion and awhile." Unwelcomed by the local citizenry and unable to find lodgings in town, members of the 29th lived in tents on the Boston Common. How Betty Smith subsisted among the troops is a matter for speculation.

After her cohabitation with Bill Pynchon and members of the 29th Worcestershire, Betty experienced her first serious brush with the law. "The next news of her," continued Anna, "was, that she was got into gaol for stealing: from whence she was taken to the public whipping post."

The crime was perpetrated on December 20, 1770. Her victims were twenty-five-year-old retailer Peter Sigourney and his wife, Celia Loring. Betty somehow managed to gain access to the Sigourney household, perhaps working there as a servant or appealing to the family for charity. Betty succeeded in making her first known theft a major haul. Among the scores of items she stole from the Sigourneys were silk gowns, linen aprons, a large tablecloth, children's clothing, flannel blankets, and a cloak. Betty was quickly detected in the crime and pleaded guilty; she was ordered to return all the stolen goods, pay Sigourney more than £20, and meet the costs of her prosecution. In addition, she was sentenced to twenty stripes on her "naked back" at the public whipping post, a punishment in the middle range of severity for the period.

Street punishment in late-eighteenth-century Boston as experienced by Betty Smith was best described by Samuel Breck in his memoirs:

> The large whipping-post, painted red, stood conspicuously and permanently in the most public street in town. It was placed in State street, directly under the windows of a great writing-school which I frequented, and from them the scholars were indulged in the spectacle of all kinds of punishment, suited to harden their hearts and brutalize their feelings. Here women were taken from a huge cage, in which they were dragged on wheels from prison, and tied to the whipping post with bare backs, on which thirty or forty lashes were bestowed amid the screams of the culprits and the uproar of the mob. A little farther in the street was to be seen the pillory, with three or four fellows fastened by the head and hands, and standing for an hour in that helpless posture, exposed to gross and cruel insult from the multitude, who pelted them incessantly with rotten eggs and every repulsive kind of garbage that could be collected. These things I have often witnessed, but they have given way to better systems, better manners and better feelings.

Betty's "next adventure," recalled Anna, "was to the Castle, after the soldiers were removed there, for the murder of the 5th of March last." Betty's stay at Castle William did not last long. When she was turned away from the Castle, she returned to town "and soon got into the workhouse for new misdemeanors." The brick workhouse building was opened in Boston in 1739 as a facility for "the idle and the poor" of the town; it was located at the southwest end of the house of correction or bridewell. Life at the workhouse did not agree with Betty and she quickly fled it. According to Anna, she then "set up her old trade of pilfering again, for which she was put a second time in gaol, there she still remains." Betty's most recent "pilferings" included the theft in October 1771 of £10 worth of goods from Samuel Whitwell, owner of a hardware store, and in February 1772 the theft of a large and valuable assortment of clothing belonging to one Mary King.

During her stay in jail, Betty and her jailmates attempted to burn down the building in order to escape. Anna recalled that "about two months agone (as well as I can remember) she and a number of her wretched companions set the gaol on fire, in order to get out, but the fire was timely discovered and extinguished, and there, as I said she still remain to this day." Setting the jail on fire in order to perpetrate a jailbreak was something of a tradition in Boston. In February 1767, a prisoner in the old wooden jail burned a hole in the ceiling of his cell through which he attempted to flee. He was recaptured and transferred to the new stone jail, "from whence," the *Boston Gazette* reported, "'tis said, he will find it very difficult again to escape." The new stone jail, however, was not immune to fire. Bostonian John Boyle noted in his diary another such attempt in January 1769 that led to a major conflagration:

> The large, elegant new stone gaol was discovered to be on fire. . . . The fire got to such a height before it was discovered, that the flames spread rapidly through every apartment & in a few hours entirely consumed the same, leaving nothing standing but the bare walls. The prisoners lives with great difficulty were saved— some of them were much burnt. It was set on fire by a soldier and another lad, in one apartment, in order that they might make their escape.

Betty and her accomplices failed to burn their way out of jail, and there she remained until her trial in March 1772. In Anna's letter to her mother, she reported that there were rumors Betty might be found innocent: "I heard somebody say that as she has some connections with the army no doubt she would be cleared, and perhaps have a pension into the bargain." One of Anna's friends told her that "the way of sin is down hill, when persons get into that way they are not easily stopped."

A DIALOGUE

BETWEEN

ELIZABETH SMITH, and JOHN SENNET,

Who were convicted before his Majesty's Superior Court, *Elizabeth Smith* For *Thievery*, and *John Sennet* for *Beaftiality* ! and each fentenced to Set upon the Gallows for the fpace of one Hour, with a Rope round their Necks *Elizabeth Smith* to receive Twenty Stripes upon her naked Back, And *John Sennet*, Thirty-nine.

Smith. SEE here the knave expos'd to publick view,
　　　And for his wickednefs receives his due :
While all the crowd behold him with difdain,
And laugh to fee him thus expos'd to fhame.

Sennet. No doubt you thought your crimes would lie
Forgot and hidden from the *partial* eye ;
But now you know that " *Ropes* and *Lines*" can fee
Crimes of a fmall, though not a large degree.

Sennet. Though Murd'rers pafs with crimes of deeper hue,
Thieves and houfe-breakers always have their due.
Cufhing has eas'd the former from their fate,
But vengeance always does on Villains wait.

Smith. You know your fault is far more bafe than mine,
The moft unnatural of any crime ;
A deed of *Beaftiality* you know
Is what expofes you to publick fhow.

The laws divine and human you have broke,
And took upon yourfelf a heavy yoke :
For know, O man ! the Lord your maker faith,
He that lies with a Beaft fhall fuffer death.

Sennet. O dare you lift your head to fenfure me,
You know your crime is of the firft degree ;
Convicted twice of theft, you have your due,
If all the croud fpare me to punifh you.

A thief, the moft detefted of mankind,
How can you e'er a moment's comfort find ?
Your guilt will follow you where e'er you go,
And turn your joy into moft deadly woe.

Smith. You know, O *Sennet*, you deferve to die,
According to the laws of God moft high :
You have expos'd your wife and children dear,
To forrow, to difgrace, and black defpair.

Sennet. Now ceafe your talk, think on one fcene that's paft,
Behold your husband ftruggle out his laft !
Frail wicked breath, when drove unto defpair,
The Gallows eafed him of all his care.

Both as one. Now both of us not only fet a fhow,
But we muft hugg the poft that ftands below ;
Let therefore yeung and old be warn'd by us,
Left when it is too la　　　's a curfe.

A Dialogue Between Elizabeth Smith, and John Sennet, *1772*
broadside. Courtesy of the Historical Society of Pennsylvania.

The rumor that Betty Smith would be acquitted through military connections did not prove true. On March 10, 1772, at her second conviction, she received a more serious sentence. She was to be set upon the gallows with a rope around her neck for the space of one hour, receive twenty stripes, and pay treble damages to Mary King for an amount above £40. If she was unable to meet the debt, Mrs. King would be entitled to "dispose of her in service to any of his Majesty's liege subjects for the term of ten years."

Betty's punishment occurred when she and a fellow convict, John Sennet, were transported to the gallows on Boston Neck to be punished in full public view. Anna, who seems to have witnessed the event along with scores of Bostonians, later recorded in her diary that Betty had "behaved with great impudence" when set upon the gallows. The cases aroused sufficient public curiosity for a printer, probably Richard Draper, to publish a satirical broadside to commemorate the joint punishment. A *Dialogue Between Elizabeth Smith, and John Sennet* presents an imaginary exchange between the prisoners in which they criticize each other and make allusions to their respective cases. In one instance, Sennet says, "You know that '*Ropes and Lines*' can see, Crimes of a small, though not large degree," a thinly veiled reference to judges Nathaniel Ropes and Benjamin Lynde Jr., who heard her case. The broadside is also notable in that it implies that Betty was a recent widow. In his final passage in the spoof, John Sennet states that her husband has struggled out his last breath from despair at her sentence. In court records, Betty was presented as a "single woman" or "spinster"; no husband was identified.

Betty Smith, having made her mark on Boston as a thief and infamous convict, disappeared from view after receiving her punishment. Her chronicler, Anna Green Winslow, continued her Boston diary for at least several more months. Her acquaintance with scandal appears to have left her relatively unaffected. The day after Betty's trip to the gallows, Anna recorded having danced a minuet and "country dances," probably at Mr. Turner's dancing school. Sadly, according to family lore, Anna had all too brief a life, dying of consumption at Marshfield in the fall of 1779.

Chapter 18

Piracy on the High Seas:
The Mysterious, Inexplicable Affair
of Ansell Nickerson
1772

WHEN THOMAS NICKERSON and his crew set sail from Boston on November 14, 1772, there were no signs that this routine voyage home to Chatham on Cape Cod would end in an episode of terrible violence, leaving three men dead, one missing, and the sole survivor facing charges of piracy and robbery on the high seas. By early the next morning the decks of the fishing schooner *Abigail* were awash with blood and the only crewman left alive, Ansell Nickerson, was telling an almost unbelievable tale of piracy. This unlikely story of "pirate murders" on a vessel somewhere between Chatham and Nantucket circulated quickly and aroused deep suspicions in many, including Governor Thomas Hutchinson. Before long, Ansell Nickerson found himself in Boston on trial for the atrocity, which some believed he committed in order to steal the captain's money. Opinions on the sensational case appear to have fallen along party lines—Boston's Whigs generally believed Ansell to be innocent and the Tories thought him guilty. Ably defended by John Adams, Ansell was acquitted, but the incident has long been, to use the charmingly redundant words of Adams, a "mysterious, inexplicable affair" in New England maritime history. Boston newspapers at the time went considerably further, calling it "the most surprising event which has happened in this and perhaps any other age of the world."

On this voyage the twenty-eight-year-old master of the ill-fated *Abigail,* Thomas Nickerson, was joined by four men: his older brother

Sparrow, his brother-in-law Elisha Newcomb, a thirteen-year-old boy, William Kent Jr., and his cousin Ansell Nickerson, who was just short of his twenty-second birthday. Ansell, the son of Ansel and Bathsheba Nickerson of Chatham, had originally been called "Levi" but was renamed Ansell (or Ansel) after his father's death. The circumstances by which Thomas Nickerson accepted Ansell as a crew member will never be known, but as a young man of few options from a humble Cape Cod family, the opportunity aboard his kinsman's fishing vessel was a good one. Ansell also had a practical consideration in mind; he joined the crew in order to earn money to buy a suit of clothing.

Ansell's version of the gory events began with the *Abigail* under sail toward Chatham, the crew probably weary and looking forward to their arrival home. At about two o'clock on Sunday morning, November 15, 1772, Ansell alleged that the *Abigail* encountered an unfamiliar topsail schooner. A party from the larger craft boarded the fishing vessel and after questioning its master or crew, the strangers departed. Shortly thereafter four boats with armed men returned to the *Abigail*. At this point Ansell, who apparently had not been noticed by the first visitors, sensed danger. Fearing that he was about to be impressed into service as a sailor, Ansell scrambled to the *Abigail*'s stern. Attempts at impressing American men into the king's service were not unknown at this time, so such a fear would have been understandable. True story or not, raising the specter of impressment was sure to gain him a sympathetic audience. Using a rope, Ansell dropped over the side of the schooner and, hanging by his hands to the taffrail, propped his feet on the molding under the cabin windows below. From this unwieldy position Ansell claimed that he clung to the *Abigail* and listened as horrifying events unfolded on the decks above him. All three of his kinsmen, Thomas Nickerson, Sparrow Nickerson, and Elisha Newcomb, were, he later reported, systematically killed by the trespassers and thrown overboard. Young William Kent was spared and, according to Ansell, "carried away alive, as they said, in order to *make punch for them.*"

He then heard talk by the pirates of burning the *Abigail,* but rather than destroy all evidence of their crimes they "finally agreed to leave her to drive out to sea with her sails standing." If the pirates had torched the *Abigail* at night, other nearby vessels or people on shore might have seen the conflagration and their getaway would then have been cut short. Ansell, still grasping the taffrail, listened as the strangers violently lashed the helm and plundered the vessel, stealing among other items a "considerable quantity of cash"—perhaps recent earnings taken by the Nickersons at Boston. During the looting the pirates moved throughout the vessel, leaving bloody track marks in the cabin and hold as they pilfered the *Abigail*. They broke open chests and boxes and smashed the top off a barrel of rum, carelessly spilling most of its contents. Curiously, the pirates failed to carry off some of the vessel's best provisions, including fresh beef, butter, cider, and other supplies. Eventually they departed with their booty and when danger had passed, Ansell climbed back on deck to find wreckage and blood. He put up a distress signal and awaited discovery by another vessel.

At about ten o'clock in the morning, Captain Joseph Doane Jr., who was sailing from Chatham, spotted the *Abigail* in distress. Once onboard, the captain found a vessel "all stained with blood, the decks reeking with blood." In fact, there was so much blood that it trickled out of the scuppers and down the side of the boat. Captain Doane discovered Ansell onboard in a "great fright." Shaken, the young man recounted the terrifying events of the previous night. Doane immediately returned to Chatham with the survivor and promptly communicated Ansell's account of the horrendous acts of piracy and murder to Edward Bacon of Barnstable, a local justice of the peace. Bacon, in turn, fearful for the public safety with a marauding pirate vessel in the vicinity, hastily sent Ansell's account by express to Governor Thomas Hutchinson in Boston.

The following day, Bacon went to Chatham to question Ansell himself. He was satisfied with what he found and sent a further report to Governor Hutchinson. Ansell had by now been examined by two justices of the peace and even questioned in the presence of Thomas Nickerson, father of his two murdered cousins and father-in-law of Elisha Newcomb. After these interviews, all accepted Ansell's gruesome account and Chatham authorities dismissed him without further delay. Ansell's retelling of the pirate incident was soon printed in the

Boston newspapers and immediately created a sensation in town. John Adams, who would later play a key role in Ansell's trial, noted in his diary that "the conversation of the town and country has been about the strange occurrence of last week, a piracy said to have been committed on a vessel bound to Cape Cod, 3 men killed, a boy missing, and only one man escaped to tell the news." Meanwhile, according to Governor Hutchinson, public suspicions began to fall upon a king's schooner expected at about this time from Rhode Island—a scorching political accusation—but in the end nothing came of it. The man-of-war *Lively* was dispatched from Boston in search of a pirate vessel, but returned within ten days having made no such sightings.

Governor Hutchinson had, from afar, grown doubtful of Ansell's "incredible" story and after consulting with commissioners for the trial of piracies, decided to issue a warrant to apprehend the young man for further questioning. The warrant did not arrive at Barnstable until midnight on November 20, and was issued afresh the next morning. After a further interrogation, Ansell—swiftly changing in status from survivor to suspect—was jailed there. In retrospect, it may have appeared odd to some that the *Abigail*'s rum barrel had been opened or spilled while her food went untouched. Was a more plausible explanation for the events that a drunken celebration by the crew had turned into a deadly brawl? Adding to the suspicions was the fact that Ansell had disappeared briefly after returning to Cape Cod, during which time some believed he might have been attempting to hide monies stolen onboard the *Abigail*. Two days later, guards moved Ansell from Barnstable to the Province House in Boston, where he was questioned from seven to eleven o'clock at night by a deputation of senior provincial officials, including Governor Hutchinson, Admiral John Montagu, Lieutenant Governor Andrew Oliver, and Secretary Thomas Flucker. Whatever Ansell said during the course of the four-hour interview did not help him, and at the close of the session, he was committed to jail in Boston to await trial on the charge of piracy and robbery on the high seas. Governor Hutchinson was later criticized for the manner of this interrogation.

Ansell's trial in a Special Court of Admiralty for the Trial of Piracies—a court tried by appointed officials rather than a regular jury—

John Adams, engaged as an attorney by Ansell Nickerson. Portrait by Benjamin Blyth, 1764. Courtesy of the Massachusetts Historical Society.

commenced on December 16, 1772. The crown government's use of an admiralty court without a regular jury did not sit well with Boston's patriots, who would later play a role in attempting to prove Ansell's innocence. In fact, admiralty courts held overseas were considered so loathsome in America as to be mentioned as a grievance in the Declaration of Independence, "for transporting us beyond seas to be tried for pretended offenses." Unfortunately, the records for this unusual court no longer exist and information on the trial must be pieced together from other sources, such as newspaper reports and notes in the legal papers of John Adams. As the special court gathered in mid-December, Boston merchant and diarist John Rowe noted that it was composed mainly of Ansell's earlier interrogators, namely "The Governour, Lieut Govr, The Secretary of the Province, The Admirall, The Judge of Admiralty, Mr. Fisher the Collector of Salem, Mr. Waldo, the Collector of Falmouth Casco Bay." Ansell pleaded not guilty, and in the hope of gaining more information on the alleged pirate schooner, his counsel pressed for a delay in the trial. The court granted an adjournment of six months. Governor Hutchinson later noted that rumors were rife in town about a large armed schooner that had left Boston bound for the coast of Guinea at about the same time as the *Abigail*. In February 1773 diarist Simeon Perkins in Nova Scotia offered another scenario: "It is thought that Ansel Nickerson, suspected of piracy, will be cleared, as intelligence says some neutral French did piratical acts, and a man-o-war is gone in pursuit of them." This search was evidently fruitless.

The court was scheduled to reconvene in early June 1773, but due to outside events was delayed until the end of July. In the meantime, Ansell had at some point that summer been questioned about "money being found, suspected to be hidden by him" after Captain Doane brought him ashore. Governor Hutchinson later noted that during this time Ansell was "often visited in prison by some of the most active persons in the opposition" and that the "sons of liberty took part with him, and professed to make no doubt of [the pirate vessel] being a man of war schooner." Just after the special court was convened on July 28, Ansell engaged John Adams as one of his attorneys. Adams later noted that Nickerson had "requested my assistance and it was given. He had nothing to give me, but his promissory note, for a very moderate fee." The note promised Adams payment of six pounds and thirteen shillings. Josiah Quincy Jr. joined Adams in Nickerson's defense.

On August 3, 1773, after three days of witness examinations by both sides of the case, Advocate General Samuel Fitch opened the Crown's arguments. Fitch evidently argued that Ansell's motive was greed—

that he killed his relatives in order to steal their money, camouflaged the murders as a pirate raid, and later returned to the schooner to retrieve the hidden cash. The defense by John Adams and Josiah Quincy followed in the afternoon, and throughout the next day they vigorously fought a case that was almost entirely circumstantial.

One of the difficulties of the Crown's case was that, since the special court was convened in Boston, Ansell could be charged only with piracy and robbery. Governor Hutchinson later explained that a more serious felony charge, namely murder on the high seas, would have required the special court to "send the prisoner to England for trial there," which would have been impractical in the extreme. John Adams's legal notes yield some clues as to the arguments he used in the case and also reveal some areas of concern, such as comments about Ansell's strange disappearance after his return to Chatham— "Conduct after he came ashore—wandering God knows where," John Adams wrote, "all night absent going to his grandfather's. He pretended he was lost." While the selection of Adams as his defense counsel was an astute one, Ansell also benefited from a fundamental disagreement among the eight judges that ultimately led to his freedom. Four judges believed that to be found guilty of piracy, "the murders would also have to be proved. Hutchinson did not agree, but the equal division of the judges resulted in acquittal." Governor Hutchinson deeply regretted the acquittal on this basis, stating in his history that Ansell had "escaped punishment of a murder, which may be ranked among the most atrocious ever committed." After nearly ten months of imprisonment, Ansell was free, and he thanked "the honorable Court—and GOD—for my Deliverance!"

Ansell's liberation on August 6, 1773, did nothing to end the controversy. There was a strong public sentiment that he was guilty and that the case had become a political battle rather than a case of sound jurisprudence. In contrast to those sentiments, the next day a broadside sympathetic to Ansell but with no clear political point of view was printed in Boston with new revelations that had transpired since the close of the trial. Entitled *The Following Circumstances Relating to the Famous Ansell Nickerson,* the sheet was printed for the benefit of "an ever curious public" and attempted to accomplish several things:

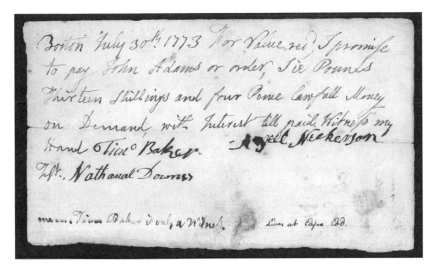

Promissory note from Ansell Nickerson to John Adams, 1773.
Courtesy of the Massachusetts Historical Society.

provide news of an apparently corroborative account of the pirate schooner on the date of the murders, report the rumored arrival in Martha's Vineyard of the kidnapped boy, William Kent Jr., and offer an unnamed magistrate's assurances of Ansell's innocence in the affair. Further, the broadside was meant to quell an angry public that greeted his acquittal with disbelief:

> *The public in general are not fully satisfied with the judgment lately given in by the honorable judges, some of whom are as remarkable for their thorough knowledge of the law, as they are for their tender regard for the life of the subject: but we are, in our early lessons, taught to know, "That it is utterly impossible to please everybody."*

It had been a "very arduous and difficult trial," according to the broadside's author, and "a more impartial one, perhaps, was never known in America, or elsewhere."

With regard to the alleged pirates, the broadside claimed that men from a vessel like that seen by Ansell had boarded a ship belonging to two mariners leaving Boston on the same night as the *Abigail* and robbed them of a quantity of wood:

> *Two men who belonged to a sloop that was bound to Seaguin, at the eastern parts of this province, have testified, that on the night of the 14th of November last, (which was the very time the bloody deed was perpetrated, for which Mr. Nickerson has so long stood in an unfair light to the world) on their passage from this place home, they were boarded by a topsail schooner, who had four boats, two of which was on deck, the others alongside the schooner: they took a quantity of wood off their deck and made off. The above agrees with Nickerson's description of the vessel he saw, whose people came on board the schooner* Abigail *and killed her men, which deed, he, the said Nickerson, was suspected to have perpetrated.*

A more sensational aspect of the broadside was the claim that William Kent Jr. had survived the plundering of the *Abigail*. The broadside offered two rumors on the missing youth: first, that he, "*they say,* is arrived in Martha's Vineyard," and another "report in town" that Kent had recently been seen aboard an armed schooner. Kent's survival, however, seems doubtful, as it would have undoubtedly corroborated Ansell's account of events; such an unexpected development could have lifted any remaining cloud of suspicion and would almost certainly have been noted by John Adams or Thomas Hutchinson.

Finally, the broadside offered that no one was more determined to find the real culprits than Ansell Nickerson, who, it alleged, was "in search to find every man that lately came home in the Guinea-man, which sailed at the time the murder was committed . . . and expects soon to give the public convincing proofs of his entire innocence in this important and interesting matter." The "proofs" gathered by Ansell never seem to have materialized. John Adams, for one, appears to have been ambivalent with regard to his client's guilt or innocence: "This was and remains still a mysterious transaction. I know not to this day what judgment to form of his guilt or innocence. And this doubt I presume was the principle of acquittal." Adams lost contact with Ansell, stating, "I have heard nothing of him, nor received anything for his note, which has been lost with many other notes and accounts of a large amount, in the distraction of the times and my absence from business." Ansell was never pressed to meet his obligation to Adams.

THE FOLLOWING
CIRCUMSTANCES
Relating to the Famous

ANSELL NICKERSON,

And concerning the BOY, (mentioned in the Trial to be carried away by the PIRATES) who, they say, is arrived at *Martha's-Vineyard* : Also, the Testimony of Two Men, belonging to *Seaguin,* who were ROBBED by a Top-sail Schooner with four Boats, on the Fourteenth of *November* : To which is added, the Declaration of a Justice of the Peace, respecting Mr. NICKERSON's Innocence of the Murder and Robbery in *Nov.* All which particulars have transpired since his Trial and Acquittal.

BOSTON, *Saturday, Aug.* 7, 1773.

THESE Circumstances may not, perhaps, be unentertaining to the ever curious Public at this Time, especially when an Affair of such Moment is in Agitation, which concerns the Lives of such a Number of our Fellow-Men, who undoubtedly are in imminent Danger ; as they are now, we trust, they will be agreable at least to those who live more remote from the busy Metropolis ; and probably may serve to elucidate many Doubts that have arisen in the Minds of a considerable Body of the Community, with respect to Mr. *Nickerson's* Innocence of the bloody Transaction in the Night of the Fourteenth of *November* last, although there was nothing but circumstantial Evidence that was offered on the Trial to prove him guilty of the Crime alledged against him. The Public in general are not fully satisfied with the Judgment lately given in by the Honorable JUDGES, some of whom are as remarkable for their thorough Knowledge of the Law, as they are for their tender Regard for the Life of the Subject : But we are, in our early Lessons, taught to know, " That it is utterly impossible to " please every Body." However, it must afford infinite Satisfaction to those worthy Gentlemen, if they can say within themselves, which we would not be supposed to doubt, that they have done that which they thought to be strictly RIGHT : Then let the noisy Clamor among either Party rage with Impetuosity, it will only soothe the Mind of the *honest* MAGISTRATE, when conscious that he is actuated by the Dictates of his own Conscience, and is influenced by the Principles of solid Reason and Equity, and has not suffered himself to be led away by Faction and Party-prejudice, which is thought by many to have been the unhappy Case in some of the Trials which have happened here in late Years, and it is to be wished both Parties could exculpate themselves from this Imputation. It is humbly recommended to every candid Mind to suspend their Judgment for the present on this unaccountable Affair, in hopes that a Time will come, when the Perpetrators of so shocking and bloody an Action will meet with their Deserts in this World, and not suffered to remain alive to disgrace the human Species, but may be made public Examples of, in order to be a Terror to others from committing such outragious and enormous Crimes in future. This we are certain of, That that GOD who tireth the reins and searcheth into the utmost recesses of Men's Hearts can, by his penetrable Providence, discover and bring to Justice the Murderer or Murderers; until that Time shall come, may we all submissively acquiesce in what hath been already done concerning this truly affecting and melancholy Affair, and not thirst to spill the Blood of the innocent, as every Man surely must be thought to be so, (according to the present happy Constitution ─, which all must acknowledge when ─ *English* Laws are with Re- ─ until the

The STORY that is now current in Town, is, TwoMen who belonged to aSloop that was bound to *Seaguin,* at the eastern Parts of this Province, have testified, That on the Night of the 14th of *November* last, (which was the very Time the bloody Deed was perpetrated, for which Mr. *Nickerson* has so long stood in an unfairLight to the World) on their Passage from this Place hous, they were boarded by a Topsail Schooner, who had four Boats, two of which was on Deck, the others along side the Schooner : They took Quantity of Wood off their Deck and made off. The above agrees with *Nickerson's* Description of the Vessel he saw, whose People came on board the Schooner *Abigail* and killed her Men, which Deed, he, the said *Nickerson,* was suspected to have perpetrated.

Mr. *Nickerson* is now in search to find every Man that lately came home in the Guinea-man, which sailed at theTime the Murder was committed, and is inHopes to gain someIntelligence from them, at least, that they saw said Topsail Schooner, if they were not hailed or stopped by them. And expects soon to give the Public convincing Proofs of his entire Innocence in this important and interesting Matter.

It has been publicly declared by a certain *Magistrate,* not more remarkable for his honesty, than for his tenacious Regard for the Rights and Liberties of the Subject, " That it is his Opinion, that Mr. *Nickerson* is not the Man that committed the Murder and Robbery he lately stood charged with ;" for which could many have had their Will, he would possibly have suffered the most cruelDeath that could possibly have been inflicted, without Benefit of Clergy ; although there was only circumstantialEvidence could be procured on theTrial; some of which was invalidated by counter Evidence, at the same Time. And could the Public form any Judgment from Mr. *Nickerson's* Behavior at the Time he was first taken up and examined at *Barnstable* ; and when he was examined before his Excellency ; during his Confinement in Goal ; and, in short, through the whole Course of the Trial ; his unvaried Testimony on every Examination ; and the Connection that must naturally be formed between himself and the Persons that were killed, as two of them were his Brothers, and the other his Cousin. Add these Things together, and it must be acknowledged by every unprejudiced Person in *America,* that he is not the Man that committed the late Murder : Then they will fully acquiesce in the Judgment lately given in by the Honorable JUDGES of the Court of Admiralty, who were lately appointed to this very arduous and difficult Trial ; a more impartial one, perhaps, was never known in *America,* or elsewhere.

" The worstOppression who, ah ! who could bear,
" If Virtue, hov'ring Angel, was not near."
" Conscious Virtue ever vindicates itself."

Monday, Aug. 9th.

There are other Reports in Town, one of which is, That the Lad, mentioned in the Evidence given in on the Trial, has been seen on board an armed Schooner. Another Report is, that he has actually ─ *Martha's-Vineyard.* But whether ─

The Following Circumstances Relating to the Famous Ansell Nickerson, *1773 broadside. Courtesy of the Historical Society of Pennsylvania.*

The unredeemed note remains to this day among John Adams's legal papers at the Massachusetts Historical Society.

Ansell, who had married Mary Smith a few years before, presumably returned to Chatham after obtaining his freedom. He and his wife raised at least four children, one of whom was named "Deliverance" —perhaps an echo of his reaction to the court's acquittal. Sometime prior to 1790, Ansell is said to have met an untimely death in Martinique.

Before he died, however, Ansell allegedly confessed that he had murdered the crew of the *Abigail*. Like so many aspects of Ansell Nickerson's story, this claim by a chronicler of Nickerson family history—who described Ansell as "a bold, bad man" and "desperate character"—is possible but cannot be verified. Another source, William C. Smith's *History of Chatham,* states simply that he was lost at sea. Unquestionably, Ansell was a pawn of the political tensions of pre–Revolutionary War Boston. Was he guilty of a triple or quadruple murder or just the hapless survivor of an unspeakable crime? We will never know.

Chapter 19

Tempted by the Devil:
The Criminal Career of Levi Ames
1773

HIS YOUNG LIFE consumed by petty thievery, heavy drinking, and cavorting with wanton women, twenty-one-year-old Levi Ames committed his last crime in August 1773. Arriving in Boston after a lengthy, rambling spree of minor thefts in surrounding towns, Levi turned his attentions to committing a more profitable robbery. His wishes were advanced by a chance meeting with a like-minded young man, Joseph Atwood, at the marketplace in town. Forming a fast friendship, the two decided to collaborate in stealing money from the house of Atwood's former employer, the prosperous auctioneer Martin Bicker. The theft was executed at night and netted more than £60 in silver and gold coins for the youthful burglars. But before long, Levi was detected with some of Bicker's money and arrested. He was tried and sentenced for a nighttime burglary, a crime more serious than a daytime break-in and then punishable by death. The case prompted unprecedented attention and resulted in the publication of a flurry of didactic broadsides, poetry, and sermons, making him an exemplar of sinful, unclean living. Shortly before his execution, a repentant Levi dictated his own *Last Words and Dying Speech* to jailer James Otis for posthumous publication. (The complete document appears at the end of the chapter.) According to diarist John Rowe, his public hanging at Boston Neck on October 21, 1773, was witnessed by thousands of spectators and, oddly, fulfilled for Levi a premonition that his life would end at the gallows.

Levi, who hailed from a respectable Groton family and later lived in Newton, began his criminal career at the tender age of seven with the theft of a neighbor's eggs. Before long, he abandoned an apprenticeship and "opened a wide door to temptation" by going on the road as a laborer. His principal means of support, however, came through a string of at least seventeen robberies committed in small towns throughout eastern Massachusetts, Connecticut, and Rhode Island. Apprehended on several occasions, Levi suffered jail time, two brandings, and at least two or three public whippings.

Among his victims were two officeholders in Waltham, Jonathan Hammond and Jonas Dix, from whom he stole, respectively, a "quantity of money" and a hat. He had a partner for the Hammond theft—the "infamous" Thomas Cook, who, according to Boston diarist John Boyle, was soon apprehended. Not only did the pair rob Hammond, but they turned cattle into his cornfield, causing considerable damage to the gentleman's crops. One of Levi's most unlikely crimes occurred when fellow inmate Abraham Merriam told him where to find some money in the Lexington house of his elderly father-in-law, Daniel Simonds. Merriam expressed no desire to share in the proceeds; rather, he abetted Levi to exact revenge upon a father-in-law who had seen to his imprisonment for debt.

The most influential person Levi robbed outside of Boston was the Reverend Jonas Clarke, fifth minister of the First Congregational Society in Lexington. The valuables stolen included a silver tankard, more than a dozen spoons, a pepper box, and two pairs of sugar tongs, all from a silver service brought to the parsonage by Clarke's wife. Jonas Clarke reportedly later visited Levi in prison, where they prayed together. Levi did not even spare his jailers from small thefts.

Silhouette of the Rev. Jonas Clarke, a burglary victim of Levi Ames. From Charles Hudson, History of the Town of Lexington.

In one of his first imprisonments, a jailer in Cambridge brought Levi a silver spoon to eat with. Levi promptly stole it. Levi resembled other pre-Federal-era rogues in at least one respect: he for a time adopted an alias. In Newburyport, Levi called himself "Isaac Lawrence" and during his interlude there stashed several articles of clothing at the home of a black man, Scipio Burnam.

What might have become Levi's most legendary crime never came to pass. After arriving in Boston in June 1773, he was invited by a pock-marked Irishman, Thomas Smith, to break into Governor Thomas Hutchinson's mansion to steal "a considerable quantity of money." Smith, who had probably already stolen a watch from the governor, claimed he had an accomplice among Hutchinson's servants and that he would relieve His Excellency of a "chest of dollars." Smith intended to commit the burglary armed with swords and pistols. Refusing to participate in such a risky and potentially violent scheme, Levi later claimed that he "had never thought of murdering any man" in his crimes.

Subject to a guilty conscience after some of his robberies, Levi on more than one occasion secretly returned stolen goods to their rightful owners. Distraught citizens who had been robbed one day might awake the next morning to find the pilfered goods sitting at their doorstep. Guilt was not Levi's only misgiving. During one of his excursions a more disturbing feeling overcame him—he had a premonition of his death upon the gallows:

> I passed the gallows on Boston neck with some stolen goods under my arm; when my conscience terribly smote me, and I tho't I should surely die there, if I did not leave off this course of life. What I then feared, is now come upon me.

Levi's mixed feelings about his occupation were not strong enough for him to change his life course. After meeting up with Joseph Atwood, a virtually penniless former servant, he set about his greatest crime yet. A nocturnal burglary upon the house of Martin Bicker was a per-ilous undertaking for the pair. The crime constituted a capital offense and if caught, one or both men were likely to be sentenced to death. The break-in (recalled in Levi's *Last Words and Dying Speech*) took place between midnight and 3 A.M. on August 27, 1773. Within a day of the robbery, Levi was identified by Martin Bicker as one of the culprits and arrested. John Boyle noted that he was "detected with part of the money and committed to gaol." Once in jail, Levi fingered Joseph Atwood as his accomplice, but Joseph had already absconded northward. On September 4, Joseph was arrested in Portsmouth, New Hampshire, and returned to Boston.

The young men's trials occurred a few days later. In his trial, Joseph alleged that only Levi had entered the house—a claim that might have saved his own life but, if believed, would probably cost Levi his. Joseph's version of events differed considerably from Levi's; in particular, he claimed to have been little more than a watchman as the break-in took place. Joseph said that he first met Levi the day before the theft at Martin Bicker's auction rooms and then again later at the marketplace. Levi was apparently eager to recruit him as an accomplice and attempted to ingratiate himself by treating Joseph to a warm meal and plenty of drink. After an excursion to Charlestown, the young men returned to Boston for more drinking:

> They went over to Charlestown together; returned; went to the house where they drank after dinner and got more drink; then took another walk: About nine o'clock that evening they came by Mr. Bicker's house; as they came by Ames told Attwood he had seen Mr. Bicker take a large sum of money that day, and had watched where he put it, and that if he would watch him, he would rob Mr. Bicker of the money and give up part of it; Attwood says, he at first told him he would not; upon which Ames said he was very fearful, or words to that purport, and that he (Ames) had done things ten times more dangerous than that.

The pair strolled through Market Square and into the North End where in a shipyard they decided to sleep on some planks. At about 2 A.M., according to Joseph, they awoke and, after sharing a few more swigs of liquor, Levi asked if Joseph would accompany him to Mr. Bicker's house. This time the answer was yes, and the two set off for the auctioneer's home. Joseph claimed that a window was partly open and that Levi climbed in. A quarter of an hour later Levi emerged with Bicker's money and the two proceeded to his lodgings at Captain Dickey's house where, because everyone there was asleep, they could not get in.

At this moment, Levi supposedly handed Joseph an assortment of coins and said, "This is for watching for me," and the two parted.

The jury believed Joseph's version of events and found him "guilty in part—guilty of the theft but not of burglary." Receiving the comparatively light sentence of a whipping of twenty stripes, he was also required to meet the cost of prosecution and an award to Martin Bicker of treble damages.

Levi's trial followed. For his apparent leadership in the crime and for burgling the Bicker house at night, he was convicted of a capital offense. Chief Justice Peter Oliver presented the sentence of death aloud, according to one published account, stating emphatically, "[You are] to be hanged with a rope by the neck until you are dead! Dead! Dead!" In his *Last Words and Dying Speech,* Levi contradicted Joseph's assertion that he was the only one who climbed through the open window. He also used the opportunity, however, to forgive his former cohort "from his heart" for a lie that resulted in a death sentence. The execution was originally scheduled for October 14, but was later stayed for an additional week. In the meantime, printer Ezekiel Russell published a broadside, *A Prospective View of Death,* which gave details of the case from Joseph's view and tantalized the public with the possibility that a reluctant Levi might publish a full confession. "Should a full relation of the life and actions of this young man be obtained for publication," wrote Russell, "it is thought it would open such a scene of iniquity to view as was never perpetrated by any one man in America."

Some time after being sentenced, Levi entertained thoughts of escaping from jail. Later, when this impulse faded, he began to regret his past conduct and accept the Gospel. His conversion did not come quickly enough to escape the censure of diarist John Boyle, who in October 1773 noted that while Levi, "the unhappy person under sentence of death for burglary, attends public worship every Sabbath . . . he does not appear to have that anxious solicitude respecting a future state, which might be expected from one in his situation." Levi was by this time under the constant pastoral care of several Boston ministers who, according to Boyle, were taking "infinite pains" to "enlighten his mind in the knowledge of divine truths."

On the evening of October 19, Elhanan Winchester and a large gathering of townspeople arrived at the prison in Boston to sing an "execution hymn" specially composed for the occasion. Several ministers, including Samuel Mather, Andrew Eliot, and Samuel Stillman, gave considerable attention to the condemned man and before large gatherings delivered execution sermons that were later published. The Reverend Samuel Stillman, minister of Boston's First Baptist Church, visited Levi on the morning of October 21, 1773, to prepare him for his execution later that day. The clergyman spent several hours with Levi discussing the state of his mind and at eleven o'clock conducted him to the old brick meetinghouse where the Reverend Dr. Samuel Mather preached on the execution. At three o'clock that afternoon, Levi was transported in a cart to Boston Neck, a traditional spot for executions in Boston. Shortly before his hanging, he "gave convincing proof of his dying a true penitent," evidently to the satisfaction of Boyle and other Bostonians. According to *The Dying Penitent*, Levi's final speech given that morning ended with the following words:

> *Let no idle Eye my Fate behold*
> *Nor my Tale by babling Gossips told;*
> *May each Spectator that surrounds my Cart*
> *Think on my End with Melancholy Heart,*
> *Lord! Let them profit from my Death and Pain,*
> *Then shall not I, poor Ames, expire in vain.——*
> *Now once for all, I take my final View,*
> *And bid the transient Scenes of Life Adieu!*
> *Full of my Saviour, all compos'd I die,*
> *And to his precious Arms with Rapture fly.*

Levi's life story, as told to jailer James Otis and published by Ezekiel Russell after his death, recounted the saga of his criminal life and its ultimate consequences in detail. At least eleven broadsides were published in Boston to commemorate the events—one of the largest responses of its kind to a trial in pre-Federal New England. Among Levi's final words was a request to the public regarding the welfare of his relatives in Groton. He asked that "no person, old or young, would ever reflect on my poor dear Mother, or Brother, or any of my relations on account of my shameful and untimely death." After his

The SPEECH of DEATH

T O

LEVI AMES.

Who was Executed on *Boston*-Neck, *October* 21, 1773, for the Crime of Burglary.

I DEATH, Poor *Ames*, pronounce your Fate,
Thus grining grimly through your Grate.
Remember all the Crimes you've done,
And think how early you begun.
Loft in the grand Apoftacy,
You were at firft condemn'd to die ;
In adding Guilt you ftill went on :
I doubly claim you for my own.
How often you the Sabbath broke !
GOD's Name in vain how often took !
A filthy Drunkard you have been,
And led your Life with the Unclean :
No Thoughts of GOD you ever chofe,
But chas'd them from you when they rofe :
In Idlenefs you did proceed,
And took fmall pains to learn to read ;
With vile Companions, your Delight,
You often fpent the guilty Night :
Your Lips fcarce ever breath'd a Prayer,
You gave your Tongue to curfe and fwear :
You've been to all your Friends a Grief,
And from your Infancy a Thief ;
You know the Truth of what I tell,
No Goods were fafe that you could fteal ;
How many Doors you've open broke !
And windows fcal'd, and Money took :
Round Houfes you all Day have been,
To fpy a Place to enter in ;
Thence in the Night, all dark and late,
You've ftole their Goods and Gold and Plate.
Imprifon'd, whip'd, yet you proceed,
The Life you led you ftill would lead.
Your Confcience cry'd, " you'll be undone."—
You ftifl'd Confcience and went on.
And now, behold ! my poifon'd Dart,
I point directly at your Heart.

The Halter and the Gallows view,
Death and Damnation is your due.
Darknefs, and Horror, Fire, and Chains;
Almighty Wrath, and endlefs Pains.
—But lo ! I fee the Preacher come,
Salvation fpeaks——I muft be dumb.

The Preacher fpeaks—Behold I come,
A voice from Heaven to call you home.
Though you the chief of Sinners were,
I bring the Gofpel ; don't Defpair.
Nor death, nor Hell, fhall do you hurt,
Be JESUS only your Support.
To you he holds His Righteoufnefs,
He bled and dy'd to buy your Peace,
Pardon and Life are His to give,
'Tis thine, Poor Sinner, to believe.
Let Death in all it's Dread appear,
Though public Execution's near,
Of Wrath Divine He bore the Weight,
He fuffer'd too without the Gate,
He betwixt Heaven and Earth was hung,
He conquer'd Hell, and death unftung.

Now let the Guilty fee and hear,
And all the Congregation fear ;
This Spectacle your Hearts imprefs,
And do no more fuch Wickednefs ;
Hear fuch important Truths as thefe,
Ruin advances by Degrees :
The youth with lefler Crimes begins,
And then proceeds to groffer Sins,
From Step to Step he travels on,
And fees himfelf at once undone :
Surpriz'd ! unthought on ! finds his Fate,
His Ruin final, and compleat.

The Speech of Death to Levi Ames, *1773, with a woodcut by Paul Revere.*
Courtesy of the Historical Society of Pennsylvania.

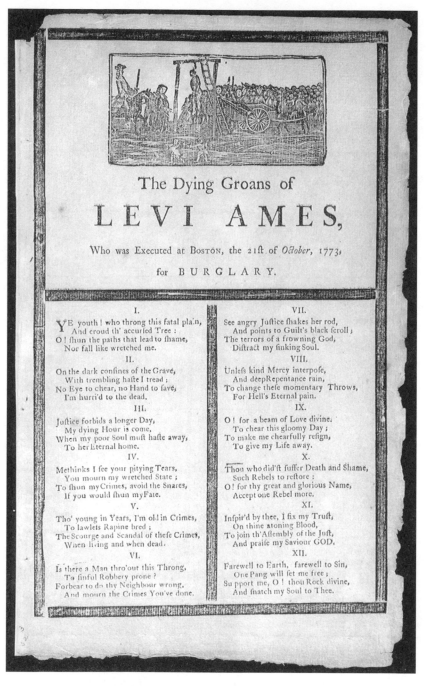

The Dying Groans of Levi Ames, *1773 broadside.*
Courtesy of the Historical Society of Pennsylvania.

execution amid throngs of onlookers, Levi's lifeless body was transported to Groton for burial by his family.

The last WORDS and Dying SPEECH of Levi Ames, who was Executed at Boston, on Thursday the 21st day of October, 1773, for BURGLARY. Taken from his own Mouth, and Published at his desire, is a solemn Warning to all, more particularly Young People. THERE IS A WAY THAT SEEMETH RIGHT UNTO A MAN, BUT THE END THEREOF ARE THE WAYS OF DEATH. PROV. 14.12.

I Levi Ames, aged 21 years, was born in Groton, in New England, of a credible family, my father's name was Jacob Ames, who died when I was but two years old. I am the first of the family who was ever disgraced. My prevailing sin, and that for which I am soon to suffer death was thieving; to practice which I began early and pursued it constantly; except at certain intervals when my conscience made uneasy, and I resolved to do so no more.

My first thefts were small. I began this awful practice by stealing a couple of eggs, then a jack-knife, after that some chalk. But being detected and reproved for the crime, I thought to repent and reform; but found myself powerfully urged to repeat this wickedness by the temptations of the devil; with which I again complied. My tender Mother seeing me take such horrid courses, and dreading the conse quences, often entreated and pleaded with me to turn from my evil ways, and I as often assured her that I would. Had I followed her good advice and council, I should never have come to this shameful and untimely end. But I am now made to feel the anger of God against me, for my disobedience to my parent! God will not let disobedient children pass unpunished.

Having got under my mother's eye, I still went on in my old way of stealing; and not being permitted to live with the person I chose to live with, I ran away from my master, which opened a wide door to temptation, and helped on my ruin; for being indolent in temper, and having no honest way of supporting myself, I robbed others of their property.

About this time I stole a gun at Woburn, from Josiah Richardson, and a large silver spoon from one Mr. Howard of the same town. I then broke open the shop of Mr. Edward Hammond, in the county of Plymouth, and took out a piece of broad-cloth, and some money. I stole between twenty and thirty dollars from another person, whose name I have forgot. I broke open the shop of Mr. Jonas Cutler, of Groton, and took from him a good piece of broad-cloth, a quantity of silk mitts, and several pieces of silk handkerchiefs. I also stole a quantity of money from Jonathan Hammond, of Waltham, and a hat from Jonas Dix, Esq; of the same place; and when in gaol at Cambridge, I stole a silver spoon which was brought from Mr. Braddish's the goal-keeper [sic] for me to eat with. I robbed the Reverend Mr. Clark of Lexington, of a tankard, twelve teaspoons, one large ditto. a pepper box, and two pair of sugar tongs. I also stole from Mr. Keith at Natick, two coats and jackets, with which I dressed myself when I came to Boston; I gave John Battle twenty dollars to make up the matter with Mr. Keith, being part of the money I stole from Mr. Hammond of Waltham. I stole ten or eleven dollars from Mr. Symonds of Lexington, whose son in law, Mr. Meriam, while I was in prison, informed me where the money was and how to get it, but he never received any of it; I supposed he gave me this information thro' envy against his father in law, thro' whose means he was then confined for debt. I stole a pair of silver buckles, and a pair of turned pumps out of a pair of saddle bags at Leason's tavern in Waltham; the buckles were marked I.D. which I delivered to a man at Marlborough, a blacksmith, to make up with him for some stockings I took from him; his name I do not remember. I twisted a padlock and entered the cellar of a Minister's house at Marlborough, I then went up the cellar stairs, lighted a candle in order to get some victuals. I have several times taken sundry articles off of lines, hedges, fences, bushes, apple trees, grass, &c. but cannot recollect the owners. Tho. Cook and I stole two great-coats and sold them. I have left three shirts and several pair of stocking at Scipio Burnam's at Newbury-port; I then went by the name of Isaac Lawrence. I stole an ax out of a cart and hid it in a stone wall between Watertown and Boston, (the night before I took the money from Mr. Hammond) in Little Cambridge, near to Mr. Dana's tavern, there I left it with a design to sell it when I came back. I broke open the house of Mr. Rice in Marlborough, on the Lord's Day, while the people were gone to public worship, having been advised to it by Daniel Cook, when we were in Concord Goal [sic, for gaol throughout]; was taken in the house and returned the things to the Owner.

Sometime last fall, I saw Tho. Cook who told me he had seven pounds of plate hid, viz. a tankard, a number of table spoons, and one soup ditto; these he dug up while I was with him; we carried them away from that place and hid them in a stone wall, near a barn, close to the sign of the bull on the Wrentham road, but he never informed me where he got them, or how he came by them: he offered me half if I would dispose of them, but I was afraid to do it.

Last June an Irishman who called his name Thomas Smith, of middle stature, much marked with the small-pox, told me that he knew of a watch which was taken from his Excellency some time ago, and I suspected that he was the person who stole it, because he said he knew the governor's house well: He also assured me that his Excellency had a considerable quantity of money in the house, and asked me to go with him to get it. I denied, knowing that the governor had many servants, which I urged as a reason why I would not join him. He said he had one to assist him, whose name he would not tell me, unless I would be one of the party. He farther declared that he should go well armed with swords and pistols. Upon this I absolutely refused, because I never thought of murdering any man, in the midst of all my scene of thieving. He thought to prevail on me by telling me that there was a chest of dollars in the house but I would not go with them.

In the same month, June I lodged at a tavern in Killingsley or Pomfret Connecticut government on the Lord's-day, where I sat and eat and drank and went off without paying. A few evenings after, I returned, shoved up the window and put in my hand and stole a box with a johannes, some small change, a pair of knee buckles, and sleeve buttons, for which I was apprehended, confessed the fact, returned the goods, was punished and set at liberty. The same night as above I took a horse out of Killingsley, and rode him down to the county of Worcester, where I broke a shop open about day light, and took a quantity of coppers, and a remnant of sattin: the owners have got them again. I also robbed a baker at Rhode-Island of a quantity of coppers which I found in three baskets, and spent them.

As for Atwood, in company with whom I committed that theft for which I am soon to die, my acquaintance with him began in the following

*manner——I was standing at a countryman's cart, in the market at
Boston, asking the price of a turkey; Atwood came up to me, and we
fell into conversation, he asked me to walk with him to Beacon-Hill,
which I did——We asked each other about the place of resort. I told
him that I lodged at Captain Dickeys. He said that his money was
all spent except one copper, which he had in a snuff-box. I asked him
where he belonged? He said he was born in an Island in the West-
Indies, and that his parents lived in Rhode-Island. I asked him where
he had been? he told me that he lately came from Portsmouth. I told
him that since he had no money, if he would go with me to my lodgings, I would give him some dinner——I asked him what he would do
with some silver plate, if he had any to dispose of? He told me he
knew of a goldsmith who would take it, because he had sold some to
him before. I told him I knew where there was some, and if he would
go with me, we would get it; to which he consented. We then went to
Menotemy, and found it hid in a stone wall. We kept it about us till
next morning. He told me he knew of a Vendue-master in Boston, with
whom he had lived, who had a large sum of money by him, and if I
would join him, we would get it. I asked who it was; he said Mr.
Bicker. We accordingly agreed to steal it. At night after we had slept,
we went to a joiner's shop, into which I entered and took out three
chizels; we then went to Mr. Bicker's house, and on the way were
hailed by a watchman, to whom we answered, Friends. Having come
to Mr. Bicker's house, we found a front chamber window open; we
pulled off our shoes, and Jos. Atwood with my assistance climed up to
the window, and entered the house, and opened the doors for me; we
then went together to the desk, which we broke open with the chizels.
Atwood pulled out the first drawer, and said there was small change
in it, which was all he could find. As he was going away, I pulled out
another drawer, in which I found a bag of silver coin.——After that we
came out, and went to fox-hill, near the powder-house, there we hid
the plate, which we had kept in our pockets while we were at supper,
and when we entered Mr. Bicker's house. The small change in silver,
which Atwood took were equally divided, tho' the gold which Atwood
had then secreted I knew nothing of, nor did he ever give me any of
it. Before sunset I saw him at Mr. Bell's, when he informed me that a
warrant was out for me; he went with me to Winisimit, and advised
me to go over the ferry, promising to meet me at Portsmouth the*

Wednesday following at the house in which he was taken. I returned again to Boston to see if any of my clothes were done, which I had bespoke; on Saturday I was taken by Mr. Bicker and committed to goal, and saw Atwood no more till I saw him in the prison yard after he was apprehended.

Thus I have given an account of that shocking manner in which I have filled up a short life, and of which I am now ashamed. May God forgive me my dreadful wickedness, committed both against him, and many worthy men, of whom also I would ask forgiveness, it being not in my power to make restitution, which if it was I would readily do it—I also forgive from my heart Joseph Atwood, who swore on my tryal that I entered the house of Mr. Bicker first, and let him in, when he knows in his conscience that he entered first and let me in. I die in charity with all mankind. But though I lived such a wicked life, it was not without some severe checks of conscience. For after I had stolen, I have been so distressed at times, as to be obliged to go back, and throw the stolen goods at the door, or into the yard, that the Owners might have them again. —And not long before I was taken for this last robbery, I passed the gallows on Boston neck with some stolen goods under my arm; when my conscience terribly smote me, and I tho't I should surely die there, if I did not leave off this course of life. What I then feared, is now come upon me.—

Having thus given an account of my dreadful life of wickedness, I would also mention the manner in which I have conducted, and my mind has been exercised during my confinement in goal, since the awful sentence of DEATH was passed upon me.

At first I had secret hopes of escape; that I should by some means get out of prison. When I saw that it was impossible, I endeavored to reconcile myself as well as I could. My conscience made me uneasy—I thought I had been so wicked that I should certainly go to Hell. And when I considered how short my time was, I knew I could not do good works to go to Heaven. To Hell then I was sure I should go. And I seemed to have such an awful sight of Hell and the Grave, that I was very much terrified indeed—I then took to drinking strong liquor in order to drown my sorrow. But this would not do—I left that off and took to reading my bible; my conscience became so uneasy, that I could have no rest, O! a wounded conscience who can bear? I tried to pray; but it came into my mind that the prayers of the wicked would not be heard. Yet I could not help crying for mercy. I was at times ready to despair of the mercy of God. But the ministers who visited me, assured me that the blood of Christ was sufficient to cleanse me from all sin, which gave me a little encouragement to go on crying to God. I now began to understand something of that law of God which I had broken, as condemning me for the wickedness of my heart as well as life—I saw that I was undone, that my heart and life were bad beyond all account. I saw that if God should damn me a thousand times he would be just, and I should have nothing to say. In this condition I was a week before the time first fixed for my execution—The loss of body and soul made me tremble; though I could not freely tell all that I felt to all who came to see me. I thought that if I should be executed in this condition, I must be dragged like a bullock to the slaughter.

But God's name be blessed forever; on that Friday evening the 8th instant, I turned over a little book which was put into my hands, in which I saw, Ezek. 36. 26, 27. A new heart will I give you, and a new spirit will I put upon you: and I will take away the stony heart out of your flesh, and I will give you a heart of flesh. And I will pour out my spirit upon you; &c. This at once surprized me: I knew that I wanted this new heart; and could not help looking on this as God's gracious promise to me: and I tho't that as I knew God could not lie, if I would not believe this, I would believe nothing: my mind at once felt easy. I now saw that I had sinned against God all my life with as much envy, as ever I killed a snake; which I always hated.

After this I had, and now have such a view of the way of salvation by Christ, that I felt and do feel my soul rest on him as my only hope of salvation. Since which I have found peace of mind, anger against myself for sin, and a desire to be made holy. At times the terrors of death seem to be removed: at other times I am full of fears lest I should deceive myself. Yet I cannot but hope that Christ has freely pardoned me. On him I desire to rest living and dying; and to give him all the praise.

And now as a dying man I mention the following things, viz.

1. To keep your doors and windows shut on evenings, and secured well to prevent temptation. And by no means to use small locks on the outside, one of which I have twisted with ease when tempted to steal. Also not to leave linnen or clothes out at night, which have often proved a snare to me. Travellers I advise to secure their saddle bags, boots, &c. in the chambers where they lodge.

2. Parents and masters I entreat who have any concern for, and connection with children, to have an eye over their actions; and to take special care for their precious and immortal souls.

3. All Persons whether old or young, who may see these lines, spoke as it were by a poor, dying, sinful man, now bound in chains, and who has but a short space of time before he must launch into an endless eternity; guard against every temptation to sin. If at any time you are tempted to do any thing like the poor soul who now speaks to you, earnestly pray to God for strength and resist the temptation, as well as for repentance for your past sins.

The youth more especially I would solemnly caution against the vices to which they are most inclined—Such as bad Women, who have undone many, and by whom I have also suffered much; the unlawful intercourse with them I have found by sad experience, leading to almost every sin. I also warn them to guard against the first temptation to disobedience to parents. Had I regarded the many kind entreaties and reproofs of my tender Mother, I had never come to this shameful and untimely death.

Profane cursing and swearing I also bear my dying testimony against, as a horrid sin, and very provoking to God.

Nor must I omit to mention gaming, to which young people are much inclin'd, and which at this day prevails to the ruin of many. For when a youth hath gamed away all his money, he will be tempted even to steal from his master or parents, in order to get at it again. Besides, this sin leads to drunkenness another dreadful vice.

There is one sin more I must warn all persons against, and that is, a profanation of the Lord's day, and of public worship. Oh! How many such days I have despised, and while others have been engaged in serving God, I have been employed in wickedness, which I now confess with grief of heart.

4. I have one request more to make from the borders of the grave, a compliance with which is earnestly desired by a poor dying mortal: which is, That no person, old or young, would ever reflect on my poor dear Mother, or Brother, or any of my relations on account of my shameful and untimely death, who could not prevent my wickedness, and have trouble too much to be borne, by the life I have lived, and the death I am to die.

I desire sincerely to thank all the good ministers of the town, who have taken great pains with me ever since the sentence of death was past upon me, to convince me of my unhappy situation, of my lost and undone condition by nature, of my aggravating sins by practice, and of the infinitely free rich grace and mercy of God, only thro' the minutes and mediation of my dear savior Jesus Christ. I also thank all the good people both of town and country, who, I have reason to think, have offered up many prayers at the throne of grace for me. I also thank Mr. Otis, the goal-keeper and his family, who have all been very kind to me during my confinement in goal.

And now may Jesus Christ forgive me, the worst of sinners, as he did the thief on the cross, if he does not, I am forever undone in soul and body!

Levi Ames
Attest, Joseph Otis,
Dept. Goal-keeper
Boston: Printed and Sold at the Shop
opposite the Court-House in Queen Street.

Part Four

Family Skeletons, Dangerous Liaisons, and Black Sheep

"THE PROPER BOSTONIAN," observed social historian Cleveland Amory, "feels that if certain of his ancestors were distinguished, so much the better, but they do not have to have been." Portraits of black sheep, Amory mused, were just as likely to be displayed in the homes of Boston's *crème de la crème* as those of "stern-faced ancestors whose ways were more tried and true." For the descendants of Boston's earliest residents, family skeletons abound, bearing witness to untold tales of infidelity, bigamy, illegitimate births, broken engagements, miserable relationships, divorce, and suicide. Members of prominent families sometimes escaped the consequences of these actions. For others, such human failings often resulted in public censure or punishment.

The "first families" of the Massachusetts Bay Colony were not exempt from personal scandals. Female descendants of Governor Thomas Dudley, for example, had a propensity for conducting extramarital affairs, giving birth to illegitimate infants, and pursuing separations or divorces. At least seven of the governor's progeny over three generations were involved in one or more of these actions. Thomas Dudley's daughter, Sarah, was divorced from Major Benjamin Keayne after behaving disreputably and was subsequently excommunicated by the First Church of Boston. Sarah's daughter, Anna Keayne, was, in turn, divorced from Edward Lane in one of the most convoluted divorce sagas of the colonial period. Another granddaughter of the governor, Margaret Dudley, bore an illegitimate daughter by Francis Pafat.

Rebecca Dudley, a daughter of Governor Joseph Dudley and a grand-daughter of Thomas, had an acrimonious separation from her husband Samuel Sewall Jr., and in 1716 gave birth to an illegitimate male child. Finally, in 1773, a great-granddaughter, Ann Dudley, sued her husband, John Lovell Jr., for a separation from bed and board, an arrangement just short of divorce that would allow her to live independently.

Other Dudley descendants demonstrated the same behavior. Anne Cotton, a granddaughter of Governor Simon Bradstreet and a great-granddaughter of Thomas Dudley, was one of the few in the family brought to justice for her transgressions. In 1685 she became preg-nant by a man other than her husband. Samuel Sewall made a brief mention of the story in his diary: "Mr. Stoughton also told me of George Carr's wife [Anne Cotton] being with child by another man, tells the father, Major Pike sends her down to prison." Anne was fined twenty shillings in 1688 in York, Maine, for committing fornication with William Johnson, a man who later became her second husband. In the court record, Johnson was presented as the "reputed father" of Anne's child. He was fined in the same amount as his future wife and also ordered to pay maintenance for the child's care.

One of Thomas Dudley's other great-granddaughters, Dorothy Wade, married Boston housewright Jonathan Willis. In June 1712 Samuel Sewall noted in his diary that "Mrs. Mercy Wade sends her complaint against Jonathan Willis, her daughter Dorothy's husband, for his inhu-mane actions; hateful expressions, as well as murderous threatenings towards his wife." Willis countered that the complaint should have come from his wife, not his mother-in-law, and requested its dismissal. In the meantime, Mercy Wade's complaint attracted the support of her uncle, Governor Joseph Dudley, who Sewall remarked was "very hot in his niece's cause." Finally, after two days of procedural bickering, Dorothy endorsed her mother's complaint, and the hearing was adjourned for a month. Sewall made no further references to the con-tretemps in his diary. One possible cause of conflict in the marriage was the birth of Dorothy's daughter, Phebe, whose paternity appears to have been in question. Jonathan Willis does not seem to have embraced the girl as his own. In his 1748 will he identified "Phebe Willis alias

Phebe Potter" as his "reputed daughter" by Dorothy, bequeathed her only twenty-five shillings, and otherwise "utterly excluded" her from his estate. In a journal filled with references to his family, Jonathan Willis made no mention of Phebe. Another of Thomas Dudley's great-granddaughters, Dorothy Dunster Page, in 1739 "absconded" from her husband, Solomon Page, in Hampton, New Hampshire, leaving him "four small children" and obstinately refusing to live with him.

Accounts of "unclean dalliances" and "wantonness" are common in early Boston records. In the summer of 1645 John Winthrop recorded in his journal one of the greatest adultery scandals in town. The "sad business," as Winthrop put it, began more than two years earlier when William Hudson, a vintner and innkeeper, embarked for England to serve in a military company during the English Civil War. Before leaving town, Hudson asked a friend, Henry Dawson, to watch over his family and business in Boston. A young man "of good esteem for piety and sincerity," Dawson agreed. A laborer whose own wife was abroad at the time, he began looking after Hudson's business. Before long, however, he began looking after Hudson's wife, Anne, as well. One night, two of Anne Hudson's servants "being up, perceived him go up into their dame's chamber." Word of the nocturnal visit slowly wound its way to the authorities, reaching them about three months after Anne's husband returned from England. Anne promptly told her husband what had happened. She had "used the best arguments" to dissuade Dawson from sharing her bed. He did not touch her, Anne claimed. She, in turn, had not "cried out" at the time because he had been so helpful to her and she was unwilling to "bring him to punishment or disgrace." In spite of Anne's protestations, the incident was brought before the magistrates to adjudicate and the principals were questioned. Dawson confessed "not only that he was in the chamber with her in such a suspicious manner, but also that he was in bed with her," an admission that made a capital adultery trial inevitable. Winthrop continued his account:

> Both denied any carnal knowledge and being tried by a jury upon
> their lives by our law which makes adultery [punishable by] death.
> The jury acquitted them of the adultery, but found them guilty of
> adulterous behavior.

Winthrop wrote that the case weighed heavily upon the minds of the magistrates and elders, who favored the death penalty, but in the end it was determined that only "suspicion of adultery" existed and, as such, a lesser punishment would be administered. Henry and Anne were sent to the place of execution and halters were placed around their necks for one hour; they were also whipped and fined. Henry Dawson was summarily "cast out" of (excommunicated from) the

Governor Joseph Dudley, circa 1682–1686, by an unidentified artist.
Courtesy of the Massachusetts Historical Society.

First Church of Boston for his "wanton dalliances." The following year, after his narrow brush with death, Dawson openly expressed his penitence and was restored to membership in the church.

ONE OF THE MOST detailed accounts of marital discord in provincial Massachusetts, the saga of Samuel "Sam" Sewall Jr. and Rebecca Dudley, featured all the ingredients of a soap opera: bitter unhappiness, an acrimonious separation, an extramarital affair, the birth of an illegitimate child, and perhaps most surprisingly, an unexpected reconciliation. Sam and Rebecca started their marriage with much promise. As a match between the twenty-one-year-old daughter of the governor of the Massachusetts Bay Colony and the twenty-four-year-old son of a prominent jurist, the union undoubtedly attracted much interest among the worthies of Boston. But in spite of such an auspicious beginning, just over a decade later the marriage was in deep trouble. Rebecca was receptive to the attentions of another man and Sam, dissatisfied with his treatment at home, eventually separated from his wife in January 1715, noting in his diary he "went to Boston intending to live at my father's until I could find better treatment in my own." The situation culminated in 1716 in a scandal, when Rebecca gave birth to an illegitimate son by an unnamed man. Headed for almost certain collapse, the marriage at this point appeared to be beyond salvation.

The deteriorating situation between Sam and Rebecca was aired between Judge Sewall and Governor Dudley in October 1716, when the senior Sewall went on foot to Roxbury to discuss the matter. One of the major issues Sewall undoubtedly intended to raise was the disturbing news that Rebecca was pregnant by a man other than Sam. The conversation appears to have been one-sided, with the Dudleys "reckoning up" the offenses of Sam on one hand and the virtues of Rebecca on the other. By the end of the visit, Samuel Sewall was pessimistic about reconciliation and said he "saw no possibility of my son's return."

On December 19, 1716, Samuel Sewall noted the news that "Mrs. Sewall of Brookline was brought to bed of a son last night." Some months later, after Sam insisted that the illegitimate boy not be made "chargeable to his estate," Joseph Dudley acknowledged the infant's unknown paternity, saying "nobody knew whose twas." No further record of Rebecca's illegitimate son has been ascertained, and the mystery of his paternity may be answered only by an undecipherable abbreviation in Sewall's diary.

A turning point in the saga occurred about six months later. In July of 1717 Rebecca came to Boston to seek her husband's forgiveness. In his own diary Sam recorded that "my wife came to see me at my father's and confessed her faults with tears. With promises of an amendment. The Lord instruct me in my duty and give me a heart to perform it." In time, a reconciliation was brokered and the following March Sam's horse carried him back to Brookline and to Rebecca— closing a chapter in the domestic troubles that had plagued the young couple for just over five years. Finally, on March 8, 1720, a son, Henry, was born to the reunited Sewalls, one of provincial Boston's most unlikely reconciliations.

Another spectacularly unhappy marriage was found in the union of Katherine George and Nathan Howell, the scion of a prominent Long Island family who became a Boston merchant. The Reverend Cotton Mather, Katherine's stepfather, loathed Nathan and considered him "an exceedingly wicked fellow" and "the worst husband upon earth." Not only was Nathan given to "insupportable tyrannies," but, according to Mather, he was a spendthrift whose financial indiscretions could bring "a noble to nine-pence." Believing Nathan to be a threat to his family, the minister set about trying to manifest his death by fervent prayer. To Mather's surprise, his efforts were rewarded in May 1716 when Nathan died. "God smote the wretch," Mather wrote, "with a languishing sickness, which no body ever knew what to make of."

Divorce was a solution for ending some unhappy marriages, and Bostonians were not averse to this remedy in spite of the notoriety. One of the town's most sensational cases occurred in the early 1670s and involved Katherine Wheelwright Nanny Naylor, a daughter of the religious dissenter Reverend John Wheelwright. A man who impregnated a servant girl and regularly tormented his wife and family, Robert Naylor was a disagreeable character given to sexual dalliances and violent outbursts. His lewd conduct was observed on one occasion by a woman who, looking through the crack of a door, saw him "slip down his britches and go to bed" with Mary Moor. Naylor made harsh and excessive demands on Katherine and abused their children. Other members of the household were not exempt from his erratic behavior. When a servant did not appear quickly enough for him one night, Naylor impatiently fired a gun into the garret to speed her along. In due course, the Court of Assistants set Katherine at liberty. (Centuries after her death, Katherine made headlines in Boston when her privy, or outhouse, was excavated during the Central Artery/Tunnel Project, the "Big Dig.")

An equally scandalous case was heard before the Governor's Council almost a century later. In 1767, Mary Lawrence Fairservice sued her husband, Boston merchant John Fairservice, for a divorce. Mary married her husband in 1755 and since that time had borne him several children. By the late 1760s the marriage had soured. Not only had John Fairservice shown Mary "signs of fixed hatred and aversion," but his behavior, she alleged, consisted of one unprovoked abuse after another. In addition to striking and pushing her, John, she claimed, was verbally abusive. During her most recent pregnancy, John was reputed to have said that he "hoped in God he should see her carried out feet foremost," meaning, of course, that he wished she would die. On other occasions, he was heard calling her "bitch" and "whore." At some point in the marriage, John struck up a relationship with another woman, Hannah Stockbridge, alias Sally Rogers—a liaison that appears to have resulted in the birth of two illegitimate children. Mary's most damaging assertion was that she had barely escaped the marriage with her life: she charged that, in his efforts to be rid of a wife he detested, John had attempted to poison her.

The poisoning occurred during an illness, when her husband gave her some pills. After swallowing them, she detected a strange copper taste in her mouth and soon became violently ill. Patience Munday, a nurse or midwife, testified that she had requested that John obtain the pills, but that when he returned to the house he acted secretive about the medicine. In a cross-examination by John Fairservice, the nurse addressed the matter of the strange pills:

> *I desired you to go for the pills. You would not let me see them, nor allow your wife to see them, saying that if she did, she would not take them, and I told you that, live or die, I would never give her another without seeing them. I knew there was a difference between them about Sarah Rogers.*

One of Mary's witnesses, Dorothy Wharton, stated that John Fairservice admitted some culpability to his wife. When asked what he would have done if she had died, John replied that he "would have buried her in six hours." Other testimony suggested that John rolled the pills in toxic verdigris paint. Dorothy Wharton stated that John was actually pleased that his suspicious actions aroused attention and "thanked God" that his conduct "might be a means of parting them." If he could get rid of Mary, he could then "live like a king."

On another occasion, Mary was so frightened by her husband's behavior one night that she knocked on the door of a lodger, Nathaniel Young, and said, "Don't go to sleep for I don't know what my husband will do to me before morning." Young testified that John was eager for a divorce and said that he would "lie with a woman before a number of witnesses if it would procure a divorce."

John Fairservice strenuously denied Mary's most serious charges and presented himself to the council as a decent provider wronged by a complaining wife. He did acknowledge some faults. Mary greatly offended him by saying she would make him "fly from the country" and that he should be "set on the gallows with a rope about his neck and be branded" for his actions against her. She added that he was widely thought to have "the gallows in his face" and that people pointed at him as he went along the streets. These comments, John admitted, put him in a passion and he bestowed "a light blow on that mouth that had so notoriously abused him." He claimed he never hit her again.

After deliberations, the council appears to have granted Mary a separation from her husband. Some time later, a surprising turn of events occurred: the couple reconciled, but the misguided reunion was short-lived. In 1770, Mary submitted a new petition for divorce to the Governor's Council. In her statement, Mary explained that after the 1767 divorce suit, a repentant John Fairservice came to her and begged forgiveness for his "former folly and wickedness" and that he made "repeated protestations of love and kindness." After carefully laying the groundwork for reconciliation, John prevailed upon Mary to return to him. One of his likely motivations was the sizable inheritance due Mary from the estate of her mother—a bequest from which, Mary stated, he secured "thousands in cash." Before long, John returned to his cruel ways. Among Mary's new charges were that John had deprived her of food, turned her outdoors, and threatened to strip her. He also promised to quit Boston and leave her and their children to fend for themselves. Snubbing the council's summons to appear before them in the matter of divorce, John instead recklessly submitted to that body "a paper containing a high contempt and false and injurious reflections" upon its members. The council promptly ordered his arrest. The ultimate outcome of the troubled relationship between the Fairservices has not been traced, but it is possible the couple reconciled again: John Fairservice's 1799 estate names a Mary Fairservice as his widow.

Another colorful divorce proceeding took place a few years after the Fairservice flap. Martha Barron in 1773 sued her husband, Boston joiner Adam Ayer, for divorce, claiming that for several years he had neglected to support her, had "greatly abused and evil treated her," and had cohabitated with "divers other women." Miserable in her present circumstances, Martha presented witnesses Mary Angell and Abigail Galloway to help confirm her husband's "wicked and profligate conduct." Mary Angell, the couple's next-door neighbor, stated that only a thin partition divided her home from the Ayers, who lived in quarters rented from Andrew Johonnot. She often heard Martha screaming as Adam beat her. She also recounted an incident during which she and Abigail Galloway were walking in the street and heard noises coming from a nearby house. Looking through an open window, they discovered Adam Ayer having intercourse with another woman. The two indignant women stood in silence for a few moments before confronting him:

> We heard a noise in the house and the window being open, I saw the
> said Adam Air in the act of copulation with one Priscilla Brickford,
> a girl who formerly lived in this town. On seeing this we went into
> the house and stood behind them as they lay on the floor, and after
> observing them some time, the said Abigail Galloway spoke and asked
> him if he was not ashamed to act so when he had a wife at home.

Priscilla scurried out of the room and Adam, standing naked before the
women, answered that "one woman was as good to him as another."
This incident was not the only infidelity Mary witnessed. She claimed
that on another occasion she observed Adam fornicating with a sol-
dier's wife. Andrew Johonnot, the couple's landlord for six years,
testified that Adam was a troublesome tenant: "I have heard of many
disturbances." Johonnot had also seen Martha with a black eye. The
evidence presented appears to have been sufficient for a divorce. Having destroyed his marriage to Martha, Adam Ayer apparently married
again the following year.

Sometimes as marriages disintegrated, men sought to protect their
assets by placing advertisements in the newspaper disavowing potential debts incurred by runaway wives. In early 1728 Josias Nottage
began running the following notice in the *Boston News-Letter:*

> WHEREAS *Elizabeth Nottage, the wife of Josias Nottage of Boston,
> housewright, hath brought disgrace upon her husband; which hath
> occasion'd very unhappy differences between them, and upon which
> she hath eloped from her said husband: these are therefore to desire
> all persons not to trust her with money or goods; for he shall not
> pay any such debts.*

In 1760, John Bedson advertised in the same newspaper that his wife,
Mary, had run away from him about a year and a half earlier, and in
Albany taken up with "a regular Sargeant called Taylor, with who she
cohabitated as wife for some time, and has not yet returned to Boston,
the place of my dwelling." Like the husbands of many runaway wives,
Bedson warned the newspaper's readers "not to harbor or entertain
her" at his expense: he would accept no responsibility for his wayward wife's charges.

Trade card for Jane Eustis, who divorced her husband for bigamy in 1760.
Courtesy of the American Antiquarian Society.

Bigamous situations arose with some frequency in the colonial period.
The most famous case in Boston occurred in the 1690s, when it was
discovered that ship's purser Matthew Cary already had a wife living in
England when he married Mary Sylvester, the daughter of an owner of
Shelter Island in New York. In the end, provincial laws were changed
and Cary escaped punishment. In September 1748, Jane Brewer married tinplate worker Joshua Eustis in Boston; her new husband soon
departed for Barbados, where, without obtaining a divorce, he married another woman. Jane Eustis, as she was known, claimed in her
1760 divorce petition that Joshua married Mary Webb in December
1749 and supposed that they were still living together as man and
wife a decade later. Her divorce was eventually granted and, not
allowing herself to be marginalized in Boston mercantile society
because of Joshua's misconduct, she continued in her career as one
of the town's most visible businesswomen. Located next door to the
Town-House, Jane's shop was for many years a thriving enterprise.
In 1761, the year after her divorce, she advertised the arrival of the

latest imported fashions and an array of luxurious fabrics, ribbons, trims, and toiletries. When he heard the news of her death while she was abroad in 1770, merchant John Rowe noted in his diary that Mrs. Eustis was greatly lamented in town.

Sometimes scandals occurred even before a marriage took place. Facing the shame of a potential marriage that would have reduced her station in life, Martha Coggan—one of the most prominent women of her day in the Massachusetts Bay Colony and the widow of three men, including Governor John Winthrop—became upset and died under suspicious circumstances, possibly involving poison, in Boston in 1660. The episode might have forever remained a mystery if not for a letter exchanged between the Reverend John Davenport of the New Haven colony and Martha's stepson, John Winthrop Jr., that survives. Davenport's letter offers a second- or third-hand version of events he had heard from a man who had recently been in the colony, Anthony Elcock. If true, Elcock's account sheds some light on the reason for the apparent suicide of one of the colony's "first ladies."

Two and a half years after the death of her last husband, merchant John Coggan, Martha appears to have become restless about her marital status, a situation that drove her into actions she would regret. According to the story Elcock heard, Martha was "discontented that she had no suitors." Having spent most of the prior twenty-five years as a married woman, she looked close to home for a prospective fourth husband. Elcock said that Martha "encouraged her farmer, a mean man, to make a motion to her for marriage." The farmer, whose identity has not been established, responded to her overtures and proceeded to court his mistress. At some point, though, Martha had a change of heart: "Afterwards, when she reflected upon what she had done, and what a change of her outward condition she was bringing herself into, she grew discontented." We may infer that the farmer was a socially inferior man who would lower the status—her "outward condition"—accorded by her prior husbands. This predicament, according to Elcock's account, led Martha into deep despair. It was said that she took her own life by ingesting "a great quantity of ratsbane," a shocking and painful manner of suicide that must have greatly disturbed all levels of Boston society. On October 24, 1660, the magistrates sitting in town were informed of Martha's "sudden death," an event "not without suspicion of poison." A jury of inquest was summoned and impaneled to investigate. The outcome has been lost to posterity, leaving only Anthony Elcock's version of events as an explanation for the surprising death of the last wife of Governor John Winthrop.

One of Boston's most notable jilting cases occurred when Samuel Walker, a mariner, returned from a voyage in October 1729 only to find that his fiancée, Grace Brickwood, had married another man during his travels. Nine months earlier, the twenty-year-old Samuel had become engaged to Grace, a widow seventeen years his senior with a goodly estate. By the time of her engagement to Samuel, Grace had already outlived three husbands. In undertaking an active marital career, she was following something of a family tradition. Grace's mother, Mary Messenger, had a succession of five husbands to her credit, making her one of the most married Boston women of her day. The engagement of Samuel Walker and Grace Brickwood was serious enough for the couple in January 1729 to officially register their intention to marry. This was followed by the customary practice of having the marriage banns (the public announcement of an upcoming marriage) read at three public meetings in town. Samuel, as he sailed to Cape Fear and England, was undoubtedly comforted in the knowledge that when he returned to Boston all would be clear for him to take Grace's hand in marriage. Instead, he found that during his absence Grace had wed mariner Thomas Dudding in a ceremony conducted quietly at Queen Anne's Chapel in Newbury. Having been abandoned so late in the marital process, Samuel was not content to let the matter rest. Early the following year, he took Grace and her new husband to court, seeking £500 in damages. In a deposition, Samuel claimed that he had every expectation of marrying Grace upon his return to Boston. He had remained single and committed to his intended spouse in spite of receiving offers of "several advantageous matches" during their separation. Grace's conduct, he alleged, was false and deceitful and "greatly disordered" him in his "mind and business." Most damaging, perhaps, was the fact that the unexpected turn of events had put him to "very great and unnecessary charges and expense." In spite of his claims, the jury found for the defendants, but in a March 1730 appeal the verdict was overturned, and a judgment of £100 plus costs was entered by the Inferior Court against Grace and Thomas Dudding. Having restored some funds, as well as a measure of his pride, Samuel's involvement with Grace concluded. His subsequent marital history is unknown.

The family trees that stretch back to early Boston are full of colorful characters, willful women, and errant men. Some of their stories amuse us, others sadden us, but all these ancient family disturbances provide us with reassurance on one point: some things never change.

Chapter 20

By the Strength of His Affections:
Governor Bellingham's Controversial Marriage
1641

A "REMARKABLE ACCIDENT" recorded in John Winthrop's journal occurred in Boston in 1641, when Governor Richard Bellingham became besotted with a friend's fiancée, wooed the young woman away from her intended husband, and married her in a highly irregular ceremony that he appears to have performed himself. Winthrop, who occasionally sparred with Bellingham, was not given to repeating tittle-tattle and debated even including the item in his journal. However, the blatant manner in which Bellingham had conducted himself not only flouted Puritan conventions but was "contrary to the constant practice of the country." When the matter was brought before the court, Governor Bellingham's conduct was again questioned, but he managed to escape censure and the matter was ultimately dropped. Had he been anyone other than the governor, Bellingham's improprieties might have resulted in grave consequences.

Richard Bellingham was almost fifty years old at the time of his romantic misadventure with Penelope Pelham. Descended from a prominent English family and educated at Oxford and trained at Lincoln's Inn as a lawyer, Bellingham arrived in Massachusetts Bay in 1634 with his first wife, Elizabeth Backhouse. After serving in various public offices, Bellingham, by then a widower, became governor in 1641. His election to the office was evidently not an easy one, and repeated "ego clashes" with John Winthrop were an ongoing issue.

Governor Richard Bellingham, who wooed and married his friend's fiancée, Penelope Pelham. Portrait, by an unidentified artist, from Portraits of the Founders *by Charles Knowles Bolton.*

Winthrop's account of the incident does not reveal the name of Penelope Pelham's would-be husband, but offers that he was a friend of Richard Bellingham, lived in his house, and obtained permission from the governor to proceed in his courtship with Penelope. "The young gentlewoman was ready to be contracted to a friend of his," recalled Winthrop, "who lodged in his house, and by his consent had proceeded so far with her, when on the sudden the governor treated with her, and obtained her for himself." The sudden, surprising romance on the governor's part almost certainly raised eyebrows throughout town. Bellingham could only excuse himself "by the strength of his affection, and that she was not absolutely promised to the other gentleman." In spite of his explanation, Bellingham had nonetheless been responsible for breaking up a couple that was nearly betrothed. Not only had Bellingham disrupted another man's marital intentions, but worse still, he subsequently refused to have his marriage banns published, an act of defiance that, as Winthrop put it, was "contrary to an order of court." Adding fuel to the fire was the fact that Bellingham apparently conducted his wedding ceremony himself. These actions suggest that Governor Bellingham was afraid of interference by Penelope's jilted beau or even his own government, which might have prevented the marriage because his wife had been promised to another man.

After word of his extraordinary nuptials became public, Bellingham was asked to explain his actions before the rest of the council. In his position as governor, he found himself on the bench in a matter that involved his own conduct, an unusual position that, in another questionable move, he played to his advantage. According to Winthrop, the governor stubbornly refused to recuse himself even though the court "[thought] it not fit he should sit as a judge, when he was by law to answer as an offender." Bellingham rebuffed Winthrop and said he would not get off the bench unless commanded to do so. "I did command him," wrote Winthrop. Having created a brief sensation, the issues surrounding one of early Boston's most controversial marriages slowly began to fade. In spite of its improper start, the Bellingham marriage appears to have flourished. The couple had seven children, although only one survived to adulthood. Richard Bellingham died in 1672 and was buried at the Granary Burying Ground; Penelope remained a venerated widow in Boston until her death in 1702.

Chapter 21
The Madness of Mistress Hopkins
1645

HAVING FALLEN INTO "a distempered melancholy," Ann Hopkins,
wife of the second governor of Connecticut, was brought to Boston in
1645 to be assessed by doctors and placed in the care of her brother.
According to John Winthrop, Ann's mental afflictions were brought on
by intellectual pursuits conducted over many years. Reading and writing books, Winthrop believed, were activities unsuitable for a woman.
By indulging these interests, Ann ignored her household affairs and
strayed too far into a domain Winthrop believed was reserved for
men. Ultimately, Ann's treatment in Boston proved futile, and details
of her subsequent care are not known. It is likely that she returned
with her husband to England in 1651 or 1652, where he became
warden of the fleet, keeper of the palace of Westminster, and in
1656 a member of Parliament for Dartmouth in Devonshire.

Ann Yale's family connections in Britain and New England were
noteworthy. Descended from an eminent Welsh family, Ann was also
related to several prominent churchmen and merchants. Her maternal
grandfather, George Lloyd, was made the Bishop of Chester in 1605.
Her mother, also named Ann, married as her second husband the
London merchant Theophilus Eaton, later the governor of the New
Haven colony. Ann Lloyd Yale Eaton was, like her daughter later,
afflicted with mental irregularities: she was "driven to the verge of
insanity by the severity of church discipline." From this background,
Ann Yale married Edward Hopkins, a wealthy and "devout Puritan"

of comparable social stature. Unsettled by the accession of Charles I and a friend of Puritan emigrants, Edward decided to quit England and move to the colonies. The couple arrived in Boston in 1637 and quickly settled in Hartford, where Hopkins built a mansion. A few years later he was elected to the first of several terms as governor of Connecticut.

In April 1645, John Winthrop recounted in his diary the arrival of Edward and his mentally infirm wife. Ann's brother, David Yale, then a "thriving" merchant of Boston, lived in a house at the foot of Pemberton Hill (near the later site of Scollay Square), and Ann was sent to his house for possible treatment. Because so few details survive about her symptoms, the exact nature of Ann's mental distraction is unknown. The case attracted enough local comment to merit considerable attention by Winthrop. Ann was, in his estimation, a "godly young woman, and of special parts," but one whose mental fragmentation had taken place over several years. At the root of the problem, he concluded, was her intellectual activity:

> [She] was fallen into a sad infirmity, the loss of her understanding and reason, which had been growing upon her divers years, by occasion of giving herself wholly to reading and writing, and had written many books. Her husband, being very loving and tender of her, was loath to grieve her; but he saw his error, when it was too late.
>
> He brought her to Boston, and left her with her brother, one Mr. Yale, a merchant, to try what means might be had here for her. But no help could be had.

Winthrop believed that if Ann "had attended her household affairs, and such things as belong to women, and had not gone out of her way and calling to meddle in such things as are proper for men, whose minds are stronger, etc.," she might have kept her wits. By Winthrop's account, Ann was among early New England's most educated women and, as the writer of "many books," one of its earliest authors. Regrettably, none of her writings survive.

The story of Ann's mental illness was kept alive by Cotton Mather in his *Magnalia Christi Americana*. In a more detailed version of Ann's plight, Mather claimed that she had since childhood "been observable for desirable qualities." Her incurable distraction set in after her marriage to Edward and resulted in "ill-shaped ideas in her brain, as use to be formed when the animal spirits are fired by irregular particles, fixed with acid, bilious, venomous ferments in the blood." Edward, Mather stated, was a tender and affectionate husband who, seeking medical treatment for his distracted spouse, was dismayed to learn

Portrait of John Winthrop, whose journal recorded the story of Ann Hopkins and other seventeenth-century scandals. The 1834 portrait by Charles Osgood is based on the portrait by an unknown artist in the Massachusetts State House. Courtesy of the Massachusetts Historical Society.

from a physician that "no means would be likely to restore her sense, but such as would be also likely to hazard her life." Edward asked one of Ann's kinswomen what God had meant by chastising him through Ann's malady with "so sharp a rod . . . with so long a stroke." She answered, "God hath afflicted others in the like way, and we must be content with our portion." Edward, according to Mather, "wisely, meekly, fruitfully bore his heavy affliction unto his dying day."

After returning to England in 1651 or 1652, Edward soon received an appointment as a naval commissioner from Oliver Cromwell and inherited the posts of warden of the fleet and keeper of the palace of Westminister from his older brother Henry. In 1656 he was elected a member of Parliament. When he died the following year, Edward left considerable bequests to various institutions in New England, including Harvard College, which used some of the funds to purchase the township later named Hopkinton. In a strange epilogue that mirrored the heartbreak of his wife's long mental illness, Edward's body was opened after his death. His shrunken heart was found to be so brittle that when touched it "presently dropped in pieces." Ann died more than thirty years later, in 1698, at age eighty-three at her ancestral home in Wales. It is sad to think that her intellectual potential may have been punished and devalued as she was pressured to accede to Puritan norms.

Chapter 22

Heiresses Adrift:
Two Generations of Marital Misadventures
in Boston's Puritan Elite
1647 & 1659

ECLIPSED IN HISTORY by the renown of her father, Governor
Thomas Dudley, and her elder sister, poetess Anne Bradstreet, Sarah
Dudley made an impression all her own in mid-seventeenth-century
Boston. Sarah's precipitous fall from grace was sparked by a controver-
sial habit of preaching and "irregular prophesying in mixed assemblies"
and exacerbated by her lewd behavior with a man from Taunton.
These missteps led to her excommunication from Boston's First
Church in 1647, a disgrace that came on the heels of a reputation-
tarnishing divorce, one of the colony's first, from merchant Benjamin
Keayne. What followed for Sarah was a disreputable life at the fringes
of the Puritan elite. Her lapses, however, were only a prelude to an
even more indecorous story. Sarah's daughter, Anna Keayne, brought
a new level of sordidness to family affairs in a marital saga virtually
without parallel in colonial New England.

Born in 1620 in Lincolnshire, Sarah Dudley was a young girl when
she and her family took passage with the Winthrop Fleet and arrived
in the Massachusetts Bay Colony. At about age nineteen she married
Benjamin Keayne, eldest son of the affluent merchant Robert Keayne,
a founder of the Artillery Company and its first captain. The union of
the daughter of one of the young colony's most important magistrates
to the son of a prominent merchant was undoubtedly seen as eminently fitting. But within a decade the marriage fell apart. Sarah's
habit of preaching and prophesying in public, and other "unnatural"

behavior, began sometime after the birth of her daughter, Anna, in about 1640, although the impetus for this activity and the nature of her prophesies are unknown. Stephen Winthrop, writing from London in March 1646, reported that "My she-cousin Keayne is grown a great preacher."

The apparent escalation in Sarah's religious activities in the mid-1640s coincided with the breakdown in her marriage to Benjamin Keayne. By early 1646 or 1647, Benjamin left Boston for London, where he was engaged as a cloak seller at Birching Lane. Later he wrote to his father-in-law, Thomas Dudley, to report his wife's shameful behavior and to make their split permanent. The letter was not his first on the topic, and although he offered no details of her misconduct, Benjamin asserted that Sarah had "unwived" herself from him. "That you and myself are made sorry by your daughter's enormous and continued crimes, is the greatest cause of grief that ever befell me," began Keayne to his father-in-law, "and the more because [of] her obstinate continuance in them . . . I am certain I never gave her the least just cause or occasion to provoke her to them." Benjamin expressed his grief that Sarah had "run so fast from that height in error in judgment to that extremity of error in practice . . . that she has not left me any room or way of reconciliation." At his father-in-law's request, Benjamin committed in writing his desire to separate permanently from Sarah. He also communicated his dismay at the thought of supporting her any further:

> [A]s you desire, I do plainly declare my resolution never again to live with her as a husband. What maintenance yourself expects I know not. This I know (to my cost and danger) she has unwived herself and how she or you can expect a wife's maintenance is to me a wonder.

Evidently at some point Sarah had followed Benjamin to London. In a June 1649 letter to John Winthrop from England, Brampton Gurdon Sr. recounted a story, presumably by then old news, that Sarah had come to England to join her husband. In her passage, she encountered some sort of disaster and, according to Gurdon, "all her goods miscarried and she escaped only with her life." After this brush with death, Sarah returned to New England and, to Gurdon's great disapproval, "resolves there to take another husband. I hope your laws will not tolerate such wicked actions."

In September 1646, Sarah's controversial conduct as a "preacher" came to a head at the First Church of Boston, when Elder John Leverett admonished her in open assembly for "irregular prophesying in mixed assemblies." Eleven months later she was again rebuked by the church for "falling into odious, lewd, and scandalous unclear behavior" with Nicholas Hart, an excommunicated merchant of Taunton. Sarah was noted in the church records as a divorced woman and was excommunicated for her transgressions. Sarah's divorce was also highly controversial. In November 1647, the Reverend Ezekiel Rogers of Rowley wrote to John Winthrop to inform him "that there is not a little discourse raised, and by some offence taken, at the late divorce granted by the Court." Rogers considered the action a "weighty business" that could result in damaging rumors as far away as England.

In time, Sarah married again, this time Thomas Pacy, a man of whom little is known and who was unable to reverse her marginalization. Her aged father was sympathetic to Sarah and in spite of her earlier alarming behavior, she was named among the old governor's beneficiaries when he died in 1653. However, Sarah remained a disreputable woman in Boston. In July 1654 the merchant John Floyd was fined five shillings for "receiving Mrs. Pacey into his house as inmate." In February of the following year, Sarah was admitted as an inhabitant of Boston only on the condition that several prominent gentlemen give security "to save the town from all charges that may arise by her." Five years later, having apparently made no further waves in town, Sarah died intestate in Roxbury, leaving her daughter Anna little more than the embarrassing legacy of a shunned woman. Among Sarah's possessions at the time of her death were household furnishings, crockery and utensils, and an assortment of fine apparel (including a red petticoat with black lace and one "horse flesh petticoat") valued at just over £36. The estate was beset by many debts, however, including amounts owed to Goody Knap "for keeping her," six shillings to Goody Haile for washing, and £2 to James Johnson "for his trouble," meaning, presumably, his efforts in arranging the funeral and preparing the estate inventory. In the end, Anna was left with about £10 from her mother's estate.

Anne's marital misadventures exceeded even those of her mother. When he died around 1656, Robert Keayne left a substantial bequest—with numerous strings attached—to his sixteen-year-old granddaughter. His massive, 158-page will left specific instructions regarding Anna's future. In particular, he required the overseers of his will to ensure that Anna marry appropriately. He desired that a match be made with a God-fearing man who valued his granddaughter more than her estate so that she would not "cast away herself for want of counsel and watchfulness upon some swaggering gentleman." Further, as Anna's age for being courted approached, Keayne in his will speci-fied that she "dare not set her affections upon any" without the advice, counsel, and help of his designees. Anna's marriage, in other words, would be arranged by others and in keeping with the terms of her grandfather's will. The will also pointedly excluded Anna's mother, Sarah, who was then still living. Robert Keayne specified that Anna's bequest should not be used to assist her "unworthy mother," a woman he identified as "sometimes the unnatural and unhappy wife of my son, that proud and disobedient daughter-in-law to myself and wife." Sarah, who had "walked so unworthily," was not fit to receive maintenance "in her pride and contempt from anything that ever was accounted mine." In spite of this position, Keayne advised Anna not to fall into "rebellion, stubborn or undutiful carriage" toward her disgraced mother, who Keayne prayed would show "unfeigned repentance for all her former evil carriages" and be worthy of pity. In that case, he wrote, Anna would be left "to her own liberty" to assist Sarah. Nonetheless, in the matter of any dealings with her mother, Anna would be subject to the advice of her father and the overseers of the will or risk losing her entire inheritance. Anna's father, Ben-jamin Keayne, never entered the story again and, at some point after Robert Keayne's death in Boston, presumably died in England.

Given Anna's elevated financial position, it is likely that a number of single men in Boston might have fancied their chances with the youthful heiress. If any local candidates made an attempt to court her, however, none was successful. Within months of Robert Keayne's demise, though, a prospective suitor unexpectedly arrived on the scene. An affluent merchant from London, Edward Lane was some twenty years older than Anna. Perhaps his maturity and worldliness made him especially attractive to a sheltered young gentlewoman. The circumstances of how they met after his arrival in Boston on the *Speedwell* in July 1656 are unknown, but he soon prepared to take the intricate steps required to court Anna. Edward first set about impressing her grandmother that he was an appropriate candidate for Anna's hand. Mrs. Keayne, who was also named Anna, was agreeable to this prospect and granted permission for Edward "to make trial for the gaining of my grandchild's affections as to marriage." The courtship was, according to custom, conducted to some extent by proxy: a friend of Edward's, presumably Richard Cooke, visited Anna regularly to communicate the London merchant's interest in her. Among the tokens of affection conveyed to Anna during this ritual were pieces of gold. As one author has written, these mementos were "doubtless, to remind her that he was a man of wealth, worthy to be her suitor." The courtship proved successful, and Anna and Edward became engaged.

Before marrying, there was family business to settle. Administration of the complicated Keayne estate weighed heavily upon Anna's grandmother. Willing to accept an offer of assistance from her granddaughter's fiancé, Mrs. Keayne turned over the executorship of her husband's estate to Edward Lane. The will contained at least one provision that Edward found disconcerting. If Anna were to die before reaching the age of eighteen, her widower would lose part of her share of the estate. On the basis of this point and other issues in the will, Edward pressed for an agreement that would assure him a sizable portion of Robert Keayne's fortune in exchange for his services to the estate. Mrs. Keayne agreed to this arrangement and also granted Edward the sum of £50 to arrange for "the more contentful and comely appareling" of her granddaughter. She further specified that Edward would need to oversee the details of the impending nuptials and approve whatever "he sees meet to lay out for the marriage solemnity so that the said Anna the elder may be freed from all troubles in making provision for the same." With the Keayne estate in order and an assortment of "comely apparel" selected for his bride, Edward married Anna on December 11, 1657, in a ceremony performed by Governor John Endicott.

At some point shortly after the wedding, Anna realized that her marriage was in trouble. Edward Lane, she discovered, was impotent and the union remained unconsummated. Anna, by her later account, kept quiet about this embarrassing problem for months. In due course, however, rumors began to spread in Boston about his condition. In the meantime, Edward consulted a physician, William Snelling, "who practiced upon him with forcible medicines" but without success. Somehow the problem was brought to the attention of the overseers of Robert Keayne's will, who, in their capacity as advisors to the family, recommended that he seek further medical attention. Edward went in turn to three more doctors, including Simon Ayres and John Clark, and for seven months underwent treatments. None of the medical experts were able to help, and Edward remained "incapable of performance of the marriage covenant." This state of affairs greatly upset Anna, who chose not to "impart her grief" to even her "nearest friends." After fifteen months of marriage, Anna concluded that she had been deceived in her marriage and decided, perhaps on the advice of the overseers, to petition the Court of Assistants for a divorce. The remedy of divorce in colonial Massachusetts was rare, and two generations of successive divorces in one family was unprecedented. In March 1659 Anna's petition was presented at a meeting of the Court of Assistants. She claimed that her marriage to Edward was based upon "an essential mistake" and having given herself "as a wife" expected that her spouse would give himself in "the performance of a husband." Edward, she stated, had "from first to last" been "altogether deficient." Edward Lane was summoned and, "after a considerable pause," acknowledged that he had not "performed the office of husband." Having heard from both parties, the Court of Assistants determined that there was sufficient cause for the dissolution of the marriage and declared Anna and Edward to be divorced.

Edward Lane, now divorced and widely known in Boston as an impotent man, decided to extricate himself from the tangled affairs of the Keayne estate. After various legal maneuverings, and over the protests of Anna's grandmother, Mrs. Keayne, he eventually succeeded in removing himself as executor and recovered £650, plus other charges he had incurred or was due from his work on behalf of the Keaynes. In the meantime, Anna was informed that her inheritance would not be as large as had been expected. Edward told his former wife that due to losses, her legacy would "fall short by more than two thirds."

At this point, the story took an unexpected path. After the divorce, Edward continued to see physicians about his sexual dysfunction. To everyone's surprise, the treatments apparently began to work. A newly invigorated Edward began calling upon his ex-wife at Mrs. Keayne's house. Anna's grandmother was appalled by this turn of events. She "several times" found Anna alone with Edward and his friend Richard Cooke in her house. Mrs. Keayne alternated between anger and grief. Cooke persuaded her to leave the former spouses alone, saying that she should let Anna again "try him for he is a man." Cooke also raised the issue of Edward's new potency, an "immodest" subject that offended Mrs. Keayne. Edward's renewed calls upon Anna became more than a reacquaintance of former spouses; before long the two were again courting and in December 1659, nine months after their divorce, they approached Governor Endicott with the request that they be allowed to remarry. The governor explained that the Court of Assistants had separated them and it was "not for him to join them together" again. Instead, the governor proposed a more novel solution: if the cause of their separation had been removed, then the nullification of their marriage was void. Edward and Anna left his house having successfully reinstated their marriage without any further formalities.

The following morning Edward Hutchinson and Peter Oliver called upon the "newlyweds." The visitors were evidently curious to know how the quasi-wedding night had gone. Perhaps sensing that the subject of Edward's infirmity was no longer taboo with Anna, Oliver enquired if she was satisfied that the impediment to her happiness had now been removed. Anna, according to Hutchinson, answered that "it was now otherwise with him than before; and she was satisfied with his sufficiency as a man." In keeping with the happy tenor of their reconciliation, Edward resumed his executorship of the Keayne estate. In due course Anna gave birth to two children—a girl, Sarah, named after her wayward mother, who died as an infant, and a boy, Edward, who later died in Holland while at university there. In spite of these improved appearances, great troubles were again brewing just beneath the surface in the Lane household. The reinstated marriage was not what it appeared to be, and Anna was keeping a major secret.

Anna's story took a dramatic turn in 1664, when she decided to embark for England without Edward. Shortly thereafter Edward died in Boston, ending one of the town's most talked-about marriages. Anna did not return to her native land for another two years and when she did, she faced the fight of her life. At the crux of her new problems was that while in England, Anna had married Captain Nicholas Paige, a Boston merchant. The timing of that act was now in question. It was rumored that she had married (or had had an affair with) Nicholas some time prior to Edward's death. Before long, a grand jury in Boston began looking into the matter and, having found some evidence, indicted Anna for adultery. At this point, however, even more sensational news surfaced. Richard Cooke, Edward Lane's friend, revealed that before she left for England he had heard Anna admit that her children had not been fathered by Edward Lane but rather had resulted from an affair with Nicholas Paige that had begun long before her journey to England. This claim was now substantiated by Edward Lane, as if from beyond the grave. Richard Cooke produced a deposition by Edward dated December 6, 1663, in which he admitted that the couple's reconciliation had been a sham, that he had never known Anna "carnally," and that they maintained separate beds. The purpose of the document was for Edward to "utterly disown" Anna and "never more to maintain her or look at her as any relation to more than a friend." In the same instrument, Edward conveyed to Anna a pasture that had formerly belonged to Robert Keayne. In a separate document prepared during his final illness, Edward granted Anna the Keayne mansion. The use of the house would soon emerge as another battleground.

We can only imagine how the individual magistrates responded to this muddled, unseemly state of affairs, but after much deliberation the General Court concluded that Anna's behavior had been egregious and found her "guilty of much wickedness." The court gave Anna the opportunity to repent, which she promptly did, an act of contrition that undoubtedly spared her punishment as an adulteress. This, however, was not the last to be heard of Anna.

The coat of arms of Nicholas Paige, who eventually married Anna Keayne after allegedly fathering two of her children while she was wed to Edward Lane. From the Gore Roll of Arms, courtesy of the New England Historic Genealogical Society.

Before dying, Edward Lane conveyed his property, including various assets that had belonged to Robert Keayne, to two Bostonians: his longtime friend, Richard Cooke, and John Wiswall, a local ironmonger and shopkeeper. In making this arrangement, Edward pitted Richard Cooke and Anna against each other for control of various Keayne family interests. It now appeared to Anna that Cooke had deliberately orchestrated all her troubles: he, apparently, performed the original courtship gestures on behalf of Edward Lane; later brokered the sham reconciliation; and, finally, gathered evidence against Anna after she left for England to join Nicholas Paige. Anna certainly believed Cooke was her nemesis, and Cooke took no pains to conceal his disdain for her. When told by two local women that Anna was poised to return to Boston with her new husband to recover her property, Cooke claimed that he "would see her hanged if she tried to do it." Anna was later informed that Cooke was spreading the rumor that she had attempted to poison Edward Lane. Never one to back out of a potential dispute, Anna brought to the General Court a case against Cooke and Wiswall for conspiracy. That body, however, was, as Edmund S. Morgan put it, "weary of this eternal squabble over Robert Keayne's property and refused to believe the story which to Anna was so obvious."

Having failed to convince the General Court that Richard Cooke had conspired to gain control of part of her inheritance, Anna allowed the matter to rest. Instead, over some years, she regained her former stature in town—a position she had nearly frittered away by her unconventional behavior. Now, as the wife of a prominent business and military man, Anna was accepted back into the highest echelons of Boston society. In keeping with his status as a prominent gentleman, Nicholas Paige adopted a coat of arms, and the couple resided at their Rumney Marsh estate outside of town. Finally, fate moved to Anna's side in the matter of the Keayne assets. Through political influence exercised by her husband and her uncle, Governor Joseph Dudley, the legacies intended for Anna by her grandfather were, through a convoluted series of actions, eventually restored to her.

Late in life, Anna undoubtedly savored the victory of regaining her birthright. In an epilogue that mirrored the actions taken by her grandfather in his famous will, Anna prepared a document with similarly unusual provisions. As their son had died many years earlier, Anna and Nicholas had no direct descendants and decided to make a significant bequest to a relative, Martha Hobbes, with the caveat that she be "very careful" in how she married. As if echoing the words of her grandfather, Anna directed Martha that the legacy "not be thrown away" in her match. When Anna Keayne Lane Paige died on June 30, 1704, the painful legacies of two generations of marital misadventures in Boston began to fade from memory.

Chapter 23

Reversal of Fortune:
The Scandalous Affair of Ruth Read
and Augustin Lyndon
1673

RATHER THAN LEADING a quiet and unremarkable life in England, Ruth Crooke Read appears to have followed an older sister to the Massachusetts Bay Colony where, in 1673, she was tried and convicted for adulterous misconduct and banished from the colony. For Ruth, a married woman with at least ten children who had led a respectable life in Puritan Boston for most of her adult life, the price of her sordid affair with mariner and shipwright Augustin Lyndon was a steep one. In 1669 she abandoned her husband, traveled to England, and for several years remained abroad, where she and her paramour pretended to be married, adopted false identities, and proceeded to have an illegitimate son. In time, Ruth came to regret her actions and returned to her family in Boston. Before long, her scandalous conduct became common knowledge and she was tried and convicted before the Court of Assistants. Ruth was given a choice of punishment: she could accept a whipping of thirty stripes and face public ridicule in the town marketplace or she could leave the colony forever. She chose the latter option, abandoned her family a second time, and eventually drifted into obscurity in Connecticut. For Augustin Lyndon, the affair resulted in an acrimonious divorce from his fourth wife, Mary Sanderson, during which his patterns of deception and barefaced womanizing over many years were revealed. The ensuing public disgrace appears to have driven him to remain in England, where he died years later.

When Ruth's father, Roger Crooke, died, he left bequests to his children, including a girl born about 1632 named Ruth. Ruth and her sisters, Mary and Rebecca, were given the lease of Sir John Cotton's house with the stipulation that their elder brother, Walter, financially maintain them. How long the Crooke daughters retained the lease of the house is not known, but one of the girls, Rebecca, quit England altogether and by 1646 made her way to Massachusetts, where she married Peter Gardner.

The first record of Ruth Crooke in Boston occurred in January 1654 when she married William Read as his second wife. In William, Ruth found a mature husband of substantial quality. Their union was a prolific one, with at least ten children born between 1655 and 1669. But in 1669, some time after the birth of her daughter, Elizabeth, Ruth's life took a turn that would change its course forever, shock the people of Boston, and bring shame upon her family. For reasons that may never be fully known—perhaps on an excuse of Crooke family business or some other contrived reason—Ruth returned to England without her husband or children. During part of what became a four-year sojourn abroad, Ruth carried on an adulterous relationship with Augustin Lyndon.

At some point during Ruth's visit in England, the couple attempted to conceal their identities by adopting the names Rebecca Rogers and John Rogers. "Rebecca" was a curious choice as an alias for Ruth, as it was the name of her older sister. For a period of three months, Ruth and Augustin lived together in the guise of man and wife. In due course Ruth gave birth to a son, whom the couple named John. When Augustin later left on a return voyage to New England, he wrote to Ruth with "great respect and affection" and urged her to keep a low profile and stay in good spirits by keeping herself "private and cheerful." He reassured her that "all would be well" and that he would "return to her with all possible speed." For her care during his absence, he left Ruth with about £20. He arrived in Boston by November 1672.

During Augustin's absence, Ruth suffered from a guilty conscience. By now "convinced of the evil of her ways," she decided to return to

New England, rejoin her family, and face the judgment of her husband, authorities, and the public. She departed for Boston, not waiting for Augustin's return. As it happened, he had left Boston to rejoin her, and the two would never see each other again.

During his wife's long absence, William Read despaired that she would ever return to her family. When she arrived in 1673 after an absence "above four years," the joy of her unexpected reappearance was tempered by the shock that she was accompanied by a two-year-old boy sired by another man. Shortly thereafter, William asked two townsmen, Job Laine and Richard Collicott, to come to his house to talk with her. He might have wanted to ensure that Augustin would be responsible for providing financial maintenance for the "bringing up of a child which she brought with her from England." During her interview with Laine and Collicott, Ruth confirmed that Augustin Lyndon was the father of her son. She also acknowledged that they had lived together in England under assumed names. Perhaps to complete her act of penitence, Ruth revealed that she had in her possession four or five letters from "John Rogers" that could confirm her version of events. The letters were produced, and Job Laine, who had done business with Augustin, recognized the mariner's handwriting.

Ruth's revelations and the presence of her illegitimate son in Boston provided ample evidence for her prosecution by the Court of Assistants. She was sent to prison and subsequently

> brought to the bar to answer for that having been absent from her
> husband and bringing with her a child of about two years old . . .
> affirming that she received it at Branford in England that Augustin
> Lyndon who changing his name to John Rogers & herself by the name
> of Rebeckah Rogers as she also affirmed between whom several letters
> wickedly (as if man and wife[)] had passed between them which are
> on file, and that John Rogers told her the child's name was John
> Rogers, and most impudently returning to these parts imposing the
> said child on her husband William Read.

The Court of Assistants found Ruth guilty of adulterous misconduct. Her sentence was either banishment from the Massachusetts Bay

Colony within two months or a more public punishment: to stand in the marketplace on a stool for one hour with a paper affixed to her breast reading **THUS I STAND FOR MY ADULTEROUS AND WHORISH CARRIAGE**. Further, she would receive a public whipping of thirty stripes—the maximum generally given in this period to female felons—after the next lecture day in town. Instead of submitting to these degradations, Ruth accepted banishment and hastened out of Boston for haven in Rhode Island. Rather than divorcing Ruth, William Read appears to have forgiven her. Accordingly, he petitioned the Court of Assistants in 1674 to set aside its sentence and allow Ruth return to Boston. The petition was refused. Defeated in his request, William Read soon thereafter disappeared from Boston records. After a time, a presumably widowed Ruth, along with more than one of her sons, appears to have moved from Rhode Island to New London County, Connecticut. There she married a man named Percy. Then she, too, faded from view.

During the affair in England, Augustin Lyndon also abandoned a spouse in Boston, but unlike Ruth Read he was a veteran of a lengthy marital career. He was widowed three times before marrying his fourth wife, Mary, the widow of goldsmith Joseph Sanderson. In the aftermath of Ruth Read's scandalous return to Boston, Mary Sanderson Lyndon decided to obtain a divorce from her rakish husband. During the protracted legal proceedings, Mary was rendered nearly destitute by a fire that destroyed her home. To make matters worse, deponents in the case revealed that Augustin's dalliance with Ruth Read was not his only indiscretion. In fact, his pursuit of younger women remained unabated even after the Ruth Read scandal became public knowledge in 1673. During his overseas voyages, Augustin remained a world-class roué, preying on younger women in and around London.

The most detailed account of Augustin's conduct after his affair with Ruth Read came from Boston mariner Thomas Berry. In his deposition, Berry recounted an incident that occurred at a London tavern in February 1678. He was asked by Francis Therwit about an "old man" (meaning Augustin Lyndon) he had transported to Barbados four or five years earlier. Therwit explained that Augustin was courting his young sister and "would feign marry her and would have been in bed with her before they were married." Berry replied that Augustin already had a wife and touched upon his notorious affair with Ruth Read:

> *I answered that he was a married man and had a wife in New England when came from thence and not only so but that it was supposed that he had a child by another woman one Reed which was some trouble about in the court and I had seen the copy of several letters that he wrote to her in England calling his wife Rogers.*

Berry called Augustin "an old rascal" who he recalled "made his wife wait upon him at table." As to Augustin's financial position in England, Berry affirmed that "to the best of my knowledge he has three hundred pounds in the hands of Mr. Glover, merchant, in London where of one hundred and fifty pounds I paid to him at the said Glover's."

After her husband's infidelity with Ruth Read became common knowledge, Mary Lyndon petitioned the Suffolk County Court to protect her financial position. In April 1674 the court responded favorably given "what hath been charged upon the said Lyndon by Ruth Read." It ordered that Augustin's attorney, Deacon Henry Allen, a housewright of Boston, restrict Lyndon's assets for the benefit of Mary and her children. The couple was beyond reconciliation, and in time Mary pressed for a divorce. In October 1679 her petition was finally heard by the Court of Assistants. Mary, stressing her "poor, desolate, and distressed condition," beseeched the court to set her free from her husband "since he hath in so many particulars broken covenant with her" and requested the settlement of her savings and two-thirds of a land parcel. Her petition emphasized Augustin's "vicious and debauched" life and stated that he had absented himself from her for more than six years, written a letter renouncing her as his wife five years earlier, and that he had attempted to marry two other women in London.

On top of her marital woes, Mary had other problems. In early 1674 her house was burgled on a Sabbath day by Thomas Carr, who filched more than £13 in cash. Carr, who previously had stolen £6 from another local woman, was apprehended, tried, and sentenced to be branded with the letter *B* (for *burglar*) on his forehead, to have an ear cut off, and to pay treble damages to his victims. Having come through the ordeal of a burglary, Mary's misfortunes contined when some time later her house burned down, destroying all her possessions and leaving her in an "uncomfortable and miserable condition" with little more to call her own other than two firkins of nails. The court granted the divorce and "set her at liberty to marry another man." Mary promptly reverted to her prior married name of Sanderson.

Owing to partial deafness, Mary had not understood some matters raised in the divorce hearing, in particular the whereabouts of money put aside during Augustin's time abroad. The funds had been held in safekeeping at various times by John Leverett, his wife, Sarah Sedgwick, and Augustin's attorney, Henry Allen. Mary sought clarification of her claims, stating that she was "thick of hearing" and had misunderstood the disposition of her funds. Further, she wanted to make certain that her earnings made during Augustin's absence would safely go to her and her heirs as well as a "small piece of land." The settlement was granted, and in 1681 Mary Sanderson took as her third husband the merchant William Ardell.

His standing in Boston considerably diminished, Augustin Lyndon apparently remained in England. In his will, proved in August 1699, Augustin made bequests to his son Josias, then living in Rhode Island, including his house and lands near the town dock in Boston—but he made no mention of "John Rogers," his son by Ruth Read.

Chapter 24
Bigamy in Boston
1698

"I AM YET ALIVE," wrote a distraught Elizabeth Cary from London in a November 1693 letter to her husband, Matthew, in Boston, "and through mercy I stand to bare all the base abuses and affronts that your sister or her master the devil can put upon me." Elizabeth Cary had cause to be upset. Her husband had a few months earlier married another woman in New England, perhaps in the belief that Elizabeth was dead. Matthew's new wife, Mary Sylvester (the "sister" in league with the devil in Elizabeth's letter), was the daughter of a prominent New York family, owners of Shelter Island. When Mary's brother Giles Sylvester learned of the dubious nature of her marriage, he began gathering evidence and ultimately moved to have Matthew charged with bigamy. In spite of Elizabeth Cary's scornful letters and Giles Sylvester's legal maneuverings, Matthew and Mary Cary continued to cohabitate and have a family in Boston. And even as questions about the legality and morality of their union swirled, provincial authorities entrusted Matthew Cary with several important and perilous assignments during this period, including a 1695 mission to recover New England captives redeemed and left in Quebec. In due course, Cary was acquitted of bigamy, and the case appears to have been instrumental in the legislative softening of the colony's laws with respect to the waiting period for remarriage when a spouse has been missing or absent.

Some details of Matthew Cary's life before arriving in Boston in the spring of 1692 can be reconstructed. On April 16, 1685, he married the widow Elizabeth House, whose brother-in-law, William House, was a witness to the London nuptials. In about 1692 Matthew was appointed purser of the ship *Nonesuch*. Through this occupation he dabbled in the trade of furs, cranberries, and other merchandise between New England and England after the frigate's arrival in Boston in May 1692.

In the single surviving letter from Matthew to Elizabeth, dated September 29, [1692?], and written aboard the *Nonesuch*, he wrote about his business ventures and his plans to return to England in another year. In what he described as his fourth letter since arriving in New England, Matthew thanked Elizabeth for sending him a chest of clothing by the ship *Samuel & Henry*. He showed the tenderness of a loving husband, who after a long absence longed for Elizabeth's "dear company." He regretted that one of her recent letters with its "affectionate writing" had been miscarried. Matthew went on to describe his purchases of assorted furs, including bear, otter, beaver, sable, and mink and the shipment to Elizabeth of crates of these skins and other goods worth hundreds of pounds. He provided directions for their dispersal, including making several of the most select items gifts to various officials. For Elizabeth's own pleasure, he suggested she keep "the best and blackest" otter skin.

Touching upon Elizabeth's affairs in London, Matthew agreed with her plan to sell her house. He emphasized his desire to return to her in a better financial position: he hoped "to make a voyage sufficient to maintain us. I desire but one year more to get money by thy dear company I shall gladly want this winter." Not knowing where his wife would move after selling her house, he said he would direct future letters to her friend Mrs. Evitt, who would know how to find her. Finally, Matthew commented upon the witchcraft hysteria raging in Massachusetts, noting that even "ships at sea" might not be safe from its destructive effects:

> The lord is pleased to afflict the people with a great judgment for the devil is . . . loose among them for they destroy one the other by witchcraft; several hundreds now accuse with many already put to death; both ministers and other outwardly seeming godly people . . .

> *come in that freely confess themselves baptized by the Devil and*
> *accuse many . . . under his banner and show by what ways they have*
> *to destroy and afflict both Christians and beasts, ships at sea and*
> *many other wickedness.*

While Matthew's letter sheds some light on his business affairs and his desire to provide for Elizabeth, it offers no foreshadowing of the surprising turn of events that would occur within a year. The details of how Matthew Cary and Mary Sylvester met and married remain unknown, but considerably more has been established about Mary's background. She was one of eleven children of Nathaniel Sylvester and Grizzell Brinley, who settled at Shelter Island, New York, in 1652. By the time Mary met Matthew Cary, both her parents had been dead for a number of years. Mary was likely living in the household of her brother Giles, who in time would become a fierce opponent of her marriage. Since all Mary's siblings married individuals with Boston associations, it seems probable that the family spent some time in Massachusetts.

On August 1, 1693, Matthew Cary married Mary Sylvester at Bristol, Massachusetts. Several possibilities may explain why he took a second wife. Perhaps after the sale of her London house he had lost touch with Elizabeth. It is also entirely possible that he knowingly entered into a bigamous marriage. However, there is some reason to believe that he may have received an erroneous account of his first wife's death. Mrs. Evitt (or Evat), who was to forward Matthew's letters to Elizabeth after the sale of her house, later denied a rumor that she was the source of such a report:

> *I hear Mr. Carey has reported that I, Susan Evat, have sent him word*
> *of his wife's death which I declare before God and you I never writ a*
> *word to him for his wife is alive and well and too good for so false a*
> *fellow as he.*

It did not take long for word of Matthew's New England marriage to reach Elizabeth Cary in London. In what Elizabeth indicated was her eleventh letter to Matthew, dated November 1, 1693, she lamented that she had not been "worthy of one line" from her errant husband. She called herself a "faithful wife and friend" and expressed wonder that

Matthew "being a man of so good an understanding" should have so leveled his principles in the execution of such a grievous sin. His bigamous conduct, she claimed, dispossessed her "of all comforts in this world." In closing, she challenged Matthew and Mary to respond to her letter:

> *Sir, my sorrow is great that it makes me so bold to write to you but since it is your sister that hath willfully and knowingly done me this evil, I can do no less and if you or the Jezebel your sister has anything to say to me either in defense or offense, I am ready to make you an answer so long as I live. Direct your letters to William House's, barber, in Shoreditch, London. Sir, I am yours to command.*
>
> *Elizabeth Carey*

The tenor of Elizabeth's next surviving letter, dated January 2, [1694?], remained highly pitched. "You have given away my husband to a whore," she proclaimed. Once again making a biblical analogy, Elizabeth compared Matthew to "those which injured Judas." In spite of her miserable state, she remained her husband's "humble servant" and was prepared to accept his return:

> *I think it too little for me to beg your pardon since you have knowingly done me this injury but if I live to hear your coming home I shall be ready to wait on you though you are the man that hath disturbed my rest.*

Although by now several individuals probably knew that Matthew Cary had two living wives, it took until 1698 for Giles Sylvester to bring the matter to the attention of provincial authorities. Between 1693 and 1696 Giles gathered various depositions and brought them to the Boston offices of attorney John Valentine.

In spite of the growing controversy, Matthew and Mary began their family and in February 1694 purchased the house and land of cordwainer John Adams in Boston. Matthew also remained purser of the *Nonesuch* under the command of Captain Richard Short, a reckless and frequently drunken man who was constantly at odds with Governor Sir William Phips and for a time imprisoned at Castle William. In 1693 Matthew was twice dispatched by Governor Phips to Piscataqua to apprehend deserters from the *Nonesuch,* and on the second occasion he was held there for a time by New Hampshire authorities. In August 1695 Governor William Stoughton and his council requested that Cary recover English prisoners held in Quebec. His efforts in Canada were at least partly successful. For his time and troubles in recovering twenty-two prisoners, he was amply rewarded.

The matter of Matthew's marriage to Mary Sylvester finally came to a head on July 18, 1698, when Giles Sylvester made a formal complaint, charging that Cary had broken the law under statutes concerning adultery and polygamy:

> With great sorrow of heart gives your honor to understand and be informed that one Matthew Cary now of Boston, barber-periwig maker, commonly called purser Cary, having a wife in London (to whom he is married) whose name is Elizabeth Cary and well known to be living in the said city, yet hath presumed to marry to one Mary Sylvester, sister of your complainant, and doth continue to live with her after the manner of a man and his wife and hath several children by her to the great dishonor of almighty God and contempt of his Majesty's laws within this his province enacted and in force against adultery and polygamy—wherefore your complainant prays your honor (the premises considered) to grant the warrant for convening the said Mathew Cary before yourself or some other of the honorable council to the end that he may be obliged to answer the same.
>
> Giles Sylvester

The complaint had its desired effect, and after merchant Timothy Clarke posted £20 as surety, Giles Sylvester was bound over to appear at the next session of the Superior Court to press his case. On October 25, 1698, Matthew Cary was indicted on charges of bigamy as a result of "having at once two wives." The indictment alleged that Matthew "wickedly and feloniously unto one Mary Sylvester was married and as husband and wife the said Matthew Carey with the said Mary doth live and cohabit." Brought to the bar, Matthew was shown his 1692 letter to Elizabeth Cary written onboard the *Nonesuch* and admitted it was authentic. Details of Matthew's defense are unknown, but he may have alleged that Elizabeth Cary had died some years earlier. At any rate, the outcome was a victory for Matthew—the jury found him innocent for "want of evidence." This did not sit well with Giles Sylvester, who once again sought the intervention of the General Court. In a letter to Governor Stoughton dated November 17, 1698, Giles pressed for further action:

> Although it did manifestly appear that the said Matthew Cary had two wives living at one and the same time, [the jurors] were forced to return not guilty by which meant the said Cary doth still continue to cohabit in an adulterous manner the sister of the petitioner contrary to the laws of God and man.

The cohabitation of the couple, Giles alleged, brought "great grief and shame" to him and his family. He asked the General Court to prevent the couple from living together at least until Matthew could receive "certain intelligence from England [to] prove that the other wife there is dead."

Matthew Cary, instead, almost certainly did not have to prove Elizabeth's death. In a surprising move eight days later, the council and representatives meeting in assembly decided to revise the adultery and polygamy laws of the colony. On November 29, 1698, they passed an act significantly changing the law—an action that appears to have been prompted, at least in part, by Matthew Cary's case. The act dictated that the former seven-year waiting period for those with spouses "continually remaining beyond the seas" to be declared unmarried was "excessive" and "inconvenient." The new law ordered the waiting period reduced to three years, and those who "have lately or shall hereafter" cross the seas shall, after the waiting period, be considered "single and unmarried." It is likely that this new law effectively derailed Giles Sylvester's attempts to prosecute his brother-in-law and closed forever the case of Matthew Cary and his questionable second marriage.

The fate of Elizabeth Cary in London is not recorded; Matthew and Mary Cary remained in Boston and had at least four children, of whom little is known. Matthew Cary was buried in December 1706 and his wife, Mary Sylvester, died the following month, closing forever the story of one of early Boston's most controversial marriages.

Chapter 25

Misconduct in Such a Glaring Light: The Reverend Benjamin Colman's Disobedient Daughter 1737

BOSTON SOCIETY WAS scandalized in 1737 by the news that the Reverend Benjamin Colman's only surviving daughter, Abigail or "Nabby," had eloped to New Hampshire with Albert Dennie, the dashing but disreputable son of a Boston merchant. No one was more upset than Colman, minister of the Brattle Street Church, who fervently opposed the union and initially challenged its validity. After returning to Boston, a defiant Abigail proceeded to rewed Albert Dennie in a second ceremony against her father's wishes. In Colman's eyes, the restless and headstrong Abigail never matched the dutiful and devout example set by her recently deceased elder sister, Jane Turell, and her choice of a husband, considered unsuitable by Colman, made the disparity between the siblings seem even greater.

Abigail's matrimonial saga began on September 9, 1737, when, according to diarist Benjamin Walker Jr., she left Boston in order to marry Albert Dennie outside the sphere of her disapproving father's influence. Walker recorded that on that date Abigail "went or run away from her father's house this morn and went a-long with Albert Denny, a young man and very awkward beau." Dennie, who has also been described as a "handsome, charming and resistless" rake, offered the minister's daughter the promise of a more exciting, perhaps even romantic, life. There was clearly a physical attraction between the two and in subsequent years Abigail lovingly recalled the "rich cordial of his lips." Abigail accompanied her suitor to Kingston, New Hampshire, "and there was married to said Denny, contrary to her fathers and friends consent and by parson Brown a priest of the Church of England." In Walker's estimation, the officiating parson, probably Arthur Browne of Portsmouth, had undertaken a "villainous, base action" in marrying the two. Walker's reaction undoubtedly reflected the prevailing sentiments about the elopement in Boston. He also noted the unsavory rumor that Dennie had induced the parson to perform the ceremony by offering him a bribe of twenty pistoles of gold.

The couple did not return to Boston for more than a week, arriving in town on the evening of September 20 in the midst of a downpour. Soaking wet, they headed to Dennie's lodgings in Cornhill above

The Reverend Benjamin Colman, father of the disobedient Abigail.
Engraving by Peter Pelham, after the portrait by John Smibert;
courtesy of the New England Historic Genealogical Society.

William Blinn's shop, where their first evening in Boston together was about to be rudely interrupted. Walker noted that Abigail had already "got to bed" and Dennie was in the process of "undraping to lie with her" when suddenly their chamber door was violently forced open by two men. The men, almost certainly dispatched by Colman to retrieve his daughter and interrogate Dennie, were Jacob Wendell, a prominent merchant and a colonel in the Ancient and Honorable Artillery Company, and constable John Blower, a local mason and bricklayer. After apprehending a disrobed Dennie, the two men marched him to Justice Habijah Savage for questioning about the marriage. The young man produced what appeared to be a valid marriage certificate, and Savage, according to Walker, stated "he could do nothing with him; he could not part man and wife." Nonetheless, suspicions lingered that the certificate—and the marriage—might be a sham. In spite of Savage's reluctance to intervene, Colman's henchmen parted the couple and escorted Abigail back to her father's house while a frustrated Albert Dennie returned alone to his quarters.

Benjamin Colman did not have the upper hand for long. Once again defying her formidable father, and perhaps in an attempt to short-circuit his investigation of the first nuptials, the couple were wed a second time the following day. The ceremony was again conducted outside of Boston, this time in Charlestown where, curiously, the bride's name was recorded as "Abigail Turell"—possibly an error but more likely an attempt by the couple to disguise the real name of the prominent bride. As "tongues began to wag" in Boston about her latest misadventure with Dennie, Abigail's father and friends were sharply pained.

Benjamin Walker concluded his diary account of Abigail's marital woes by noting that a truce was reached: "I hear Wednesday September the 28, 1737, Denny and wife are to lie at her father's house." The truce, if one actually occurred, was short-lived. Colman, who believed his daughter's errors were the result of "her early sins of reading novels and idle poems," never accepted his raffish son-in-law. The marriage was an uneasy one, with Dennie moving to Connecticut and traveling overseas for stretches of time. In a letter to Sir Richard Ellis around 1740, Colman called Dennie a "miserable man" on whom Abigail had thrown away her life. Abigail, together with her young son by Dennie, eventually returned to her father's house to live. Benjamin Colman did not welcome his son-in-law to do the same despite Dennie's pleas and promises of repentance for misdemeanors that have been lost to time. Abigail never returned to her husband and, as one author put it, adopted the mantle of a "great tragedienne" who worried that she had become the "butt of Boston society ladies." Affected by distress and languishing illness, Abigail died in her father's house in May 1745. Colman marked her passing by writing that a "gracious God had set her misconduct in such a glaring light." His daughter Jane, he noted, "never offended anyone," but Abigail, he lamented, "made the greatest breaches on me, and had given scandal and offence to all in point of filial duty." Dennie, who released custody of his son by Abigail to Colman, apparently never repented to his father-in-law's satisfaction and died himself about ten years later.

Chapter 26
John Lovell Jr.:
The Blackest Sheep of Boston
1773

FREQUENTLY ILL AND WORN DOWN by the appalling
behavior of a husband who had led her and her children into poverty,
Ann Lovell in 1773 made a most unusual and desperate request—she
petitioned for a separation that would free her from a man she
claimed was dissolute, idle, and living the life of a vagrant. Ann's husband, John Lovell Jr., was a member of a well-known local family and
son of the master of Boston's South Latin School. However, he had
not only refused to work or support his family, but also actively prevented Ann from taking in work. He accepted no responsibility for
the couple's youngest daughter, Polly, and worse still, according to
witnesses, committed at least two scandalous acts: he publicly threatened the life of John Hancock and later made a half-hearted suicide
attempt on the Boston Common. John in time became the most infamous ne'er-do-well in town. During the Revolution, he achieved further notoriety as an outspoken Loyalist involved in several intrigues in
Boston. He claimed to have stolen documents from the Sons of Liberty and, after the British evacuated Boston, was imprisoned for several years. He later fled to England and unsuccessfully petitioned the
government for major losses suffered during the war. In this last
effort, as in most of his other ventures, John was a failure and a
nuisance.

In 1760 Ann Dudley married twenty-four-year-old John Lovell Jr.
in a ceremony performed in Roxbury by the Reverend Dr. Samuel

Cooper of the Brattle Street Church, the most fashionable Congregationalist minister in Boston. Nineteen-year-old Ann was marrying respectably but, as the granddaughter and great-granddaughter of governors of Massachusetts (Thomas Dudley and his son, Joseph), the match was at least a notch below her own social position. Ann's husband, John, was the son of schoolmaster John Lovell, a noted disciplinarian with whom he had an uneasy relationship. The younger John was originally on a educational track that might have led to college. Instead, he began his career as an apprentice to a Boston merchant and later worked as a clerk for the merchant (and fellow Loyalist) Commodore Joshua Loring. His association with Loring was fruitful enough for John to start his own business with the merchant's assistance.

In the first flush of success, the Lovells lived well enough to maintain a house with two maids and a manservant. Later, when his fledgling enterprise collapsed, John blamed his former employer and attempted to sue him in England. This became a pattern for John: he claimed he had been wronged and that others were responsible for his misfortunes. Failing in his endeavor against Loring, a defeated John returned to Boston. He was by this time, in the words of a contemporary commentator, "in very low circumstances and was obliged to seek the shelter of his worthy father . . . while his wife returned to her friends." He received a cool reception from his wife, according to his mother, Abigail Lovell, when he arrived in Boston. Ann's refusal to see her husband on the morning of his humiliating return from England troubled John for years to come. He cited the incident to his sister, Abigail Walker, as the starting point of all his "misfortunes afterwards." In 1769 he went bankrupt, broke up his household, dismissed his servants, and moved with two of his three surviving children back into his father's house. Signs that John might be mentally unbalanced soon began to emerge.

At about the time of his bankruptcy, John became agitated over a financial dispute with John Hancock. According to Dr. James Lloyd, also a Loyalist, John admitted having stalked Hancock at his house on Boston Common with the intent of killing him: "[John] walked up and down the Common several times with pistols expecting to meet

John Hancock, whose life was threatened by John Lovell Jr. Portrait by John Coles Sr.;
courtesy of the New England Historic Genealogical Society.

Mr. Hancock and if he did not comply with his demands with respect to some money matters, he was determined to put him to death."

While John appears to have broadcast his threat against Hancock to members of his extended family, little more about this strange incident is known. In any case, he did not fire at or kill the man who a few years later would boldly sign the Declaration of Independence and serve as governor of Massachusetts.

One of the main difficulties in John and Ann's marriage appears to have been his refusal to allow Ann to help support the family during financial shortages. This issue emerged shortly after the couple married and even extended to Ann's willingness to undertake housework. Elizabeth Scarborough, who knew the couple, recalled John becoming "uneasy and angry" when Ann labored in any way. "It was not her business," Mrs. Scarborough later remembered John saying, "to employ herself in that way; such business ought to be done by her maid or servant." Catherine Clark, a servant who lived with the Lovells until they broke up housekeeping, recalled an incident during which John became enraged by his wife's attempt to earn a bit of money. Catherine recounted a time when Ann undertook a small tailoring job: "Mrs. Lovell went out one evening and bought a shirt to make up for somebody." Upon finding Ann with the shirt, John asked his wife if she was trying to take in work. She said "she thought it her duty to do something to support her and her children." John claimed that he "had always maintained her and always would and that she had no business to take in work," and that she should mend only her own family's clothing. According to Catherine, Ann snapped back that she "had neither thread or money" to do as he suggested. John then became angry and "twitched the shirt out of her hand and threw it to the other end of the room." Calling Ann a "low-lived bitch," John threatened that if the garment was not immediately taken out of his house he would burn it by morning.

Other witnesses in 1773 reported on the Lovells' breakup. Margaret Clemens, who had lived with the family for nearly two years, stated that while John had been verbally abusive to Ann, cursing and damning her and calling her a "bitch" and "hell ghost," she had never seen him actually strike her. Mary Fulton, a nurse, claimed that in about 1768, as Ann awaited the birth of a child, John was in a particularly bad humor. "Whenever he came into the room he cursed and swore at her and treated her with the most abusive language," Mrs. Fulton alleged. "She was at this time very ill." The day before John left to return to his father's house, Ann made her own permanent exit from their home, saying, according to John, that she was going to visit her sister Catherine Johonnot. Eventually, she found refuge at Elizabeth Scarborough's house. On one occasion when she was ill, Mrs. Scarborough recalled that John did nothing to help: "He gave not as much as a copper to me for her support."

At some point, Ann moved to her friend Mary Jackson's house, where she lived for about thirteen months. There she supported herself, perhaps working on tailoring jobs, and made ends meet by accepting the charity of friends and relations. Mrs. Jackson recalled John's visits to her house as unpleasant. She found John "very harsh" and although he did not strike Ann in her presence, he threatened violence by promising to make her "appear as black as the Devil." Mary Jackson had taken Ann in when she appeared at her door, ill, destitute, and begging to have "a bed to lay on." Ann also pleaded with Mrs. Jackson to let her daughter Polly join them there, an arrangement to which her friend consented. During an illness, John visited Ann and Mrs. Jackson urged him to find employment. John responded that he would not move his family out of town for a job, even as near as Salem.

Polly Lovell's care continued to be an issue during Ann and John's estrangement. John steadfastly refused to make any arrangements for his daughter, stating that "she was entirely her mother's ward." When she was not with her mother at Mary Jackson's house, Polly lived for a time with the Clemens family. John Lovell told James Clemens that he would not take care of his daughter until he found employment.

Having lost his business and gone adrift, John's inactivity earned the scorn of his wife, father, and others in town. His family arranged for him to be committed to Boston's workhouse after his suicide attempt on the Boston Common in the summer of 1771 or 1772. The episode was evidently sparked by an argument between John and his father, who, tired of his son's unpredictable temper, may have asked him to move out of his house. Having swallowed poison, John headed to the Boston Common, where he intended to lie down and die. On his way to the Common, John encountered Joseph Green, the Loyalist satirical verse poet who lived near the Lovells on School Street. Green recalled the incident several years later:

> He told me he had been so ill used by his father that morning he had taken arsenic and mentioned the quantity, which I do not remember, but it was so large that if he had really taken it, it must have put an end to his life; he told me he was going to lay himself down on the Common expecting to die and desired that I would acquaint his friends where they might find him.

John's first known suicide attempt failed because he did not ingest enough poison, a hint that the episode was a desperate attempt to shock his family and upset or humiliate his father. The incident was one of the reasons John's family decided to seek help from town authorities. The family approached Samuel Partridge, an overseer of the poor, with a complaint stating that John was "idle and indigent and did no business for a livelihood." Partridge found the complaint well founded and committed him to the workhouse. Once safely confined there, the overseer observed John to be "very calm" and ready to acknowledge that he had taken arsenic and laudanum in "great quantities." He recognized that "his own impudence had put him upon those violent attempts upon himself."

Meanwhile, Ann felt she could not keep Polly indefinitely at Mrs. Jackson's house and, perhaps because of the existing burden on their household with two grandchildren already there, the senior Lovells did not invite Polly to live with them. John again balked at the possibility of caring for his youngest daughter. If anyone attempted to send Polly to him, he "would absent himself from the town to avoid her." She was nonetheless sent to him in July 1773, apparently at the same time he was confined to the workhouse. John harshly "told her to get along" and "refused her all manner of protection." The following day Samuel Partridge placed Polly in the adjacent almshouse. John quickly sought out Partridge, saying that he had found a place for his daughter in the country, but the overseer refused the offer, "detailing his neglect of her in the past." John responded to Partridge's rejection by stating that he "would never ask again for her."

During John's lengthy period of unemployment, attempts were made to find him work. Ann's brothers-in-law John Cotton and Peter Johonnot visited him at the workhouse with the news that they believed they could find him a position in "a gentleman's store" for a salary of £50 or £60 a year. To their surprise, John rebuffed the offer, replying "with great emotion that he would sooner lay down on his floor and die than accept such a place." The gentlemen were "astonished at this unexpected answer . . . knowing him at the time to be in a state of real poverty." In due course, John was released from the workhouse. At some point he found work, apparently for the wealthy merchant and customs collector Robert Hallowell, and stated in the presence of his wife and Mary Jackson that it was paying him well. At this remarkable news, Ann begged him to take care of Polly, but John replied that "he would not touch her until he got satisfaction of his father."

Having sustained years of aberrant behavior and long stretches of neglect by her husband, Ann in September 1773 petitioned for a "separation from bed and board"—a quaint-sounding term signifying a marital arrangement that would allow the couple to live in permanent separation with distinct finances. During the action, John appears to have acted as his own attorney, asking questions of witnesses and charging that Ann's claims were "caprice and conjecture." He stated that he was willing "to procure a small tenement and cohabit with her, nourish and cherish her as he ever hath done while in flourishing circumstances." John acknowledged that he had experienced "heavy losses" in business and had been unable to support a wife and family in the "comfortable manner" they had previously enjoyed. He vigorously denied that he was a vagrant or had ever received alms from the town of Boston. Moreover, he was critical of Ann for not selling some of her Dudley family lands to help support the family. By refusing to sell properties from which she collected a small income, Ann was, argued John, complicit in his failure. During the course of the case, it emerged that John had refused several job offers made to him during his idle periods. Charles Paxton, customs commissioner and arch Loyalist, stated that he had offered him two posts as a "weigher"—one in Wilmington, Delaware, at a rate of £40 a year and one in Boston for £25 a year. In total, John refused at least three "unprofitable posts of honor" Paxton had extended to him.

During the proceedings, testimony unflattering to Ann came from John's mother, Abigail. She characterized her daughter-in-law as acting like a young person "inexperienced in family affairs." Her behavior toward John could be "irritating and provoking to the highest degree" and she "seemed to take pleasure in doing it," claimed Mrs. Lovell. When asked how Ann had been so annoying, Abigail Lovell recounted Ann's tendency to repeat rumors hurtful to John:

> One instance I recollect which I think bad and vile is about the time of his confinement for debt; she often went abroad and on return home would acquaint him with what she had heard to his disadvantage; upon his desiring not to hear any of these story, she answered 'I will acquaint you with what people say;' which I looked on as harsh and cruel.

Overcoming John's initial protests, on November 2, 1773, an agreement between Ann and John to separate was made. The agreement called for Ann to

> enjoy her own estate and also such other estate as she may earn or acquire during such separation and shall not run him in debt or any way put him to charge for her maintenance or support and he shall in no way meddle with her person or estate or in any manner molest her during said separation.

As part of the agreement, John was required to sign a £1,000 bond to ensure his compliance with its terms. For Ann, the victory of obtaining a separation from her wayward husband was short-lived. In 1775, she died in Boston. Her three surviving children, Nancy, Polly, and John, were now motherless, and before long they would see very little of their father, who delved into the politics of Revolutionary War–era Boston and eventually served a lengthy stint in prison.

The epilogue to the story of John and Ann's marital problems came in the form of his involvement in the mid-1770s in Loyalist politics in Boston. His allegiance to the British government coincided with the views of his father, but was in sharp contrast to those held by his younger brother, schoolmaster James Lovell, who favored American independence and became a noted rebel (and later served in the Continental Congress, as receiver of continental taxes, and as collector of the port of Boston). Few noteworthy siblings in Massachusetts history have undertaken such divergent paths in life, perhaps with the modern exception of renowned politician William Bulger and his brother, fugitive and reputed Boston mob boss James "Whitey" Bulger.

During this period, John was employed by General Thomas Gage on "some private services" and became a vocal supporter of the British in Boston. On one occasion, General Gage supposedly tapped John to steal some papers from the Sons of Liberty. He successfully obtained the documents and delivered them to Gage, an act John later claimed was executed at the "risk of being tarred and feathered." During the Siege of Boston, John and another man confiscated "certain merchants' goods to prevent them from falling into the hands of the rebels." When the British abandoned Boston, John was imprisoned for this activity. When the matter was eventually dropped, John nonetheless remained incarcerated. A notorious troublemaker with a "litigious disposition," John's "abuse of the leading men" of Boston resulted in his incarceration for as long as three years. After finally being released, he slipped away to England, abandoning his children.

Once in England, John attempted to press a claim for compensation by the British government for his activities in Boston, which he said cost him serious losses. Because of his unpopularity, even among his political sympathizers, a damaging statement on John's background was prepared by an anonymous author (and supported by noted Loyalists). John, it alleged, was "a man who rates his pretensions high and in bombastic language, who was always of a low cast of character, indigent and worthless." John, however, was armed with letters of his own, including one from Sir William Pepperell in which he was described by the New England baronet as possessing the "character of a very loyal subject." Another was later procured from Harrison Gray, who stated that John was "from a good family" and "that few loyalists had suffered more." John began peppering British authorities with letters. In 1781 he wrote to Lord Hillsborough, demanding to have his case reviewed and acted upon:

> *I pray your Lordships answer to my application, for if you will not grant it, I must get it into Parliament in any way I can where I hope to find friends though I am now as destitute of able support for that purpose as when I was to meet General Washington flushed with success and left to defend myself not only against him, but an Act that might make even a Turkish Sultan blush.*

The government rejected John's claims, noting that "he seems to have received more from [the] government than he ever lost." Undeterred, John Lovell set his sights on complaining to a new body: the American Congress. Firing one of his final salvos at British authorities, John in 1782 wrote to John Robinson, secretary of the treasury, to express "his sense of his deception and ruin by the King and the late Parliament." He requested a pass in order to "depart honorably to the American Congress to seek that relief denied to him by the King and his ministers." His threats were effective. Knowing that he planned to return to his native country and being "very troublesome" and "almost insane," British authorities offered him £30 on the condition that he promptly leave England. Quieted by this trifling buyout, John's actions after the rejection of his English claims elude detection. His trail, from this point forward, goes completely cold.

A man who caused all who knew him trouble, John was shunned by his wife and family, despised by scores of Bostonians, and rejected by the British authorities he attempted to aid. Undoubtedly Boston's blackest sheep, John Lovell's conduct and character were, as one author put it, "very singular."

Acknowledgments

I AM THANKFUL TO MANY friends and associates for their assistance in the preparation of this volume. Ralph J. Crandall, Executive Director of the New England Historic Genealogical Society, was most supportive and arranged for me to have a sabbatical leave of absence from the Society in 2004 in order to work on it. Judith Huber Halseth carefully reviewed each chapter of the book and offered much encouragement. A number of other colleagues generously read individual chapters or portions of this work, including Jerome E. Anderson, Robert Charles Anderson, J. L. Bell, Martha Bustin, Cornelia Hughes Dayton, Robert J. Dunkle, Eric G. Grundset, Sally Dean Hamblen Hill, Henry B. Hoff, Thomas A. Foster, Judith Graham, Diane Rapaport, Marilynne K. Roach, Gary Boyd Roberts, Scott C. Steward, Helen Schatvet Ullmann, and Hiller B. Zobel. I am especially grateful to Michelle Morris for her transcriptions of several court records.

Others who helped in a variety of ways include Kathleen Ackerman, Robert Allison, Jeremy Dupertuis Bangs, Georgia Brady Barnhill, Amanda Batey, Henry L. P. Beckwith, Dana Berg, Elizabeth Bouvier, Esther Coke, Abbott Lowell Cummings, John Demos, Dan Duncan, Laurel K. Gabel, Robert Gormley, Lewis S. Greenleaf, Donny L. Hamilton, John A. Herdeg, Sandra M. Hewlett, Hirschl & Adler Galleries, Philip Holzer, Wheaton Hudson, Ginger Koster, David Allen Lambert, Eve LaPlante, Michael J. Leclerc, Cynthia Leveille, Barbara Luck, Bernie Margolis, Celia Cullen Martin, Robert Neer, Mary Beth Norton, Jane C. Nylander, Richard C. Nylander, Carolyn Sheppard Oakley, Julie Helen Otto, Joshua E. Palter, Betty Ring, Zachary Ross, Sharon Salinger, Melinde Lutz Sanborn, Andrew B. Searle, Eric B. Schultz, Iain Sherwood, Mary Alice Short, Susan Sloan, Frederick H. Spero, Geoff Swinfield, Maureen A. Taylor, Kevin E. Thomas, Roger Thompson, John Titford, Lora Treadwell, Laurel Thatcher Ulrich, Ruth Wellner, and my associates at the New England Historic Genealogical Society. In particular, Jean Powers offered invaluable assistance in obtaining image permissions.

I am greatly indebted to the staff of the Massachusetts Historical Society who warmly welcomed me to their library for several months in 2004. I extend my thanks to all there who made it a gainful experience, especially William M. Fowler, Jr., Peter Drummey, Conrad E. Wright, and Kim Nusco.

The curators, librarians, and staff members of a number of other institutions and repositories also deserve acknowledgment for their assistance, including the American Antiquarian Society, the Bayou Bend Collection, the Boston Athenæum, the Boston Public Library, the Bostonian Society, the Colonial Society of Massachusetts, the Colonial Williamsburg Foundation, Harvard Law School Library, the Historical Society of Pennsylvania, the Massachusetts Supreme Judicial Court Archives, Historic New England (formerly known as the Society for the Preservation of New England Antiquities), the Massachusetts State Archives, the Metropolitan Museum of Art, the Museum of Fine Arts, Houston, and the New England Historic Genealogical Society. In England, staff members of the Society of Genealogists and the National Archives were extremely helpful.

I would like to thank my friends and family who have been supportive throughout this project. Commonwealth Editions publisher Webster Bull and managing editor Penny Stratton have been most helpful to me and I am especially grateful for their kind assistance. For their important contributions, I am thankful to Sarah Weaver, copyeditor; Lida Stinchfield, proofreader; Kevin Millham, indexer; Anne Rolland, production artist; and Dean Bornstein, jacket designer. Finally, for marketing and distribution efforts, many thanks are due to Jill Christiansen and Katie Bull.

Notes

Please see the bibliography for full versions of shortened citations. I have used abbreviations for certain frequently cited works:

Boyle's Journal of Occurrences: Boyle, John. "Boyle's Journal of Occurrences in Boston, 1759–1778." *New England Historical and Genealogical Register,* vol. 84 (1930), pp. 142–171, 248–272, 357–382; vol. 85 (1931), pp. 5–28, 117–133.

Mather Diary: Mather, Cotton. *Diary of Cotton Mather.* 2 vols. New York: Frederick Ungar, 1957.

NEHGR: The *New England Historical and Genealogical Register.* 159 vols. Boston: New England Historic Genealogical Society, 1847–2005.

Rowe Diary: Cunningham, Anne Rowe, ed. *Letters and Diary of John Rowe, Boston Merchant, 1759–1762, 1764–1779.* Boston: W. B. Clarke, 1903.

Sewall Diary: Thomas, M. Halsey. *The Diary of Samuel Sewall, 1674–1729.* 2 vols. New York: Farrar, Straus and Giroux, 1973.

Sibley's Harvard Graduates: Sibley, John Langdon. *Biographical Sketches of Graduates of Harvard University.* Boston: Massachusetts Historical Society, 1873–2000, 18 vols.

Thwing Index: Thwing, Annie Haven. *Inhabitants and Estates of the Town of Boston, 1630–1800.* CD-ROM. Boston: New England Historic Genealogical Society and Massachusetts Historical Society, 2001.

Walker Diary: Walker, Benjamin, Jr. Mss. diary at the Massachusetts Historical Society.

Winthrop Journal: Dunn, Richard S., et al. *The Journal of John Winthrop 1630–1649.* Cambridge: Belknap Press, 1996.

Introduction

ix *"There fell out a great business":* Winthrop Journal, pp. 395-398, 451-454. The squabble is also covered in Thwing, *The Crooked & Narrow Streets of Boston,* pp. 119–120.

x *"Toward the end of this month":* Charles F. Adams, "John Marshall's Diary," *Proceedings of the Massachusetts Historical Society,* vol. 1, second series (Boston, 1884–1885), p. 160.

x *"false reports and defamations":* This incident is reported in *Boston News-Letter,* September 28–October 5, 1727, ibid., April 27-May 2, 1728.

x *Englishman Edward "Ned" Ward:* The full text of Ward's commentaries, in *A Trip to New-England, With a Character of the Country and People, Both English and Indians.* 1699, is available on the Internet; see www.etext.lib.virginia.edu.

xi *"well advanced in years":* Walker Diary, July 31, 1731. Courtesy of Sally Dean Hamblen Hill.

Part One: Witch's Brew

1 *Especially vulnerable to charges:* Demos, *Entertaining Satan,* pp. 93–94.

2 *"God's displeasure with the Antinomians":* Hall, *Witch-Hunting,* pp. 19–20; Winthrop Journal, pp. 253, 255, 330.

2 The principal source for Margaret's story is the Winthrop Journal, pp. 711–712.

3 *"some angry words passing between her and her neighbors":* Hall, *Witch-Hunting,* pp. 21–23.

3 *"played the harlot":* Burr, *Narratives of the Witchcraft Cases,* p. 409.

3 *"enjoined to appear":* Noble, *Court of Assistants,* vol. 2, p. 131.

3 *"I have heard the devil drew in":* Hall, *Witch-Hunting,* p. 28.

3 *Her surviving children:* G. Andrews Moriarty, "The Early Rhode Island Lakes," *The American Genealogist,* vol. 12 (1935), pp. 18–19.

4 *In 1673, Ann Martin Edmonds:* Information about Edmonds is from Noble, *Court of Assistants,* vol. 1, p. 11. See also Tannenbaum, *The Healer's Calling,* pp. 118–129.

5–6 *One of Boston's last and most elusive witch suspects:* Dunton, *Life and Errors,* vol. 1, pp. 109–110.

6 *"This day Mrs. Prout dies":* Sewall Diary, vol. 1, p. 317.

Chapter 1: Hanged for a Witch

7 *"person of superior quality in life":* Drake, *New England Legends and Folklore,* p. 29.

7 *Ann's most serious conflict:* Jerome E. Anderson generously shared with me his unpublished article, "John Crabtree of Yorkshire and Boston."

7　*An outspoken woman:* Hutchinson, *History of the Massachusetts-Bay*, vol. 1, pp. 160–161; Hall, *Witch–Hunting*, pp. 89–91; and for the case presented before the First Church of Boston, Demos, *Remarkable Providences*, pp. 262–282.

8　*Before marrying William Hibbins:* Anderson, *Great Migration*, vol. 3, pp. 315–317. Because William Hibbins and Richard Bellingham were related by marriage, various accounts have misidentified Ann Hibbins as the sister of Governor Bellingham. Their relationship was more complex. Ann was the wife (and later the widow) of the governor's brother-in-law. Robert Charles Anderson in the aforementioned source demonstrates that there were probably two men named William Hibbins in the records of early Boston and further that William Hibbins, husband of Ann, did not arrive in Boston as early as was previously believed.

8　*Trerise, later recalled by some:* Johan Winsser, "Nicholas Trerise, Mariner of Wapping and Charlestown," *NEHGR*, vol. 143 (1989), pp. 25, 29–30.

8　*"so discomposed [her] spirit":* Hubbard, *History of New England*, p. 574.

9　*Crabtree, a native of Yorkshire:* Anderson, "John Crabtree."

9　*In the end Crabtree demanded:* Demos, *Remarkable Providences*, p. 270.

9　*Merchant Robert Keayne:* All references to and quotations taken from Robert Keayne's notes on the First Church hearings are from Demos, *Remarkable Providences*, pp. 262–282.

11　*"so odious to her neighbors":* Hutchinson, *History of the Massachusetts-Bay*, vol. 1, p. 160.

12　*According to historian William Hubbard:* Hubbard, *History of New England*, p. 574.

12　*"Mrs. Anne Hibbins was called forth":* Shurtleff, *Records of the Massachusetts Bay,* vol. 4, p. 269.

12　*On May 27, 1656: Suffolk Deeds*, vol. 3, items 81–87. It is claimed that two of Ann's sons living in Ireland, John and Joseph Moore, later removed to Charlestown, Massachusetts. See Michael J. O'Brien, *Pioneer Irish in New England* (New York: P. J. Kennedy & Sons, 1937), pp. 234–235.

13　*One administrator, Joshua Scottow :* Hall, *Witch-Hunting*, p. 89n.

13　*On June 16, 1656:* Suffolk County Probate Records, vol. 3, p. 73.

13　*Among the other bequeests:* Mary Ann Everett Green, ed., *Calendar of State Papers Domestic Series, 1655–6 . . .* (London: Longmans, 1882), pp. 238–239.

13　*The second codicil:* Information about the codicils in this paragraph and later ones is from Suffolk County Probate Records, vol. 3, p. 73.

14　*"probably thrust into some obscure hole":* Drake, *New England Legends*, pp. 34–35.

14　*According to Thomas Hutchinson:* Hutchinson, *History of the Massachusetts-Bay*, vol. 1, p. 161.

15　*"You may remember":* Hutchinson, *History of the Massachusetts-Bay*, vol. 1, p. 161.

15　*"Mrs. Hibbons witchcrafts":* Hall, *Witch-Hunting*, p. 89.

15　*"It fared with her":* Hutchinson, *History of the Massachusetts-Bay*, vol. 1, p. 161.

Chapter 2: Mary Hale and the Death of a Bewitched Mariner
Mary Hale appears to have been born Mary Williams. See Suffolk Deeds, vol. 4, pp. 217–218, which includes a deposition by "Wenifreet Lyng" who was almost certainly "Winifred King," mother of Joanna Benham. I wish to thank Michael J. Leclerc for his research assistance in this case. Mary Hale's story is derived from depositions in her 1680 witchcraft trial found in Superior Court of Judicature, vol. 24, case 1972.

16　*During one smallpox outbreak: Records and Files of the Quarterly Courts of Essex County Massachusetts* (Salem, Mass.: Essex Institute, 1919), vol. 7, p. 395.

16　*Mary was found guilty: Records of the Suffolk County Court*, vol. 2, p. 818.

19　*Among the witnesses present:* Thwing Index reference code 18832. The relationship between Hannah Wakeham and James Everill was suggested to me by Robert Charles Anderson in a communication dated January 22, 2005.

19　*On the strength of his accusations:* Noble, *Court of Assistants*, vol. 1, pp. 188–189.

19　*Mary Hale's last days:* Donald Lines Jacobus, *Families of Ancient New Haven* (Rome, N.Y.: 1927), vol. 4, pp. 596–598; Burr, *Narratives of the Witchcraft Cases,* p. 395.

Chapter 3: The Pitiful Spectacles of Haunted Children
All quotes in this chapter are from Cotton Mather's "Memorable Providences, Relating to Witchcrafts and Possessions," 1689, from Burr, *Narratives of the Witchcraft Cases,* pp. 99–131. All quotes herein are from Mather's text unless otherwise noted. See also Hall, *Witch-Hunting,* pp. 265–279, Demos, *Entertaining Satan,* pp. 7–9, and Poole, "Witchcraft in Boston," pp. 142–146.

20　*The laundress's elderly mother:* Often called Goody Glover, the witch has been variously referred to as Mary or Anne. Marilynne K. Roach points to three references for unpaid jail bills in 1689 that list Mary Glover, Massachusetts Archives vol. 35, pp. 95, 96, 254. On this basis, I have accepted the witch's name as Mary.

20 *Martha Goodwin was the eldest daughter:* Wyman, *Genealogies and Estates of Charlestown*, p. 415; E. B. Huntington, *A Genealogical Memoir of the Lo-Lathrop Family. . . .* (Ridgefield, Conn.: Julia M. Huntington, 1884), p. 49.

21 *According to one source:* O'Brien, *Pioneer Irish in New England*, pp. 236–237.

22 *At the instigation of the governor:* Norton, *In the Devil's Snare*, pp. 39–40.

24 *Martha Goodwin reported:* Hall, *Witch-Hunting*, p. 266.

26 *Martha, for example, became:* Thwing Index reference code 15880.

Chapter 4: Devil in the Damsels
Unless otherwise noted, quotes in this chapter are from Cotton Mather, "A Brand Pluck'd Out of the Burning," and "Another Brand Pluckt Out of the Burning," in Burr, *Narratives of the Witchcraft Cases*, pp. 259–287, 308–341.

27 *She witnessed the brutal murder:* Norton, *In The Devil's Snare*, pp. 177–178.

27 *When her mistress:* Mary Beth Norton proposes Mrs. Thacher as Mercy's employer; see ibid.

28 *Her possession:* Janice Knight, "Telling it slant: the testimony of Mercy Slant," *Early American Lecture*, Winter 2002, vol. 37, p. 39.

28 *In 1694 she was well enough:* Thwing Index reference code 44718.

29 *found guilty of adultery and excommunicated:* Mather Diary, vol. 1, p. 261.

30 *"I do testify":* Mather, "Another Brand Pluckt Out of the Burning," p. 337.

31 *This accusation and others:* See also Silverman, *The Life and Times of Cotton Mather*, pp. 130-135.

31 *Over the course of her life:* H. Minot Pitman, "Descendants of John Snelling," *NEHGR*, vol. 34 (1954), p. 180.

Chapter 5: An Encounter with Satan
For a detailed account of Martha Robinson's story, see Minkema, "The Devil Will Roar in Me Anon," in Reis, *Spellbound*, pp. 99–118. Minkema gave Martha's surname as "Roberson," the spelling in Pitkin's diary and a variation of the more common "Robinson" used for the family in public records. I favor the latter, standard version of the name. All quotes unless otherwise noted are from The Joseph Pitkin diary, pp. 55–63, Connecticut State Library, courtesy of Richard Roberts.

32 *During a brief sojourn:* A. P. Pitkin, *Pitkin Family of America: A Genealogy of the Descendants of William Pitkin. . .* (Hartford, Conn.: Case, Lockwood & Brainard, 1887), p. 14.

32 *"I found it profitable to my soul":* Pitkin diary.

32 *innkeeper Josiah Shelton:* Thwing Index reference code 54394.

33 *Old South Church:* Martha was baptized there May 12, 1717/18, Boston Church Records, reference code 32,346.

34 *The following month:* Ibid., reference code 27,640.

34 *Gilbert Tennent:* Frederick Lewis Weis, *The Colonial Clergy of the Middle Colonies: New York, New Jersey, and Pennsylvania, 1628-1776* (Worcester: American Antiquarian Society, 1957), p. 159.

38 *"cried out, Robinson's daughter":* Minkema, "The Devil Will Roar," p. 114.

38 *"into the anonymity":* Ibid.

Part Two: Rogue's Gallery
39 *John Pierpont of Roxbury:* See Helen Schatvet Ullmann, "The Pierponts of Roxbury, Massachusetts," unpublished mss. at the New England Historic Genealogical Society, 2004.

40 *His educational career: Sibley's Harvard Graduates*, vol. 9, pp. 375–386; Bridenbaugh, *Early Americans*, pp. 121–149; Bullock, "A Mumper among the Gentle," pp. 231–258 ; Jack Lynch, "Of Sharpers, Mumpers, and Fourberies: Some Early American Impostors and Rogues," *Colonial Williamsburg*, Spring 2005, pp. 82–86.

41 *"He is a slim fellow":* Bridenbaugh, *Early Americans*, p. 135.

41 *was hanged at Kingston:* Ibid., p. 148.

41 The story of John Hill was reprinted in newspapers as far away as the *Pennsylvania Gazette*. On May 3, 1733, the *Gazette* ran a version of the story in which Hill's "wife" was called Rachel Hill alias Rachel Fig. Accessible Archives CD-ROM Edition of the Pennsylvania Gazette, Folio I, 1728–1750 (Malvern, Penn.: Accessible Archives, 1991), item 1288.

42 *On questioning the scoundrel. Boston News-Letter*, April 12–19, 1733.

42 *"A woman called Mary Kemp": Boston Evening Post*, November 29, 1736.

42 *He was so famous:* www.mysteriouspeople.com.

43 *In 1818, John Adams:* Bridenbaugh, *Early Americans*, p. 123.

43 *"a lunatic called 'Mad Tom'":* www.mysteriouspeople.com.

43 *"Mr. Carew was surprised":* Bampfylde Moore Carew, *The Life of Bampfylde Moore Carew, Sometime*

King of the Beggars; Containing An Accurate History of His Travels, Voyages, and Adventures . . .
(Philadelphia: William M'Carty, 1813), p. 86.

43   *They "persuaded him to go"*: Ibid., p. 86.

43   *In the summer of 1771:* Thwing Index reference codes 6656, 23769. Special thanks to J. L. Bell.

44   *Lendall was defended by John Adams:* Wroth and Zobel, *Legal Papers of John Adams*, vol. 1, pp.
157–161. See this source for an apparent difficulty with regard to the identification of Lendall
Pitts that suggests that there may have been two contemporaneous men of that name in
Boston. There is no other obvious second Lendall Pitts in Boston at the time and I believe that
the subject of this sketch was the well-recorded individual of that name born in or about 1747.

44   *An ardent patriot:* Francis S. Drake, *Tea Leaves: Being a Collection of Letters and Documents Relating
to the Shipment of Tea to the American Colonies in the Year 1773 . . . and Biographical Notices of the
Boston Tea Party* (Boston: A. O. Crane, 1884), pp. cxli–cxlv.

45   *"Mount Whoredom":* Whitehill, *Boston: A Topographical History*, pp. 7–8, 70–71.

45   *picking up unfamiliar women:* Communication from J. L. Bell dated January 11, 2005.

Chapter 6: Abominable Villainy

46   *Marrying the scion:* Crane, *Rawson Family*, pp. 9–12; Massachusetts Archives, vol. 39, p. 647. See
also Michael K. Ward, "Rebecca Rawson: Portrait of a Daughter of the Puritan Elite in the Massachusetts Bay Colony," reprinted from *New England Journal of History*, on www.rawsonfamily.org.

46   *Atkinson, then in his mid-sixties:* Atkinson's deposition against Thomas Rumsey is discussed in
Demos, *Remarkable Providences*, pp. 249–251.

46   *Thomas gave the Atkinsons some account:* It is possible that Rumsey's initial story was an approxi-
mation of the truth. An inventory dated September 12, 1662, for one Thomas Rumsey,
Gentleman, late of Sandwich in Kent, reveals an estate with £300 "in ready money" and
more than £1,200 in total assets. Archdeaconry of Canterbury Court, 1661–1663, FHL
1655562. See also Elizabeth French, "Genealogical Research in England: Tilden," *NEHGR*,
vol. 65 (1911), pp. 326, 332, for a Thomas Rumsey of Kent, son of Thomas and Sarah Tilden
Smith Rumsey, with New England associations.

47   *his stepmother's death:* Using the term "mother-in-law," Rumsey in this instance almost certainly meant stepmother. He later designated "Lady Hailes" as his mother.

47   *"religion did seem to wear away":* Crane, *Rawson Family*, p. 11.

47   *Within a year of arriving in Boston:* While few records document Thomas's presence in Boston,
he was among scores of men in April 1679 who took the oath of allegiance before Deputy-
Governor Simon Bradstreet. *Boston Record Commissioners*, vol. 29, p. 168.

47   *Thomas approached Hull:* Crane, *Rawson Family*, p. 11.

49   *"one of the most beautiful":* Ibid., p. 9. See also, Sullivan S. Rawson, *The Rawson Family: Memoir of
Edward Rawson* (Boston: privately printed, 1849), pp. 15–16, in which an earlier unlocated
"Memorial of the Rawson Family" by Judge Joseph Rawson, of Rhode Island [hereinafter
Memoir of Edward Rawson], is cited as the source of "the story of her marriage and death."

49   *A three-quarter-length portrait:* Louisa Dresser, ed., *XVIIth Century Painting in New England . . .*
(Worcester, Mass.: Worcester Art Museum, 1935), p. 127. See also Rev. Glenn Tilley Morse,
"Edward Rawson, Secretary of the Massachusetts Bay Colony, and His Unfortunate Daughter
Rebecca," *Old Time New England* vol. 11 (1921), pp. 123–129.

50   *Edward Rawson, the son of a "highly respectable family":* Robert Noxon Toppan, "Edward Rawson,"
Colonial Society Publications, vol. 7 (1900–1902), pp. 280-295; Morse, "Edward Rawson," p.
124; *Memoir of Edward Rawson*, p. 9. The Reverend Thomas Hooker is given as a near relative in
several sources, but according to genealogist Gary Boyd Roberts, that assertion is not correct.

50   *the pen of John Greenleaf Whittier:* John Greenleaf Whittier, *Leaves from Margaret Smith's Journal . . .*
(Boston: Ticknor, Reed, and Fields, 1849). This work has sparked an unusual blending of fact
and fiction in some subsequent versions of the story of Rebecca Rawson and Thomas Hailes.
Added to this, much of the balance of Rebecca's story is based upon Victorian-era family histories and is difficult to authenticate.

50   *Kentish "Hales" or "Hailes" families:* George E. Cokayne, *Complete Baronetage* (Exeter, England:
William Pollard, 1903), p. 79. Another Hales family in the Kent gentry is found in L. E.
Whatmore, *Recusancy in Kent: Studies and Documents* (1973), pp. 27–28.

51   *both of Peter Thacher's journal entries:* A. K. Teele, ed., *The History of Milton, Mass., 1640 to 1887*
(Boston: Rockwell and Churchill, 1887), p. 642.

51   *some authors have speculated:* Crane, *Rawson Family*, p. 10. Crane's version is drawn from
Sullivan Rawson's 1849 account, which, in turn, is derived from the unlocated family
narrative by Judge Joseph Rawson.

51   *"Being handsomely furnished"*: Crane, *Rawson Family*, p. 10.

52   *In this desolate position*: Ibid.

52   *Theodore Atkinson was deposed*: Massachusetts Archives, vol. 39, p. 647.

52   *Rebecca is said to have left her child*: *Memoir of Edward Rawson*, p. 11.

52   *The effects were particularly devastating*: George R. Clark II, "The Quake That Swallowed a City," *Earth*, April 1995, pp. 34–41.

53   *"The sand in the street"*: Michael Pawson and David Buisseret, *Port Royal, Jamaica* (Oxford, England: Clarendon Press, 1975), p. 120.

53   *A number of New Englanders:* "Thompson-Houghton-Earthquake at Port Royal, 1692," *NEHGR*, vol. 19 (1865), p. 122.

53   *"overflowed by the sea"*: Green, "Diary of Lawrence Hammond," pp. 144–172.

Chapter 7: Wolves in Sheep's Clothing

All quotes herein are from Mather's *A Warning to the Flocks Against Wolves in Sheeps Cloathing* unless otherwise noted.

54   *Recalling a passage:* Burton Stevenson, *The Home Book of Bible Quotations* (New York: Harper & Brothers, 1949), p. 391.

54   *The first "wolf" was Dick Swayn:* Mather, *A Warning to the Flocks,* pp. 17-19.

56   *Born in Wrentham:* John Ward Dean. "Genealogy of the Kingsburys of Dedham, Mass.," *NEHGR*, vol. 16 (1862), pp. 338–339.

56   *In April 1696:* "A Register of Marriages in the Town of Wrentham . . . 1681 to 1724," *NEHGR*, vol. 4 (1850), p. 85.

56   *Some time later Eleazer:* Mather, *A Warning to the Flocks*, pp. 19–20.

57   *"they were almost ready"*: Ibid., p. 21.

57   *Mather's third and final "wolf"*: Mather Diary, vol. 1, p. 313.

59   *Samuel may have been conversant:* Arthur F. Kinney, ed., *Rogues, Vagabonds, & Sturdy Beggars: A New Gallery of Tudor and Early Stuart Rogue Literature Exposing the Lives, Times, and Cozening Tricks of the Elizabethan Underworld* (Barre, Mass.: Imprint Society, 1973), p. 39, and see especially therein, Thomas Dekker's 1608 *Lantern and Candle-light* with its explanation of canting, pp. 214–221.

62   *"Go tell the Church of England men"*: Mather Diary, vol. 1, p. 318.

63   *"He would often watch opportunities"*: Mather, *A Warning to the Flocks*, pp. 47–48.

63   *"Satan being exceedingly enraged"*: Mather Diary, vol. 1, p. 338.

64   *One letter was from John Earle:* Alexander Gordon, *Freedom After Ejection: A Review (1690-1692) of Presbyterian and Congregational Nonconformity in England and Wales* (Manchester, England: University Press, 1917), p. 100.

64   *After committing some "immoralities"*: Mather Diary, vol. 1, pp. 351–352. The identification of Samuel Axel in England remains elusive. One Samuel Axel, son of a deceased husbandman of the same name, of Seavington, St. Mary's Parish, Somerset, was apprenticed to Daniel Stringer of the Feltmakers' Company in London on February 23, 1679/80. London City Apprenticeship Abstracts, 1442–1850, www.englishorigins.com. The alias "Samuel May" may have been inspired by the nonconformist London minister of that name who died there in 1694. See A. G. Mathews, *Calamy Revised* (Oxford, England: Clarendon, 1988), p 346.

Chapter 8: Sign of a Rogue

The main source for the story of Elias Purrington is the Massachusetts Archives, vol. 8, pp. 108-111.

66   *A Scotsman who later established:* Thwing Index reference code 15674.

67   *"On a Saturday night"*: Superior Court of Judicature, case 5050, courtesy of Elizabeth Bouvier. Elizabeth Corbison's deposition she stated that she dispatched her master's "negro servant girl" to find Mr. Campbell—apparently a reference to Elizabeth Domini.

69   *married John Thompson in Boston*: Boston Record Commissioners, vol. 28, p. 78.

Chapter 9: In Prospect of a Fortune

The source for Robert Palmer's story is the *Boston News-Letter,* November 15–22, 1739.

71   *Hoare was the grandson*: *Dictionary of National Biography* (New York: Macmillan Company, 1908), vol. 9., pp. 919–920. See also www.hoaresbank.co.uk/html/history_content.html.

71   *"To: Mr. Draper"*: *Boston News-Letter*, November 15–22, 1739.

72   *"very considerable" bequest*: Ibid., October 18–25, 1739; November 15–22, 1739.

72   *"[Robert Palmer] heard the news:* Ibid., November 15–22, 1739.

74   *"Hearing several vessels were fitting out"*: Ibid.

75   *"He answered, with a grave countenance"*: Ibid.

Chapter 10: Dr. Seth Hudson

The most detailed commentary on Dr. Hudson's exploits in Boston was provided by Ephraim Eliot (1761–1827), who recorded a lengthy anecdote on the subject in one of his commonplace-books. Since Eliot was too young to have been a witness to Hudson's activities, it is likely that this version of events originated with his father, the Reverend Dr. Andrew Eliot. Ephraim Eliot stated that Hudson arrived in Boston in 1762, but the doctor's arrival occurred by 1761. See Morison, "Extracts from the Common-place Books of Ephraim Eliot," pp. 40–43.

78   *The son of Seth Hudson Sr.:* Perry, *Origins in Williamstown*, p. 261. I am especially grateful to Wheaton Hudson for sharing his extensive research files on Dr. Seth Hudson and his family. Genealogists have struggled over the correct identity of the impostor and ascribed the identification to both father (b. about 1703) and son (b. 1728) of the same name. In the absence of conclusive proof, I favor the more conventional identification of the impostor as the individual born in 1728 (i.e., Seth Hudson Jr.). This is based, in part, upon two circumstantial factors: the relatively youthful appearance of the man in the 1762 engraving by Nathaniel Hurd and the greater likelihood that the man who enlisted as a seaman on the *Launceston* in 1762 was then in his mid-thirties rather than his father, a man of almost sixty years of age. Further research on the impostor may help to confirm his true identity.

79   *served as a surgeon:* Perry, *Origins in Williamstown*, pp. 223–224.

79   *Seth's military career:* Ibid., pp. 11, 223–224. Also see Bill to the Province for medical services rendered by Seth Hudson, Doctor, and Commanding Officer of Fort Massachusetts . . . , dated at Boston, April 16, 1757, courtesy of Wheaton Hudson.

79   *"The character he has sustained":* Israel Williams papers, 1728–1785, box 2, at the Massachusetts Historical Society.

79   *Further damaging reports:* Ibid.

80   *In January 1760:* www.pownal.org/PHS/Land/Charter.html citing the New Hampshire State papers.

80   *According to a study:* Information about Howe and other counterfeiters mentioned in this chapter is from Scott, *Counterfeiting in Colonial America*, pp. 222–225.

80   *"traveling for his own amusement":* Morison, "Extracts from the Common-place Books of Ephraim Eliot," pp. 40-43.

81   *"with all his sagacity":* Boyle's Journal of Occurrences, p. 157.

81   *"were very liberal":* Ibid.

81   *"a partner in villainy":* Morison, "Extracts from the Common-place Books of Ephraim Eliot," pp. 40–43.

81   *"On Thursday night last":* *Boston Evening Post*, February 8, 1762.

82   *"procuring and keeping":* Ibid., February 1, 1762.

82   *"too small for the concourse of people":* Ibid., March 8, 1762.

82   *"a very mortifying thing":* Morison, "Extracts from the Common-place Books of Ephraim Eliot," pp. 40–43.

82   *Seth's punishment:* Superior Court of Judicature, Record Book 1760-1762, pp. 315–321. Joshua's punishment of thirty-nine stripes was recorded in the *Boston Evening Post*, March 12, 1762.

82   Seth Hudson and Joshua Howe's punishment at pillory and whipping post was reported in the *Boston Post-Boy*, March 15, 1762. A copy of the broadside is included in the Andrew Eliot Papers, at the Massachusetts Historical Society. The notation mentioned on page 83 may have been by John F. Eliot, who noted his name and address on the verso of the print on April 14, 1822.

83   *noted wit Joseph Green:* Sibley's Harvard Graduates, vol. 8, pp. 42–53; Morison, "Extracts from the Common-place Books of Ephraim Eliot," pp. 40–43.

84   *"The Humble Confession of that NOTORIOUS CHEAT":* Early American Imprints, first series, no. 41274.

84   *"I do therefore affirm":* A Serious-Comical Dialogue Between the Famous Dr. Seth Hudson and the Noted Joshua How, Early American Imprints, first series, no. 41309.

85   *"The famous TOM BELL":* Ibid., p. 20.

86   *HMS Launceston:* Muster book of HMS *Launceston,* from a research report by Roger E. Nixon, London, courtesy of Wheaton Hudson.

86   *in December 1763 he returned:* Scott, *Counterfeiting in Colonial America*, p. 224.

86   *"Lately died of the smallpox":* Boyle's Journal of Occurrences, p. 252.

Chapter 11: Madam Fitch's Treasure Scheme

The story of Miriam Fitch can be found in Boyle's Journal of Occurrences, pp. 160–161. All quotes are from this source unless otherwise noted.

88   *Born in Andover: Vital Records of Andover, Massachusetts* . . . (Topsfield, Mass.: Topsfield Historical Society, 1912), vol. 1, p. 182; vol. 2, p. 158. Also see Clarence Earle Lovejoy, *The Lovejoy Genealogy with Biographies and History, 1460-1930* (C. E. Lovejoy, 1930), p. 58.

88   *Her marriage to Benjamin Fitch: Vital Records of Bedford, Massachusetts* . . . (Boston: New England Historic Genealogical Society, 1903, p. 75.

88   *saw and gristmill:* Louise K. Brown, *Wilderness Town: The Story of Bedford, Massachusetts* (Bedford, Mass., 1967), p. 12. Also see Abram English Brown, *History of Bedford, Middlesex County, Massachusetts* . . . (Bedford, Mass.: Bedford Free Public Library, 1891), p. 50.

89   *had at least nine children: Vital Records of Bedford*, pp. 23–24.

89   *Bacon, a Bedford neighbor:* Thomas W. Baldwin, *Bacon Genealogy: Michael Bacon of Dedham, 1640, and His Descendants* (Cambridge, Mass.: Murray and Emery, 1915), pp. 38–39.

89   *"she could show him a vault":* Boyle's Journal of Occurrences, p. 60. See also Suffolk Files 83626, at Massachusetts State Archives.

90   *"elated with the proposal":* Boyle's Journal of Occurrences, p. 160.

90   *marrying heiress Ann Apthorp:* Thwing Index reference code 2814.

90   *redeeming New Englanders held captive:* Emma Lewis Coleman, *New England Captives Carried to Canada*, 2 vols. (Portland, Me.: Southworth Press, 1925).

90   *The three men then paid:* Boyle's Journal of Occurrences, pp. 160–161.

92   *The court called the pair: Boston Gazette*, January 31, 1763.

92   *He died in 1766:* Thwing Index reference code 15373.

92   *Her estate:* Middlesex County, Mass., probate papers.

Part Three: A Miscellany of Miscreants

93   *merchant John Rowe:* Rowe Diary, p. 149.

94   *"resolved not to go on foot": Boston Evening Post*, February 13, 1738.

95   *she was a "high Jade": Boston Evening Post*, October 13, 1740.

95   *Governor William Shirley:* Proclamation by William Shirley for Apprehending Jabez Allen alias Mead, Early American Imprints, first series, no. 40278.

95   *"Stolen or carried privately": Boston News-Letter*, February 12–19, 1710/11.

96   *"curious ingraven map":* www.mappingboston.com; see also John W. Reps, "Boston by Bostonians: The Printed Plans and Views of the Colonial City by its Artists, Cartographers, Engravers, and Publishers," in *Publications of the Colonial Society of Massachusetts*, vol. 46 (1973), pp. 3–56. In addition, see www.oldprintshop.com.

96   *"gentleman very skillful":* Thwing Index reference code 6372.

96   *Several other skirmishes:* Evarts B. Greene, "The Code of Honor in Colonial and Revolutionary Times, with Special Reference to New England," *Publications of the Colonial Society of Massachusetts*, vol. 26 (Boston, 1927), pp. 371–375 [hereinafter "Code of Honor"]; Sewall Diary, vol. 1, p. 337.

96   *He was almost certainly the Boston merchant:* Thwing Index reference code 49008; Powers, *Crime and Punishment*, p. 412, Anderson, *Great Migration Begins*, vol. 2, p. 909.

97   *"On Friday, the moon being":* "Thomas Lechmere to John Winthrop," *Collections of the Massachusetts Historical Society*, sixth series (Boston: Massachusetts Historical Society, 1892), vol. 5, pp. 256–257; "Code of Honor," pp. 371–375.

97   *"A vessel just now from Annapolis":* "Thomas Lechmere to John Winthrop."

97   *At the time of the duel:* "Code of Honor," p. 372; Thwing Index reference codes 6669-6670.

97   *both Smart and Boydell escaped:* Sewall Diary, p. 913.

97   *This duel is cited:* "Code of Honor," pp. 372–373.

97   *In April 1749:* The story of Robert Hunt is reported in *Boston News-Letter*, April 13, 1749.

98   *More macabre forms of mischief:* The "granado" incident is recorded in Mather Diary, vol. 2, pp. 657–658; Winslow, *A Destroying Angel*, p. 56.

98   *"malicious design":* Boston Record Commissioners, vol. 20, pp. 24–25.

98   *"catalogue of young men":* Mather Diary, vol. 2, p. 235.

99   *one of the town's bawdiest women:* Stevens, *Notorious & Notable New Englanders*, pp. 156–161. See also V. C. Sanborn, "The Kirtland or Kirkland Family, *NEHGR*, vol. 48 (1894), pp. 68–69. Records for Alice at the King's Arm Tavern are in Thwing Index reference code 57481.

99   *"frequent, secret, and unseasonable entertainment":* Powers, *Crime and Punishment*, pp. 179, 231.

99   *"whipped through the street":* Ibid.

99   *"day work program":* Ibid., p. 231.

100   *"that for two pints of wine":* Suffolk Files, 2161; courtesy of Michelle Morris.

100   *Hannah Hounsell became pregnant:* Superior Court of Judicature, vol. 43, p. 864.

101   *Shopkeeper Dorcas Pringle Griffiths:* Frank W. C. Hersey. "The Misfortunes of Dorcas Griffiths," *Publications of the Colonial Society of Massachusetts* (Boston, 1937–1942), vol. 34, pp. 13–25.

101   *David Wallis fatally stabbed:* Hearn, *Legal Executions in New England,* p. 112.

101   *William Franklin was found guilty:* Ibid., p. 11.

102   *"evangelical fanfare":* Ibid., p. 125.

102   *Sarah, the seventh child:* Thwing Index reference code 57826.

102   *"rash wishes" and "mad passions":* Mather, *Pillars of Salt,* pp. 107–108.

102   *His tiny body:* Hearn, *Legal Executions in New England,* p. 106.

102   *Savage, the thirty-year-old son:* Lawrence Park, "Old Boston Families, Number Three: The Savage Family," *NEHGR,* vol. 67 (1913), pp. 205, 210–211; Thwing Index reference code 53801.

102   *"Thomas Savage junior, shopkeeper":* Sewall Diary, vol. 1, p. 399.

102   *"crimes of unchastity":* Mather, *Pillars of Salt,* pp. 107–108.

102   *After being subjected:* Sewall Diary, vol. 1, p. 400.

103   *hanged before the masses:* Superior Court of Judicature, vol. 2, pp. 199–200.

103   *within three years he began to serve:* Park, "Old Boston Families . . . The Savage Family."

103   *Rebecca was a . . . domestic servant:* Thwing Index reference code 14934. See also Hearn, *Legal Executions in New England,* pp. 124–125.

103   *"house of offal or shithouse":* Walker Diary.

104   *"concealing the birth":* Superior Court of Judicature, case 35693.

105   *John and Ann Richardson endeavored:* Suffolk Files, vol. 5, case 100378.

105   *the couple was sentenced:* Superior Court of Judicature, 1764–1765, pp. 124–125.

105   *"pelted him which was what he deserved":* Rowe Diary, p. 65.

Chapter 12: Carrying the King Away

107   *the King's commissioners:* Thwing, *Crooked & Narrow Streets,* p. 62.

107   *Arthur had expected:* Hutchinson, *History of the Massachusetts-Bay,* pp. 217–219.

108   *Knight of the Royal Oak: Illustrative of the Topography and History of New and Old Sleaford . . .* (Sleaford, England: James Creasey, 1825), pp. 113–114.

108   *"very weak understanding":* George Edward Cockayne, ed., *Complete Baronetage, 1611–162* (Exeter, England: William Pollard, 1900), vol. 1, p. 59.

108   *"Mason replied, that he thought":* This extract and the excerpts in the following paragraph are from Hutchinson, *History of the Massachusetts-Bay,* p. 218.

108   *another witness, Nicholas Paige:* Noble, *Records of the Court of Assistants,* vol. 3, p. 188.

108   *"heat of discourse":* Suffolk Files, vol. 8, p. 791.

109   *"in solemn manner":* Noble, *Records of the Court of Assistants,* vol. 3, p. 188.

110   *"I spoke unto him":* Suffolk Files, vol. 10, p. 986.

110   *petitioned the Court of Assistants:* Noble, *Records of the Court of Assistants,* vol. 3, p. 188.

110   *"highborn lady":* Lillian B. Miller, "The Puritan Portrait: Its Function in Old and New England," in Hall, *Seventeenth-Century New England,* p. 155.

110   *"the flower of Boston":* Dunton, *The Life and Errors of John Dunton.*

111   *"I remember once":* John Dunton, *John Dunton's Letters From New-England* (Boston: Prince Society, 1867), vol. 4, pp. 90–91.

Chapter 13: Death on the Common

Much of the material in this chapter is from Shaw, "The Woodbridge-Phillips Duel," pp. 239–242, and Sargent, *Dealings with the Dead,* vol. 2, pp. 557–559, 561–562, 564, 565. Background information about Henry Phillips is from *Sibley's Harvard Graduates,* vol. 7, pp. 424–429.

113   *Henry was the last-born:* Thwing Index reference codes 2604, 49486.

113   *richly furnished with desks:* Henry Phillips inventory dated October 12, 1730, Phillips Collection, Harvard Law School Library; an undated memorandum ca. 1732 by Gillam Phillips to Samuel Sewall, James Pemberton, and Joseph Marrion offering a partial inventory of his brother's estate, in the papers of the Samuel Phillips Savage Collection at the Massachusetts Historical Society.

113   *His bride was Mary Faneuil: Dictionary of American Biography* (New York: Charles Scribner's Sons, 1931), vol. 6, pp. 262–263; Abram English Brown, *Faneuil Hall and Faneuil Hall Market or Peter Faneuil and His Gift* (Boston: Lee and Shepard, 1900), pp. 56–64.

114   *Henry had a reputation: Sibley's Harvard Graduates,* vol. 7, p. 424.

114   *"for three weeks or a month":* Shaw, "The Woodbridge-Phillips Duel." pp. 239–242.

114   *Robert Handy, the so-called vile fellow:* Unless noted otherwise, specific details about the evening are from Sargent, *Dealings with the Dead,* vol. 2, pp. 557–559, 561–562, 564, 565.

116   *Henry had some minor injuries:* Walker Diary.
116   *"endeavored to appease him":* Henry Phillips Collection, item one, Special Collections Department, Harvard Law School Library.
118   *"beyond the powder house":* Walker Diary.
118   *In the morning the council:* Sibley's Harvard Graduates, vol. 7, p. 426.
118   *"Whereas a barbarous murder":* This excerpt as well as the one in the following paragraph are from *Boston News-Letter,* July 8, 1728.
118   *"decently and handsomely":* Sargent, *Dealings with the Dead,* p. 553.
119   *These sentiments culminated . . . in a paper:* After missing for more than a century, the attestation in favor of Henry Phillips is now held in the Phillips Collection at the Harvard Law School Library, item three.
121   *"[A]bout three o'clock":* Sibley's Harvard Graduates, vol. 7, p. 428. Two dates of death (May 29, 1729, and July 17, 1730) have been ascribed to Henry Phillips, but I agree with the editors of the aforementioned source that the correct date must have been the earlier of the two.
121   *In an interesting postscript:* Sibley's Harvard Graduates, vol. 7, p. 428; see Robert C. Winthrop, "Case of Phillips vs. Savage," *Massachusetts Historical Society Proceedings, 1860–1862,* pp. 65–80.
121   *"so hardy and wicked":* The Charter Granted by Their Majesties King William and Queen Mary to the Inhabitants of the Province of the Massachusetts-Bay . . . [bound as *Massachusetts Laws, 1692–1753*] (Boston: Samuel Kneeland and Timothy Green, 1742), pp. 274–275.
121   *One of the last known duels:* Ayer, *Boston Common,* p. 17.

Chapter 14: Heiresses Abducted
Much of the information in this chapter comes from the *Boston News-Letter,* September 16–23, 1736.

122   *the Clan Chattan, a federation:* Ronald MacDonald Douglas, *The Scots Book of Lore and Folklore* (New York: Beekman House, 1982), p. 187.
123   *Mackintoshes of Borlum in Inverness:* Alexander M. Mackintosh, *The Mackintoshes and Clan Chattan* (Edinburgh: James Skinner, 1903), p. 383. Information about the girls' paternal grandfather is from *Dictionary of National Biography* (New York: Macmillan, 1909), vol. 12, pp. 621–623.
124   *Lachlan was the heir:* www.myclan.com/clans/MacKintosh.
124   *he wed his great-uncle Henry's daughter:* Information about Lachlan's and Elizabeth's marriage and the birth of their daughters is from James N. Arnold, *Vital Record of Rhode Island, 1636–1850,* First Series . . . , vol. 6 (Providence, R.I.: Narragansett Historical Publishing, 1894), p. 90.
124   *Elizabeth married again:* Boston Record Commissioners, vol. 28, p. 160.
124   *In his will he directed:* Bristol County probate records, vol. 5, pp. 193–194; Edward Doubleday Harris, *The New-England Royalls* (Boston: David Clapp & Son, 1885), pp. 22–24.
125   *Within a year of their grandfather's death:* H. L. Peter Rounds, *Abstracts of Bristol County, Massachusetts Probate Records, 1687–1745* (Baltimore: Genealogical Publishing Company, 1987), p. 163.
125   *"an education suitable":* Bristol County probate records, vol. 7, pp. 46–48.
125   *The girls supposedly had a strongly unfavorable reaction:* Hoover, *The Elegant Royalls,* p. 25.
126   *When the girls rejected his offer:* Mackintosh, *The Mackintoshes and Clan Chattan,* p. 383. According to A. M. Mackintosh, after Lachlan Mackintosh's death, Shaw "appears to have assumed possession of the Badenoch estate . . . , which, not being destined to heirs-male, ought to have passed to his infant nieces in North America."
126   *"Scottish law-books are crowded":* Sir Walter Scott, *Manners, Customs, and History of the Highlanders of Scotland* (originally published 1816; New York: Barnes and Noble, repr. 2004), p. 51.
127   *"seized and taken up":* Boston News-Letter, September 16–23, 1736.
128   *"very uncommon, bold and violent attempt":* Boston News-Letter, October 28–November 4, 1736.
128   *Boston diarist Benjamin Walker Jr.:* Walker Diary.
129   *"a young lady of great merit and fortune":* Harris, *The New-England Royalls,* pp. 22–24; Jones, *The Loyalists of Massachusetts,* pp. 249–250; Drake, *Historic Mansions and Highways,* pp. 119–130.
129   *"handsome collation":* Boston Gazette, November 19–26, 1739.

Chapter 15: Villainous Papers
130   *The first directed Wells:* Schutz, *Legislators of the Massachusetts General Court,* p. 374.
130   *"execrable villainy":* Andrew McFarland Davis, "Threat to Burn Down Governor Shirley's House." *Colonial Society Publications* (1900), vol. 3, pp. 207–210, and Superior Court of Judicature, Record 1747–1750, folio 301, Massachusetts State Archives, courtesy of Elizabeth Bouvier.
131   *"soldiers who had not been equably compensated":* John A. Schutz, *William Shirley: King's Governor of Massachusetts* (Chapel Hill, N.C.: University of North Carolina Press, 1961), p. 149.

131   *Wells was an ordained minister:* Franklin Bowditch Dexter, *Biographical Sketches of the Graduates of Yale College* . . . (New York: Henry Holt and Company, 1885), pp. 71–73.

131   *"We are three gentlemen":* Davis, "Threat to Burn Down," All quotes from the letter to Shirley are from this source but have been edited for clarity. Shirley's house is today known as the Shirley-Eustis House. A Georgian mansion built 1747–1751, it is considered the only remaining country house in America built by a British Royal Governor. See www.shirleyeustishouse.org.

134   *by the end of December 1749:* Superior Court of Judicature, Record 1747–1750, folio 301.

135   *Samuel Wells died at the age of eighty:* Dexter, *Biographical Sketches,* pp. 71–72.

Chapter 16: Murder by Arsenic

A version of this chapter appeared as "Murder in Colonial Boston: The Ill-fated Greenleaf Children and Their Portraits," in *New England Ancestors,* vol. 1 (2000), pp. 11–15; vol. 2 (2001), pp. 17–19.

136   *"My dear Mrs. Rockefeller":* Letter from Katrina Kipper, Accord, Mass., to Abby Aldrich Rockefeller, courtesy of the Abby Aldrich Rockefeller Folk Art Museum (AARFAM).

136   *Dr. John Greenleaf, a Boston apothecary: Sibley's Harvard Graduates,* vol. 4, pp. 472–476. For more about the Greenleaf family, see William S. Appleton, "The Greenleaf Ancestry," *NEHGR,* vol. 38 (1884), p. 299.

137   *He was . . . an active parishioner:* William P. Lunt. *Discourse Delivered in the First Congregational Church . . . Following the Death of Hon. Thomas Greenleaf* (Boston: Little, Brown, and Company, 1854), p. 25; Theodore Thomte, ed., *James Henry Stark's Antique Views of Boston* (Boston: Burdette and Company, 1967), pp. 36–37.

137   *Dr. Greenleaf's brother William: Sibley's Harvard Graduates,* vol. 4, pp. 472–476.

137   *"a cocked hat":* Allen C. Clark, *Greenleaf and Law in the Federal City* (Washington, D.C., 1901), p. 10.

138   *"quaintness and a naïve and piquant charm":* Curator work sheet ABB 7/76, on accession number 37.100.4, AARFAM.

138   *Portraits of all three children:* The portraits by Copley of the Greenleaf children must have been posthumous. Copley expert Jules David Prown originally dated the portraits as 1755–1758, but in a letter dated February 21, 1989, stated that 1753–1754 would be a more suitable revised date for this group. Courtesy of Zachary Ross, Hirschl & Adler Galleries.

138   *"putting ratsbane several times": Boston News-Letter,* January 17, 1751.

138   *"wretched creature . . . acknowledged":* Ibid.

139   *"about fifteen months old": Boston Evening Post,* January 21, 1751.

139   *oldest child's manner of death:* Lunt, *Discourse Delivered . . . Following the Death of Hon. Thomas Greenleaf.*

141   *[Phyllis] wishing to go to the Boston Common":* Alfred Frankenstein, "Copley Portraits—The Story of the Children," unidentified San Francisco newspaper clipping, ca. 1971. Courtesy of Zachary Ross, Hirschl & Adler Galleries.

141   *Phyllis pleaded guilty:* Suffolk Files 67676.

141   *Phyllis's own mother died suddenly: Boston News-Letter,* April 11, 1751.

141   *A Greenleaf family history:* Jonathan Greenleaf, *A Genealogy of the Greenleaf Family* (New York Edward O. Jenkins, 1854), p. 9; James Edward Greenleaf, comp., *Genealogy of the Greenleaf Family* (Boston: Frank Wood, 1896), pp. 207, 210.

142   *"poisoned with laudanum":* Lawrence Park, "Joseph Badger of Boston, and His Portraits of Children," *Old-Time New England: The Bulletin of the Society for the Preservation of New England Antiquities,* vol. 13 (January 1923), pp. 99–109.

142   *"It is a complete fiction":* Alfred Frankenstein, "American Paintings by John Singleton Copley: Exhibition Review," *American Art Review,* November–December 1975, pp. 145–152.

Chapter 17: An Impudent Woman

The main source for this chapter is Earle, *Diary of Anna Green Winslow.*

143   *"Dear Mamma":* Earle, *Diary of Anna Green Winslow,* p. 36.

143   *Anna Green Winslow was born:* Ibid., pp. iii–xx, 75.

145   *Whatever the relationship: Boston Records Commissioners,* vol. 23, p. 49; Thwing, *Crooked & Narrow Streets,* p. 222.

145   *Some of the gossip: Sibley's Harvard Graduates,* vol. 14, pp. 31–48.

145   *"no sooner was the 29th Regiment encamped":* Earle, *Diary of Anna Green Winslow,* p. 36.

145   *Unwelcomed by the local citizenry:* Hiller B. Zobel, *The Boston Massacre* (New York: W. W. Norton, 1970); www.bostonmassacre.net.

145   *Peter Sigourney and his wife:* Thwing Index reference code 54656; Henry H. W. Sigourney, *Genealogy of the Sigourney Family* (Boston: James Munroe, 1857), p. 10.

146   *she was sentenced to twenty stripes:* Superior Court of Judicature, 1771, reel 15, p. 41; Hull, *Female Felons,* p. 113.

146　*"The large whipping-post"*: Scudder, *Recollections of Samuel Breck*, pp. 36–37.

146　*Betty's "next adventure"*: Earle, *Diary of Anna Green Winslow*, p. 36.

146　*The brick workhouse building:* Thwing, *Crooked & Narrow Streets*, p. 223.

147　*Betty's most recent "pilferings"*: Superior Court of Judicature, 1772, p. 39.

147　*"about two months agone"*: Earle, *Diary of Anna Green Winslow*, p. 36.

147　*"from whence . . . 'tis said"*: Boston Gazette, February 2, 1767, by courtesy of J. L. Bell.

147　*"The large, elegant new stone gaol"*: Boyle's Journal of Occurrences, pp. 257–258.

147　*"I heard somebody say"*: Earle, *Diary of Anna Green Winslow*, pp. 36–37.

149　*"dispose of her in service"*: Superior Court of Judicature, 1772, p. 39.

149　*"behaved with great impudence"*: Earle, *Diary of Anna Green Winslow*, p. 65.

149　*Anna recorded having danced a minuet:* Ibid., p. xix.

Chapter 18: Piracy on the High Seas

A version of this chapter appeared in *New England Ancestors,* vol. 6 (2005), pp. 17–21. See also Butterfield, *Diary and Autobiography of John Adams,* vol. 2, pp. 69–70; Wroth and Zobel, *Legal Papers of John Adams,* vol. 2, pp. 335–340, case 57, *Rex. v. Nickerson.* Special thanks to Hiller Zobel for sharing his expertise in this case, and to J. L. Bell for offering a host of valuable suggestions. I am grateful also to Diane Rapaport and Martha Bustin for their helpful comments.

150　*"the most surprising event"*: Boston Evening Post, August 3, 1773.

151　*the son of Ansel and Bathsheba Nickerson:* Pauline Wixon Derick et al., *The Nickerson Family: The Descendants of William Nickerson, 1604-1689, First Settler of Chatham, Massachusetts, Part III* (Nickerson Family Association, 1976, pp. 336–337.

151　*a practical consideration in mind:* Wroth and Zobel, *Adams Legal Papers,* vol. 2, p. 347.

151　*Ansell's version of the gory events:* Communication from J. L. Bell, October 6, 2004.

152　*They broke open chests and boxes:* Boston Evening Post, November 23, 1772; Wroth and Zobel, *Adams Legal Papers,* vol. 2, p. 347.

152　*"all stained with blood"*: Wroth and Zobel, *Adams Legal Papers,* vol. 2, p. 347.

152　*Bacon went to Chatham:* Boston Evening Post, November 23, 1772.

153　*"the conversation of the town and country"*: Butterfield, *Diary and Autobiography of John Adams,* vol. 2, p. 69, which indicates that the date for this entry may have actually been November 27, 1772.

153　*public suspicion began to fall upon a king's schooner:* Hutchinson, *History of the Massachusetts-Bay,* pp. 300–302.

155　*"The Governour, Lieut Govr"*: Wroth and Zobel, *Adams Legal Papers,* vol. 2, p. 338n.

155　*large armed schooner that had left Boston:* Hutchinson, *History of the Massachusetts-Bay,* p. 301.

155　*"It is thought that Ansel Nickerson"*: Derick, *Nickerson Family,* p. 336.

155　*The court was scheduled to reconvene:* Wroth and Zobel, *Adams Legal Papers,* vol. 2, p. 338.

155　*"money being found"*: Ibid.

155　*"often visited in prison"*: Hutchinson, *History of the Massachusetts-Bay,* p. 302.

155　*Nickerson had "requested my assistance"*: Butterfield, *Diary and Autobiography of John Adams,* vol. 3, p. 297.

155　*The note promised Adams payment:* The Adams Papers, Letters Received and Other Loose papers, 1767-July 1775, reel 344, at the Massachusetts Historical Society.

156　*"send the prisoner to England"*: Hutchinson, *History of the Massachusetts-Bay,* p. 301.

156　*"Conduct after he came ashore"*: Wroth and Zobel, *Adams Legal Papers,* vol. 2, pp. 335–340.

156　*"murders would also have to be proved"*: Butterfield, *Diary and Autobiography of John Adams,* vol. 2, p. 70.

156　*"escaped punishment of a murder"*: Hutchinson, *History of the Massachusetts-Bay,* p. 302.

156　*"After nearly ten months"*: Boston Evening Post, August 3, 1773.

156　*The Following Circumstances:* Paper loss on the broadside owned by the Historical Society of Pennsylvania prevents further intelligence of its account of William Kent Jr.

158　*"I have heard nothing of him"*: Butterfield, *Diary and Autobiography of John Adams,* vol. 3, p. 297.

160　*Ansell allegedly confessed:* Nickerson family records.

160　*he was lost at sea:* William C. Smith, *A History of Chatham, Massachusetts . . .* (Chatham, Mass.: Chatham Historical Society, 1947), p. 332n.

Chapter 19: Tempted by the Devil

The main source for Levi Ames's story is his autobiographical "speech" presented on pages 169–176.

161　*His young life:* Rowe Diary, p. 252; Hearn, *Legal Executions,* pp. 154–155.

162　*Levi suffered jail time:* Ezekiel Russell, *A Prospective View of Death Being A solemn Warning to inconsiderate Youth occasioned by the Trial and Condemnation of Levi Ames . . .* (American Antiquarian Society, 1773).

162　*Among his victims:* Henry Bond, *Genealogies of the Families and Descendants of the Early Settlers of Watertown, Massachusetts . . .* (Boston: New England Historic Genealogical Society, 1860), pp. 199, 271.

162   *they turned cattle into his cornfield:* Boyle's Journal of Occurrences, p. 360.
162   *Abraham Merriam told him where to find some money:* Charles Hudson. *History of the Town of Lexington, Middlesex County, Massachusetts* . . . (Boston: Wiggin and Lunt, 1868), pp. 138, 140, 213.
162   *Jonas Clarke . . . visited Levi in prison:* Sibley's Harvard Graduates, vol. 13, pp. 209–216.
163   *What might have become Levi's most legendary crime:* Unless otherwise noted, quotations from Levi Ames here and throughout are from *The Last Words and Dying Speech of Levi Ames.*
163   *The break-in . . . took place:* Massachusetts Supreme Judicial Court, case 102314.
164   *"They went over to Charlestown together":* A Prospective View of Death.
165   *"This is for watching me":* Ibid.
165   *"guilty in part":* Ibid.
165   *whipping of twenty stripes:* Boyle's Journal of Occurrences," p. 366.
165   *"the unhappy person under sentence of death":* Ibid.
166   *"Let no idle Eye":* The dying Penitent, or affecting Speech of Levi Ames, Taken from his Mouth, as Delivered by him at the Goal in Boston the morning of his Execution.
166   *At least eleven broadsides:* Nine broadsides on Levi Ames are listed in the checklist of Massachusetts broadsides published in Ford, *Broadsides, Ballads,* pp. 223–225. Two additional publications were *A Prospective View of Death* and *The Dying Penitent.*
169   *The last WORDS and Dying SPEECH of Levi Ames,* Early American Imprints, first series, no. 42401.

Part Four: Family Skeletons, Dangerous Liaisons, and Black Sheep
177   *"The proper Bostonian":* Amory, *The Proper Bostonians,* pp. 16–17.
177   *Female descendants of Governor Thomas Dudley:* Watson, *Governor Thomas Dudley,* p. 13.
178   *"Mr. Stoughton also told me of George Carr's wife":* Sewall Diary, vol. 1, p. 70.
178   *Anne was fined twenty shillings:* Robert E. Moody, ed., *Province and Court Records of Maine* (Portland: Maine Historical Society, 1947), vol. 3, pp. 273–274.
178   *"Mrs. Mercy Wade sends her complaint":* Sewall Diary, vol. 2, pp. 690–691.
178   *One possible cause of conflict:* D. Brenton Simons, "The Journal of Jonathan Willis," vol. 157 (2003), NEHGR, p. 330.
179   *Dorothy Dunster Page . . . "absconded":* Boston Evening Post, February 26, 1739.
179   *In the summer of 1645:* Winthrop's journal entries from that period are on pages pp. 609–611.
180   *"Henry Dawson was summarily cast out":* Richard D. Pierce, ed., *The Records of the First Church in Boston, 1630-1868,* Colonial Society of Massachusetts Publications, vol. 39, pp. 44–46.
181   *Sam and Rebecca started their marriage:* An excellent treatment of the marital saga is presented in Graham, *Puritan Family Life,* pp. 185–194.
181   *"went to Boston intending to live at my father's":* Sewall Diary, vol. 2, p. 705n.
181   *Rebecca gave birth to an illegitimate son:* Ibid., p. 840.
181   *The conversation appears to have been one-sided:* Information in this paragraph is from Sewall's Diary, vol. 2, p. 836.
181   *"Mrs. Sewall of Brookline":* Ibid., p. 840.
182   *"chargeable to his estate":* Ibid., p. 860.
182   *"my wife came to see me":* Ibid., p. 705.
182   *Sam's horse carried him back to Brookline:* Ibid.
182   *a son, Henry, was born:* Sibley's Harvard Graduates, vol. 10, pp. 318–320.
182   *"an exceedingly wicked fellow":* Mather Diary, vol. 2, p. 349.
182   *"a noble to nine-pence":* Ibid., p. 410.
182   *"God smote the wretch":* Ibid., p. 350.
182   *One of the town's most sensational cases:* Laurel Thatcher Ulrich, "Big Dig, Little Dig, Hidden Worlds: Boston," *www.common-place.org,* vol. 3, no. 4, July 2003. See also Noble, *Court of Assistants,* vol. 1, p. 32; vol. 3, pp. 224–226, 252–253.
183   *An equally scandalous case:* The Fairservice cases are found in Superior Court of Judicature, cases 129749 and 129756; see also Thwing Index reference code 20457. A Hannah Stockbridge was warned out of Boston in 1759; see Roger D. Joslyn, "Descendants of John[1] Stockbridge," NEHGR, vol. 135 (1981), p. 122.
185   *"greatly abused and evil treated her":* For the Barron-Ayer divorce case, see Suffolk Files, 94:129779.
186   *Adam Ayer apparently married:* Mary Kent Davey Babcock, "Christ Church, Boston, Records," NEHGR, vol. 100 (1946), p. 304.
186   *"Whereas Elizabeth Nottage":* Boston News-Letter, January 4–January 11, 1728.
186   *"a regular Sargeant called Taylor":* Boston News-Letter, December 4, 1760.
187   *Jane Eustis, as she was known:* Manuscript Book of Divorces, Supreme Judicial Court, Suffolk County, Massachusetts, p. 4; also listed in George Elliott Howard, *A History of Matrimonial*

Institutions . . .,Volume Two (Chicago: University of Chicago Press, 1904), p. 342, courtesy of Georgia Brady Barnhill, American Antiquarian Society.

187 *In 1761, the year after her divorce:* Boston News-Letter, February 12, 1761; Rowe Diary, p. 214.

188 *Martha Coggan:* The primary source for Martha's story is a letter from Rev. John Davenport's to John Winthrop Jr. See *Collections of the Massachusetts Historical Society,* vol. 10, third series. Boston: Massachusetts Historical Society, 1849, pp. 44–45.

188 *On October 24, 1660:* "Abstracts of the Earliest Wills in Suffolk County, Mass.," NEHGR, vol. 31 (1877), p. 107.

189 *One of Boston's most notable jilting cases:* A complete account of Samuel Walker's story is given in Sally Dean Hamblen Hill, "The Jilting of Samuel Walker, Mariner, of Boston," NEHGR, vol. 157 (2003), pp. 355–360.

Chapter 20: By the Strength of His Affections

The story of Richard Bellingham's controversial marriage is in the Winthrop Journal, p. 367. All quotes are from this source unless otherwise noted.

191 *Bellingham arrived in Massachusetts Bay:* Anderson, *Great Migration Begins,* vol. 1, pp. 243–250.

192 *Richard Bellingham died in 1762:* Ibid., pp. 246–247.

Chapter 21: The Madness of Mistress Hopkins

The principal sources of this story are the Winthrop Journal, p. 570, and Mather, *Magnalia Christi Americana,* p. 249.

194 *he became warden of the fleet:* American National Biography (New York: Oxford University Press, 1999), vol. 11, pp. 169–170.

194 *London merchant Theophilus Eaton:* Charles Hervey Townshend, "Yale pedigree," NEHGR, vol. 53 (1902), p. 82.

194 *"driven to the verge of insanity":* Henry B. Hoff, "Lloyd-Yale-Eaton Royal Descent," *The American Genealogist,* vol. 52 (1976), p.144, citing the *Dictionary of National Biography* and *The Papers of the New Haven Colony Historical Society.*

195 *The couple arrived in Boston in 1637:* American National Biography, vol. 11, pp. 169–170.

195 *David Yale, then a "thriving" merchant:* Thwing index reference code 62872; Rodney Horace Yale, *Yale Genealogy . . .* (Beatrice, Nebr.: Milburn & Scott, 1908), pp. 96–100.

195 *"[She] was fallen into a sad infirmity":* Winthrop Journal, p. 570.

197 *After returning to England:* American National Biography, vol. 11, pp. 169–170.

197 *"presently dropped in pieces":* Mather, *Magnalia Christi Americana,* p. 252.

197 *Ann died more than thirty years later:* Yale, *Yale Genealogy,* p. 100.

Chapter 22: Heiresses Adrift

The most comprehensive treatment of Anna Keayne's story is found in Morgan, "A Boston Heiress and Her Husbands: A True Story," *Publication of the Colonial Society of Massachusetts,* vol. 34 (Boston, 1943), pp. 499–513.

198 *"irregular prophesying":* Dunkle, *Records of the Churches of Boston,* records 2350–2359.

198 *Sarah's daughter, Anna Keayne:* Morgan, "A Boston Heiress."

199 *"My she-cousin Keayne":* Anderson, *Great Migration Begins,* vol. 1, p. 587. See also Robert Charles Anderson, John C. Brandon, and Paul C. Reed, "The Ancestry of the Royally-Descended Mansfields of the Massachusetts Bay," NEHGR, vol. 155 (2001), pp. 28–29.

199 *By early 1646 or 1647:* Suffolk Deeds, vol. 1, item 83.

199 *"[A]s you desire":* Ibid.

199 *"all her goods miscarried":* Gurdon's letter is cited in Anderson, *Great Migration Begins,* vol. 1, p. 587.

200 *"irregular prophesying":* Dunkle, *Records of the Churches of Boston,* records 2279–2283.

200 *Sarah was noted in the church records:* Ibid, records 2350–2359.

200 *Rogers considered the action a "weighty business":* Anderson, *Great Migration Begins,* vol. 1, p. 587.

200 *the old governor's beneficiaries:* "Abstracts of the Earliest Wills upon Record in the County of Suffolk, Mass.," NEHGR, vol. 5 (1851), pp. 295–297.

200 *"receiving Mrs. Pacey into his house":* Boston Record Commissioners, vol. 2, p. 120.

200 *"to save the town from all charges":* Ibid., p. 124.

200 *Sarah died intestate:* Watson, *Governor Thomas Dudley,* p. 6.

200 *Among Sarah's possessions:* Suffolk Probate Records, 227, Sarah Pacy inventory.

201 *His massive, 158-page will:* Bailyn, *The Apologia of Robert Keayne.*

201 *"cast away herself":* Morgan, "A Boston Heiress."

201 *Keayne advised Anna:* Bailyn, *Robert Keayne,* pp. 65–66.

202 *The circumstances of how they met:* Morgan, "A Boston Heiress."

206   *Edward Lane conveyed his property:* Thwing Index reference code 62389.
207   *"weary of this eternal squabble":* Morgan, "A Boston Heiress."
207   *the legacy "not be thrown away":* Ibid.
207   *As their son had died:* See Jeremy Dupertuis Bangs, "The Grave of Edward Paige of Boston, 1680," *New England Ancestors*, vol. 5 (Winter 2004), pp. 52–53.

Chapter 23: Reversal of Fortune

Sources for this chapter include Leslie Mahler, "The English Origin of Rebecca Crooke, Wife of Peter Gardner of Roxbury, Massachusetts," *NEHGR*, vol. 159 (2005), pp. 40–42; Edgar Francis Waterman and Donald Lines Jacobus, comps., *The Granberry Family and Allied Families . . .* (Hartford, Conn.: Edgar F. Waterman, 1945), p. 298 [hereinafter *Granberry Family*]; and Mary Walton Ferris, *Dawes-Gates Ancestral Lines . . .* (privately printed, 1943), vol. 1, pp. 309–310. Conclusive proof of Ruth Crooke Read's parentage has not been established, but I believe it is likely she was the daughter of Roger Crooke and the sister of Rebecca Crooke Gardner.

209   *When . . . Roger Crooke died:* Elizabeth French, "Genealogical Research in England," *NEHGR*, vol. 63 (1909), pp. 279–280. See also *Granberry Family*, p. 298; Ferris, *Dawes-Gates*, pp. 309–310.
209   *The first record of Ruth Crooke:* "Early Records of Boston," *NEHGR*, vol. 10 (1856), p. 224.
209   *In due course Ruth gave birth:* Noble, *Court of Assistants*, p. 10.
209   *he wrote to Ruth with "great respect and affection":* Massachusetts Archives, vol. 9, p. 98.
210   *"bringing up of a child":* Ibid.
210   *"brought to the bar to answer":* Noble, *Court of Assistants*, p. 10.
210   *The Court of Assistants found Ruth guilty:* Ibid.
211   *William Read soon thereafter disappeared from Boston records:* *Granberry Family*, p. 298.
211   *During the affair in England:* The Great Migration, vol. 3, pp. 568–573. For more details of Augustin Lyndon's fourth marriage, see Massachusetts Archives, vol. 9, p. 94–97.
212   *"what hath been charged":* Records of the Suffolk County Court, vol. 1, p. 439
212   *"poor, desolate, and distressed condition":* Shurtleff, *Records of the Massachusetts Bay*, vol. 5, pp. 248–249.
212   *In early 1674:* Records of the Suffolk County Court, vol. 1, p. 556–557.
213   *"uncomfortable and miserable condition":* Massachusetts Archives, vol. 9, p. 88.
213   *"set her at liberty":* Patricia E. Kane, *Colonial Massachusetts Silversmiths and Jewelers* (New Haven: Yale University Art Gallery, 1998), pp. 879–880.
213   *Mary sought clarification:* Shurtleff, *Records of the Massachusetts Bay*, vol. 5, pp. 248–249, 280.
213   *Augustin made bequests:* Will of Augustin Lyndon, Shipwright, PROB 11/452, image reference 80/71, www.documentsonline.pro.gov.uk; John Osborne Austin, *Genealogical Dictionary of Rhode Island; Comprising Three Generations of Settlers Who Came Before 1690 . . .* (Albany: J. Munsell's Sons, 1887), p. 340.

Chapter 24: Bigamy in Boston

This story is derived from Suffolk files, case 3766, Massachusetts State Archives. I wish to thank Henry B. Hoff for identifying and sharing this case with me. For their assistance, I also gratefully acknowledge Helen S. Ullmann and Jerome E. Anderson. The title "Bigamy in Boston" is suggested by an unpublished article on a different case by Jeremy Dupertuis Bangs. A version of this story appeared as "Bigamy in Boston: The Case of Mathew Cary and Mary Sylvester," *NEHGR*, vol. 159 (2005), pp. 5–11, and is reproduced here with permission of the New England Historic Genealogical Society (www.NewEnglandAncestors.org).

214   *daughter of a prominent New York family:* Details of the Sylvester family history here and elsewhere are from Henry B. Hoff, "The Sylvester Family of Shelter Island," *The New York Genealogical and Biographical Record*, vol. 125 (1994), pp. 13–18.
214   *provincial authorities entrusted Matthew Cary:* William B. Trask, "Instructions to Matthew Cary About Bringing Prisoners from Canada; Information Obtained by Him in Quebec, and Lists of the Prisoners Redeemed and Left in Canada—1695," *NEHGR* vol. 24 (1870), pp. 286–291.
214   *legislative softening of the colony's laws:* The Acts and Resolves, Public and Private, of the Province of the Massachusetts Bay (Boston: Wright & Potter, 1869–1922), vol. 1, pp. 353–354.
214   *Some details of Matthew Cary's life:* Sewall Diary, vol. 1, p. 360; John A. Garraty and Mark C. Carnes, eds., *American National Biography* (New York: Oxford University Press, 1999), vol. 17, pp. 457–458.
215   *In the single surviving letter:* The year 1692 is not given in the letter but is implied by the timeline of events.
215   *"The lord is pleased":* Suffolk files, case 3766, fifth paper.
216   *"I hear Mr. Carey has reported":* Suffolk files, case 3766, sixth paper.

217 *"Sir, my sorrow is great":* Ibid., seventh paper.

217 *"I think it too little for me":* Ibid., sixth paper.

217 *Giles gathered various depositions:* Suffolk files, case 3766, first paper, first item. The Houses's deposition was witnessed by Captain Thomas Cobbet of Newcastle, New Hampshire, and William Wheeler. In reference to Elizabeth Cary, Wheeler in 1696 stated that he was "not positive about the woman's name before marriage." Suffolk files, case 3766, first paper, fourth item.

217 *Matthew and Mary began their family:* Thwing Index reference code 14736. Numerous Boston real estate transactions are recorded for Cary in which he variously styled as "purser," "gentle man," and "barber."

217 *under the command of Captain Richard Short:* The exploits of Captain Short and his conflicts with Governor Phips are recounted in Roach, *Salem Witchcraft Trials.*

217 *Matthew was twice dispatched:* Massachusetts Archives, vol. 61, pp. 539–543, photostat copy at the Massachusetts Historical Society.

218 *Stoughton and his council requested that Cary:* For information about Cary's exploits in Canada, see Trask, "Instructions to Matthew Cary," pp. 286–290, and also Massachusetts Archives, vol. 2, p. 407. "An account of Memoirs offered by Mr. Matthew Cary unto Count Frontenac, Governor of Canada," is found in Massachusetts Archives, vol. 30, p. 377a.

218 *"With great sorrow":* Suffolk files, case 3766, second paper.

218 *"having at once two wives":* Ibid., third paper.

219 *"Although it did manifestly appear":* Massachusetts Archives, vol. 9, p. 144; original document missing, copied from photostat volume at Massachusetts State Archives.

219 *"great grief and shame"...."certain intelligence":* Ibid., vol. 47, pp. 199–201. The prior laws enacted in June 1694 are found in the Massachusetts Archives, vol. 47, pp. 152–154.

219 *Matthew and Mary Cary remained in Boston:* Thwing Index reference code 14736.

Chapter 25: Misconduct in Such a Glaring Light

The principal source of this story is Walker's Diary. Special thanks to Sally Dean Hamblen Hill for her transcriptions from this source. All quotes are from this source unless otherwise noted.

220 *In Colman's eyes:* Clayton Harding Chapman, "Benjamin Colman's Daughters," *The New England Quarterly,* vol. 26 (1953), pp. 169–192.

220 *"went or run away"..."rich cordial of his lips":* Ibid., pp. 187, 191.

221 *"villainous, base action":* Weis, *Colonial Clergy,* p. 42.

222 Information about Jacob Wendell and John Blower is from Thwing index reference codes 60752 and 6203. The Charlestown elopement is treated in Chapman, "Benjamin Colman's Daughters," pp. 169–192.

222 *Colman, who believed his daughter's errors:* Information in this paragraph is from Chapman, "Benjamin Colman's Daughters," pp. 187, 191–192.

Chapter 26: John Lovell Jr.

The source of John Lovell's story is Suffolk Files 129778; transcription and research notes courtesy of Cornelia Hughes Dayton. All quotes are from this source unless otherwise noted.

225 *granddaughter and great-granddaughter:* Watson, *Governor Thomas Dudley,* p. 29

225 *"in very low circumstances":* Jones, *The Loyalists of Massachusetts,* p. 202.

231 *In 1775, [Ann] died in Boston:* Rev. Arthur Wentworth Hamilton Eaton, "Old Families of Boston, Part Two: The Family of Capt. John Gerrish," *NEHGR,* vol. 67 (1913), p. 114.

232 *schoolmaster James Lovell:* Richard M. Ketchum, *Decisive Day: The Battle for Bunker Hill* (New York: Doubleday and Company, 1974), p. 198.

232 *"risk of being tarred and feathered":* Alexander Fraser, *Second Report of the Bureau of Archives for the Province of Ontario, Part II* (Toronto: L. K. Cameron, 1905), pp. 1139–1140.

232 *John attempted to press a claim:* Jones, *Loyalists of Massachusetts,* p. 202.

232 *"a man who rates his pretensions high":* Ibid., p. 203.

233 *I pray your Lordships answer:* Ibid.

233 *"he seems to have received more":* Fraser, *Second Report of the Bureau of Archives,* p. 1140.

233 *John ... wrote to John Robinson:* Jones, *Loyalists of Massachusetts,* p. 203.

233 *British authorities offered him £30:* Ibid.

233 *"very singular":* Ibid.

Selected Bibliography

Amory, Cleveland. *The Proper Bostonians*. New York: E. P. Dutton, 1947.

Anderson, Robert Charles. *The Great Migration Begins: Immigrants to New England, 1620–1633*. 3 vols. Boston: New England Historic Genealogical Society, 1995.

————, et al. *The Great Migration, Immigrants to New England, 1634–1635*. 3 vols. Boston: New England Historic Genealogical Society, 1999–2003.

Ayer, Mary Farwell. *Boston Common in Colonial and Provincial Days*. Boston: privately printed, 1903.

Bailyn, Bernard, ed. *The Apologia of Robert Keayne: The Last Will and Testament of Me, Robert Keayne . . .* New York: Harper & Row, 1964.

Boston Record Commissioners Reports. 39 vols. Boston, 1902–1909.

Boyle, John. "Boyle's Journal of Occurrences in Boston, 1759–1778." *The New England Historical and Genealogical Register*, vol. 84 (1930), pp. 142–171, 248–272, 357–382; vol. 85 (1931), pp. 5–28, 117–133. Cited in notes as "Boyle's Journal of Occurrences."

Bridenbaugh, Carl. *Early Americans*. New York: Oxford University Press, 1981.

Bullock, Steven C. "A Mumper among the Gentle: Tom Bell, Colonial Confidence Man." *The William and Mary Quarterly*, third series, vol. 55 (1998), pp. 231–258.

Burr, George Lincoln, ed. *Narratives of the New England Witchcraft Cases 1648–1706*. New York: Charles Scribner's Sons, 1914.

Butterfield, L.H. *Diary and Autobiography of John Adams*. Cambridge, Mass.: Belknap Press, 1961.

Cowan, Maude Roberts. *Members of the Ancient and Honorable Artillery Company in the Colonial Period, 1638–1774 . . .* National Society of Women Descendants of the Ancient and Honorable Artillery Company, 1958, rev. 1999.

Crane, Ellery Bicknell. *The Rawson Family: A Revised Memoir of Edward Rawson, Secretary of the Colony of Massachusetts Bay, from 1650 to 1686 . . .* Worcester, Mass.: privately printed, 1875.

Cunningham, Anne Rowe, ed. *Letters and Diary of John Rowe, Boston Merchant, 1759–1762, 1764–1779*. Boston: W. B. Clarke, 1903.

Demos, John. *Entertaining Satan: Witchcraft and the Culture of Early New England*. New York: Oxford University Press, 1982.

————. *Remarkable Providences: Readings on Early American History*. Boston: Northeastern University Press, 1971, rev. 1991.

Dow, George Francis. *Every Day Life in the Massachusetts Bay Colony*. Boston: Society for the Preservation of New England Antiquities, 1935.

Drake, Samuel Adams. *A Book of New England Legends and Folk Lore*. Boston: Little, Brown, 1901.

————. *Historic Mansions and Highways Around Boston*. Boston: Little, Brown, 1873.

————. *Old Landmarks and Historic Personages of Boston*. Boston: James R. Osgood, 1873.

Drake, Samuel G. *Annals of Witchcraft in New England . . .* Boston: W. E. Woodward, 1869.

Dunkle, Robert J., and Ann S. Lainhart. *Deaths in Boston 1700–1799*. 2 vols. Boston: New England Historic Genealogical Society, 1999.

————. *The Records of the Churches of Boston and the First Church, Second Parish, and Third Parish of Roxbury . . .* CD-ROM. Boston: New England Historic Genealogical Society, 2001.

Dunn, Richard S., et al., eds. *The Journal of John Winthrop 1630–1649*. Cambridge: Belknap Press, 1996.

Dunton, John. *The Life and Errors of John Dunton, Citizen of London . . .* 2 vols. London: J. Nichols, 1818.

Earle, Alice Morse. *Curious Punishments of Bygone Days*. New York: Macmillan, 1922.

————, ed. *Diary of Anna Green Winslow: A Boston School Girl of 1771*. Boston: Houghton Mifflin, 1896.

Erikson, Kai. *Wayward Puritans: A Study in the Sociology of Deviance*. New York: Wiley, 1966.

Ford, Worthington Chauncey. *Broadsides, Ballads &c. Printed in Massachusetts, 1639–1800*. *Massachusetts Historical Society Collections*, vol. 75. Boston, 1922.

Graham, Judith. *Puritan Family Life: The Diary of Samuel Sewall*. Boston: Northeastern University Press, 2000.

Green, Samuel A. "Diary of Lawrence Hammond." *Massachusetts Historical Society Proceedings*, second series, vol. 7, pp. 144–172.

Hall, David D., et al, eds. *Seventeenth-Century New England*. Boston: The Colonial Society of Massachusetts, 1984.

———. *Witch-Hunting in Seventeenth-Century New England: A Documentary History, 1638–1692*. Boston: Northeastern University Press, 1991.

Hearn, Daniel Allen. *Legal Executions in New England: A Comprehensive Reference, 1623–1960*. Jefferson, N.C.: McFarland, 1999.

History Project. *Improper Bostonians: Lesbian and Gay History from the Puritans to Playland*. Boston: Beacon Press, 1998.

Holliday, Carl. *Women's Life in Colonial Days*. Boston: Cornhill Publishing, 1922.

Hoover, Gladys. *The Elegant Royalls of Colonial New England*. New York: Vantage, 1974.

Hubbard, William. *A General History of New England*. Cambridge: Hillard & Metcalf, 1815.

Hull, N. E. H. *Female Felons: Women and Serious Crime in Colonial Massachusetts*. Urbana, Ill.: University of Illinois Press, 1987.

Hutchinson, Thomas. *The History of the Colony and Province of the Massachusetts-Bay*. Cambridge: Harvard University Press, 1936 [cited in notes as *History of the Massachusetts-Bay*].

Jones, E. Alfred. *The Loyalists of Massachusetts: Their Memorials, Petitions and Claims*. London: Saint Catherine Press, 1930.

Karlsen, Carol F. *The Devil in the Shape of a Woman: Witchcraft in Colonial New England*. New York: W. W. Norton, 1987.

Koehler, Lyle. *A Search for Power: The "Weaker Sex" in Seventeenth-Century New England*. Urbana, Ill.: University of Illinois Press, 1980.

Massachusetts Archives, microfilm at Massachusetts State Archives.

Mather, Cotton. *Diary of Cotton Mather*. 2 vols. New York: Frederick Ungar, 1957.

———. *Magnalia Christi Americana, Books I and II*. Cambridge: Belknap Press, 1977.

———. *Memorable Providences, Relating to Witchcrafts and Possessions*, in Burr, *Narratives of the Witchcraft Cases 1648–1706*.

———. *Pillars of Salt: An History of Some Criminals Executed in this Land for Capital Crimes, with Some of their Dying Speeches* . . . Boston: B. Green, 1699.

———. *A Warning to the Flocks Against Wolves in Sheeps Cloathing* . . . Boston: B. Green and J. Allen, 1700.

———. *The Wonders of the Invisible World* . . . Boston: Benjamin Harris, 1693.

Minkema, Kenneth P. "'The Devil Will Roar in Me Anon': The Possession of Martha Roberson, Boston, 1741," in Elizabeth Reis, ed. *Spellbound: Women and Witchcraft in America*. Wilmington, Del. : Scholarly Resources, 1998.

Morgan, Edmund S. "A Boston Heiress and Her Husbands: A True Story." *Publications of the Colonial Society of Massachusetts*, vol. 34. Boston, 1943, pp. 499–513.

Morison, Samuel E. "Extracts from the Common-place Books of Ephraim Eliot." *Publications of the Colonial Society of Massachusetts*, vol. 25. Boston, 1922–1924, pp. 40–43.

New England Historical and Genealogical Register, The. 159 vols. Boston: NEHGS, 1847–2005. Cited in notes as *NEHGR*.

Noble, John. *Records of the Court of Assistants of the Massachusetts Bay 1630–1692*. 3 vols. Boston: County of Suffolk, 1901–1904.

Norton, Mary Beth. *In the Devil's Snare: The Salem Witchcraft Crisis of 1692*. New York: Alfred A. Knopf, 2002.

O'Brien, Michael J. *Pioneer Irish in New England*. New York, 1937.

Perry, Arthur Latham. *Origins in Williamstown*. New York: Charles Scribner's Sons, 1894.

Pitkin, Joseph. Mss. diary, pp. 55–63, at Connecticut State Library.

Poole, William F. "Witchcraft in Boston," in Justin Winsor, *The Memorial History of Boston, including Suffolk County, Massachusetts, 1630–1880*. Boston: Ticknor, 1880, vol. 2, pp. 131–172.

Powers, Edwin. *Crime and Punishment in Early Massachusetts, 1620–1692*. Boston: Beacon Press, 1966.

Records of the Suffolk County Court 1671–1680. *Publications of the Colonial Society of Massachusetts*, vols. 29 and 30. Boston, 1933.

Roach, Marilynne K. *The Salem Witchcraft Trials: A Day-By-Day Chronicle of a Community Under Seige*. New York: Cooper Square Press, 2002.

Sargent, Lucius Manlius. *Dealings with the Dead*. Boston: Dutton and Wentworth, 1856.

Schutz, John A. *Legislators of the Massachusetts General Court, 1691–1780: A Biographical Dictionary*. Boston: Northeastern University Press, 1997.

Scott, Kenneth. *Counterfeiting in Colonial America*. New York: Oxford University Press, 1957.

Scudder, H.E., ed. *Recollections of Samuel Breck with Passages from His Note-Books, 1771–1862*. Philadelphia: Porter & Coates, 1877.

A Serious-Comical Dialogue Between the Famous Dr. Seth Hudson and the Noted Joshua How, who were lately tried in Boston, and convicted of Counterfeiting and passing Counterfeit Treasurer's Notes . . . Boston: Benjamin Mecom, 1762, collections of the American Antiquarian Society.

Seybolt, Robert Francis. *The Town Officials of Colonial Boston, 1634–1775*. Cambridge: Harvard University Press, 1939.

Shaw, Samuel S. "The Woodbridge-Phillips Duel." *Proceedings of the Massachusetts Historical Society*, second series, vol. 18. Boston, 1905, pp. 239–242.

Shurtleff, Nathaniel B., ed. *Records of the Governor and Company of the Massachusetts Bay in New England*. 5 vols. Boston: William White, 1853–1854.

———. *A Topographical and Historical Description of Boston*. Boston: Boston City Council, 1871.

Sibley, John Langdon. *Biographical Sketches of Graduates of Harvard University*. Boston: Massachusetts Historical Society, 1873–2000, 18 vols. Cited in notes as *Sibley's Harvard Graduates*.

Silverman, Kenneth. *The Life and Times of Cotton Mather*. New York: Harper and Row, 1984.

———, comp. *Selected Letters of Cotton Mather*. Baton Rouge: Louisiana State University Press, 1971.

Simons, D. Brenton. "Bigamy in Boston: The Case of Mathew Cary and Mary Sylvester." *The New England Historical and Genealogical Register*, vol. 159 (2005), pp. 5–11.

———. "The Journal of Jonathan Willis: Extracts from the Diary of a Boston Housewright, 1744–1747." *The New England Historical and Genealogical Register*, vol. 157 (2003), pp. 329–337; vol. 158 (2004), pp. 61–65, 139–144.

———. "Murder in Colonial Boston: The Ill-fated Greenleaf Children and Their Portraits." *New England Ancestors*, vol. 1 (Holiday 2000), pp. 11–15; vol. 2 (Winter 2001), pp. 17–19.

———. "Piracy on the High Seas: The Mysterious, Inexplicable Affair of Ansell Nickerson." *New England Ancestors*, vol. 6 (Winter 2005), pp. 17–21.

Stevens, Peter F. *Notorious & Notable New Englanders*. Camden, Maine: Down East, 1997.

Suffolk Deeds. 14 vols. Boston: Boston Board of Aldermen, 1880–1906.

Tannenbaum, Rebecca J. *The Healer's Calling: Women and Medicine in Early New England*. Ithaca, N.Y.: Cornell University Press, 2002.

Thomas, M. Halsey, ed. *The Diary of Samuel Sewall 1674–1729*. 2 vols. New York: Farrar, Straus and Giroux, 1973.

Thwing, Annie Haven. *The Crooked & Narrow Streets of the Town of Boston, 1630–1822*. Boston: Marshall Jones, 1925.

———. *Inhabitants and Estates of the Town of Boston, 1630–1800*. CD-ROM. Boston: New England Historic Genealogical Society and Massachusetts Historical Society, 2001. Cited in notes as Thwing Index.

Walker, Benjamin, Jr. Mss. diary at the Massachusetts Historical Society.

Ward, Edward. *A Trip to New-England, With a Character of the Country and People, Both English and Indians*. 1699. Full text at www.etext.lib.virginia.edu.

Warden, G. B. *Boston 1689–1776*. Boston: Little, Brown, 1970.

Watson, Marston. *Governor Thomas Dudley and Descendants Through Five Generations*. Baltimore: Genealogical Publishing Company, rev. ed., 2004.

Weis, Frederick Lewis. *The Colonial Clergy and the Colonial Churches of New England*. Lancaster, Mass.: Society of Descendants of the Colonial Clergy, 1936.

Whitehill, Walter Muir. *Boston: A Topographical History*. Cambridge: Belknap Press, 1968.

Williams, Daniel E. *Pillars of Salt: An Anthology of Early American Criminal Narratives*. Madison, Wis.: Madison House, 1993.

Wilson, David K. "The Forgotten Witches of Boston." *Yankee*, June 1979, pp. 63–65, 140–145.

Winslow, Ola Elizabeth. *A Destroying Angel: The Conquest of Smallpox in Colonial Boston*. Boston: Houghton Mifflin, 1974.

Wroth, L. Kinvin and Hiller B. Zobel. *Legal Papers of John Adams*. 3 vols. Cambridge, Mass.: Belknap Press, 1965.

Wyman, Thomas Bellows. *The Genealogies and Estates of Charlestown in the County of Middlesex . . . 1629–1818*. 2 vols. Boston: David Clapp, 1879.

Index